THE ERRORS OF MANKIND

Mistaking the True Conditions for Our Well-Being

A Novel by Curt A. Canfield

I no longer have the luxury of believing there are evil people and good people: these two possibilities lie very close together and this means we are all much more defenceless. You cannot simply 'screen out' the evil people. The important thing is to make sure you do not create the circumstances where this side of human nature can thrive.

~ Dan Bar-On

Extract from *Grief Encounter* by Christine Toomey

www.christinetoomey.com/2004/grief-encounter

This is the first book in the Will Barnes trilogy, followed by *"Better is the End"* and *"Manuela."*

TABLE OF CONTENTS

v

CYCLE III: *DIE NIEDERLAGE* 217

CYCLE I: THE PATH TO REDRESS

Great Lords, wise men never sit and wail their loss,
but cheerily seek how to redress their harms.

William Shakespeare, Henry VI, Act 5, Scene 4

~ 1st VISIT ~

CHAPTER 1: THE UNEXAMINED LIFE

We first met in 2017. I had recently retired and was compiling my mother's genealogy when a branch led me to Johann, a distant relative who I later learned was a 91-year-old World War II German veteran. After spending time with him, I realized that Socrates was correct when he said that an unexamined life is not worth living. However, he should have added that it could prove fatal to the lives of others.

I planned to take notes on our family history when I first visited him. But after one visit turned into several, they read more like an accounting of human nature than any type of genealogy. After my last visit, I was inspired to write this book. It was no easy task to reconcile his history with mine.

I almost gave up when a friend of mine read an early draft and wrote me a convincing note to finish the work: *Anyone who reads this from the position of a Nazi sympathizer is doing the work a disservice… For whatever reason, we as a society have lost our ability to listen and appreciate points of view that conflict with our own … Your book presents the complete opposite of that by putting people together who should hate each other but have come to appreciate a different facet of the story and events that have led to that expected hatred.*

Johann was born a year earlier than my mother. He had the same first name as her great-grandfather. Both men were born in Silesia, which was then part of Germany.

I had never heard of Silesia before. In fact, before I started my family history, I never knew my mother had German roots. She never spoke about it, and we rarely interacted with her side of the family while I was growing up.

Her descendants left Europe in 1852 from Schlawentzig, a village about eighty-four miles southeast of Breslau, which was then the capital of Silesia, a province within the Kingdom of Prussia. Prussia later united with other German-speaking states to form the modern state of Germany.

Breslau cannot be found on a map today. It is now called Wrocław. Schlawentzig cannot be found either; it is now called Sławięcice. After World War II, the Allies carved off the eastern part of Germany and gave it to Poland; all things German, including the people and place names, were removed.

When I found that Johann came to America in 1956 and lived only ninety miles away, you could have knocked me over with a feather. I quickly arranged to visit him to get information about my mother's line, but I was also interested in hearing what it was like to grow up in Nazi Germany.

I didn't know how our first visit would go, so I didn't prepare much. I spent the two-hour drive thinking about my introduction and what questions to ask him. When I arrived at the entrance to the assisted living facility, I was pleasantly surprised by the well-manicured grounds leading up to a sprawling, one-story building. Both sat inside of a luxuriant forest that circled the property.

I went inside to the reception desk, asked for him, and they escorted me to the Garden Room. They said he spent every morning there. He was sitting there reading a book. The title was *1924*. There was a picture of Hitler on the front cover. A cup of coffee was placed on the table next to him.

The nurse approached him and said he had a visitor. He stood up quickly and had only a slight slouch for a man his age. He presented a deadpan expression and extended his hand to shake mine with a firm clasp. We were about the same height. Unlike me, he had a full head of hair and a slender build. I looked down and saw he took his coffee as I did – black.

"Mr. Knoske?" I asked with what I hoped was a disarming smile. "My name is Will Barnes. My mother is Emma Knoske, and I'm researching her family history. I believe you two are related."

He looked at me nonplussed. "Have I met you before?" There was no mistaking his German accent.

"No. I found your name while researching the family tree and thought I would come up and visit you."

He told me to have a seat but didn't appear interested as I rattled off dates, places, and names. After a while, his eyes began to wander around the room, always returning to his book on the table.

It was beginning to feel like this might be a short visit when a thought occurred to me. I told him that my father was born in 1926, the same year as he, and went to Europe in late 1944 during the closing days of the Battle of the Bulge. I asked if he also served in the war.

He looked at me carefully; his eyes were clear blue and piercing. They looked as if he questioned my intentions in switching to a discussion about the war. He finally answered, saying he joined the German army when he was seventeen, fought on the Western Front and then on the Eastern Front until the war's end.

And then he clammed up. He gave no further details. He sat there and waited, eyeing me carefully. The silence became heavy between us until he leaned forward. "Were you ever in the military?"

I suppressed a chuckle. Was I ever in the military? I was in it right up to my ass, enlisting right out of high school. "I was in the Marines for three years. I served in Vietnam and came out a sergeant."

"A Marine?" He looked at me with a surprised expression, and his eyes lit up. "Your motto was *Semper Fidelis*. Always Faithful, *ja?*"

"That's right. The few. The proud. That was us."

He suddenly sat up straight while his eyes engaged mine. He turned to grab his coffee cup, took a sip, and then swiveled back to face me. "How would you like me to address you, Mr. Barnes? You can call me Johann."

I must have hit paydirt. "You can call me Will. Most people do."

He thought about that momentarily, then cocked his head and smiled. "How would it be if I called you Willi? That was the name of a comrade of mine."

"No one's ever called me that before." I was pleased that he suddenly was taking an interest in me. "I wouldn't mind that one bit."

"Well, good. It was meant to be a compliment." He paused a moment before asking his next question. "Tell me, Willi, are you religious?"

"I believe in God if that's what you mean."

"That's exactly what I mean." Johann put the cup back down on the table, smiling at me. "Did you know what the German army had inscribed on its belt buckle, Willi?"

He knocked me off balance with that question. "I have no idea."

"*Gott mit Uns*. Do you know what that means?"

I shook my head.

"No? Ach, you don't speak German—shame on your mother. Well, Willi, it means: God is with us. Does that surprise you?"

He paused, waiting for my reaction. He was right. I was surprised. I was also taken aback by it.

He quickly followed that question with another. "Tell me, do you think that a country that has been portrayed as so evil would put that on all their soldiers' belt buckles?"

I was still too confounded by his first revelation to answer. Besides, I saw it was a rhetorical question and decided to turn it around by asking him a simple question. "Was that on your belt buckle as well, Johann?"

"Well, I was not in the army *per se*," he said hesitantly. He leaned forward and whispered, "I was in the Waffen-SS, Willi. Our belt buckles had the party's insignia."

An image of the swastika appeared in my mind, and my skin began to crawl. His tone or expression was not sinister, but there was something ominous coming on that I knew couldn't be undone. I had the same queasy feeling when I signed my enlistment papers, and that experience didn't end well for me.

He sat back and continued in a normal tone. "But, even so, most of us did believe in God. Do you see any contradiction between the two, Willi?"

It was my turn to eye him carefully. I assumed he was talking about the coexistence of Good and Evil, an internal struggle that had plagued me for years. I instinctively drew away from him. I wasn't about to let the presence of evil shadow my life again.

He must have seen my face tighten up in reaction to his question. "Don't let the SS fool you, Willi. The Waffen-SS had nothing to do with the camps. We were purely a military combat unit."

I didn't care. I was disgusted with his being part of the SS and looked away, but he continued. "You know, I can already tell that we are related. We both enlisted when we were teenagers, and we both joined the best fighting units. I even became a sergeant just as

6

you did; I was an *Unterscharführer*. And we even had a motto like your Marine Corps: *Meine Ehre heißt Treue*, which translates to My Honor is my Loyalty. It's awfully close to Always Faithful, don't you think?"

His comparison repelled me, and also that he was proud of serving in the SS. He was watching me and must have sensed my feelings. His smile vanished, and his eyes latched onto mine. "We were not part of the *Totenkopf SS* if that's what you're thinking, Willi. They were a separate branch of the SS and the ones in the camps. We were on the front lines."

I never knew there were separate parts of the SS. I had brought along my notebook to record family history, but now I began to write a list of things to check out after I got home.

He watched me write as he took another sip of coffee. After I finished and looked up, he tapped his book.

"In the end, Hitler had neither loyalty nor honor, Willi. He only thought of himself." He squinted as if he had painful memories. "But, in the end, none of them did…not Churchill, not Roosevelt or Stalin."

I raised an eyebrow at his inclusion of Churchill and Roosevelt, but I didn't object; I wasn't too fond of politicians either. "I know what you mean, Johann. In Vietnam, we were left high and dry by our government. Any honor or loyalty left in that war was gone by the time I got there."

I was surprised by the bitterness that came out in my reply. I paused for a moment to let it dissipate. "Kennedy, Johnson, Nixon … none of them did our country any good in pursuing that war." A taste of bile began to rise in my throat, and my eyes moistened. Feelings returned that I hadn't had for many years, and it was unsettling.

Johann became strangely quiet. I paused to watch his face change from one of engagement to one of reflection. He seemed to be looking back on his past. I suddenly empathized with him. "Was Willi with you during the war, Johann?"

He nodded. "Yes. We were like brothers. We trained together and fought in Normandy. We were in the 12th SS *Hitlerjugend* Division. Our division was formed in 1944 from Hitler Youth groups all around the country. All the recruits were only seventeen years old."

He leaned back in his chair and slowly exhaled his memories. "Our division commander wrote a book about the 12th and mentioned one episode during the Normandy campaign when Willi was ordered to serve as the forward observer for our company's command post.

"He was placed on a slight rise under a clump of trees. He had good cover with a wide view of the ground in front of him. He took an armor plate from a destroyed Panzer to shield him. He used an opening in it to steady his rifle. He shot a number of English that day. His company commander was watching him with scissor glasses. Our division commander wrote that thirty dead British were lying in front of Willi before he ran out of ammunition. He watched as Willi stood up, smashed his rifle against a tree, and then placed his arms up to surrender."

He paused briefly to rub his eyes. "After that, the English came out. One of them went right up to Willi. He grabbed Willi's jacket in his left hand, pulled out his pistol with his right, and shot Willi in the head."[1]

CHAPTER 2: CORE CURRICULUM

I was leaning forward, listening in rapt attention, until he spoke about the fate of my namesake. I fell back into my chair, momentarily stunned, and started writing. This was far more interesting than any family history.

"Ach, Willi, he was a good man. That was no way for a soldier to die." He sighed and looked away for a moment.

I sympathized with him, but that's war. It's hard not to get pissed off when some guy shoots all your buddies and then comes out with his hands up, expecting to be treated well. But Willi was only a young kid. He probably didn't know any better, so I kept my thoughts to myself.

"There is a song in Germany used at all military funerals: *Ich hatt' einen Kameraden.* I don't suppose you ever heard of it?"

"Sorry, no. I recognize the word *Kamerad* though, that means 'friend,' doesn't it?"

"*Richtig.*" His head bobbed up and down, which I took as confirmation. "I haven't heard that song for some time now, but it leaves an impression that you don't soon forget. Let me try and translate for you."

The tone of his voice lowered and became melancholy as he read: "*I once had a comrade; you will find none better. The drum called us to battle; he walked by my side, in the same pace and step.*"

He paused to gather his thoughts and, it seemed, his dead comrades as well. *"A bullet came flying; is it my turn or yours? He was swept away; he lies now at my feet as if he were a part of me. He still reaches out his hand to me while I am about to reload. I cannot hold onto your hand. Rest you in eternal life, my good comrade."*

He brushed away the tears that began to well up in his eyes. "The music makes it even more moving, Willi. You must look it up when you get home."

I did listen to it later in German. I couldn't understand a word of it, but the pace and mournful singing made it sound like a dirge. I was almost moved to tears myself.

He knitted his white brows. "You know, Willi," he said softly, "we were always painted as evil, but we were only human, trying to save our country as best as we knew how.

"Germany was devastated by the Allies after the First World War. They took away our lands and handed them over to foreign governments. The Germans left behind were disenfranchised and persecuted for years. The Allies also occupied our country for several years.

"The 1920s were a terrible time of disruption for us until Hitler showed a way out with National Socialism. The party gave us purpose and restored our country during the Thirties while the rest of the world suffered from the Depression. Our progress was so rapid that we felt God must be with us. We had no hint of what was to come."

I didn't know how to respond. I had never heard anyone associate God with Hitler, and a cold wave of caution washed over me. I thought again about leaving before he dug any deeper into this vein.

"You look puzzled, Willi. Here's something for you to write down: *Volksgemeinschaft*. It's the term we used to define our culture and our way of life back then. It's like you saying the *'American Way'* to describe what makes you proud of your country. We used that term during the Thirties to give us unity and a sense of purpose as Capitalists started coming in from the West and Communists from the East to threaten the stability of our society, our government, and our economy. We had to sacrifice and work hard to keep them from overcoming our country."

I raised my eyebrows in disbelief. It seemed he was trying to pull me into supporting his argument for Nazism.

Johann winced as he saw my expression. "Ach, you may think I'm getting out of line here, Willi. You tell me if you think so."

I smiled in deference to his apology. "I never heard it put that way before, Johann," I admitted. His display of thoughtfulness was unexpected. It made me feel comfortable enough to stay a while longer. "Anyway, that's why I'm here, Johann, to hear your story and learn as much as I can about my mother's roots."

"Ha!" he laughed. "You remind me of my son Auggie. He is always plugging me for information about the old times." He pulled something from under his book. "Do you see this, Willi?"

I couldn't quite believe my eyes. He held up an iPad. I looked at it and couldn't help but return the wide grin on his face despite my lingering sense of discomfort.

"Surprised at the old man, huh? Auggie gave me this as a Christmas present. When I retired twenty-five years ago, I devoted myself to understanding what brought about the war. I always felt we were good people, but when I came to America, we were portrayed so badly in all the history books, television, and movies. I wanted to understand what happened to our people. I gathered so many notes and copied so many documents over the years that it became hard to find anything!

"So, Auggie bought me an Apple Mac to help me organize things. He taught me how to use it while I took a typing class. Then, he helped me move everything on paper over to the computer. But most importantly, he introduced me to the Internet. And then, this year, he got me this iPad!" He brought it back down to his lap and patted it lovingly.

"He set it up so when I came here to read and found something interesting, I can look it up on the Internet and download it. Then, when I return to my room, it syncs up with my Mac."

He leaned back with a self-satisfied expression. "So, anyway, everything I found is stored in this iPad. This is my story. Would you like to hear it?"

I nodded a cautious assent, and he slapped my knee in affirmation.

"*Gut!* Well, as I mentioned earlier, Willi, when I was growing up, Germany was in terrible condition after the first world war. Foreign systems from the East and the West were coming into our country and ruining us! Speculators from the Capitalist West squeezed whatever profits they could from our depressed economy and caused crippling inflation, while Communists from the East came in and tried to overthrow our new republic and our culture with revolution."

He leaned forward and whispered in a low, conspiratorial tone. "You might also be interested to know, Willi, that FDR was one of those speculators. He was involved in all the profiteering at our expense during the Twenties. He and the other Western investors came here, bought properties from impoverished families for a steal, and then rented or sold them at an exorbitant profit. Their activities fueled the hyperinflation that caused so much civil unrest after the war."[1]

I was jotting down notes and underlined the part about FDR profiteering from the destitute German people. This an interesting piece of history, if true. I knew he was from a wealthy family but had no idea what he did before becoming governor of New York.

"Well, you can understand that if we were ever to rebuild our economy and hold onto our culture, then both of these foreign systems had to be brought under control. Hitler said as much, but no one noticed him during the Twenties. The National Socialist party only got six percent of the votes in the 1924 national elections, which fell even lower in 1928 to two and a half percent. The Nazis didn't get anywhere until the Depression hit, and even then, they only got 18% in the 1930 elections, but we'll talk more about that later."

Later? Was he thinking that I would be coming back? While Johann paused to look at something on his iPad, I noticed an older woman in a wheelchair. She was glaring at us over her reading glasses. There was a book on her lap. It was obvious our conversation distracted her. She did not look pleased.

I quickly looked away from her. I didn't want to get drawn into any scene in an old folk's home involving the ramblings of an old ex-Nazi. It was then that I began to realize why we never spent much time with my mother's side of the family.

CHAPTER 3: BAD BLOOD

Johann must have seen me look away. "What's wrong, Willi? Am I being politically incorrect? I was just telling you how it was."

I lowered my voice in reply. "There's still a lot of bad blood around that time in history, Johann."

His face went blank as he digested my thoughts. He put his iPad down and looked at me quizzically. "You're thinking about the Jews, aren't you? Well, they are part of the story, but we'll talk about that subject later."

He reached for his coffee but then stopped. "Ach! Empty! As you can probably tell, Willi, I like my coffee. It keeps me going, and it doesn't matter whether I drink it hot or cold."

He chuckled as he picked up and swirled the empty cup. "I even drank that damned fake coffee, *muckefuck*, during the war; it was all we could get back then."

I burst out laughing when he said, *muckefuck*. What kind of word was that? His mentioning it broke an otherwise tense moment, and I decided to stay awhile longer.

He closed his eyes for a second or two, and a paternal expression spread across his face when he opened them. "I have a feeling about you, Willi. Were you in the Boy Scouts?"

I looked up from my notebook with a blank stare. Why did he ask me that? "Yes, actually I was."

"Did you know the Boy Scouts were chartered by Congress in 1916?"

I had no idea our government was involved in its organization; he caught me flatfooted. "I have to confess I didn't know that."

"*Gut!* You learned something new! I joined the *Deutsches Jungvolk* in 1936 when I was ten; it was formed by our government, just like your Scout program."

I nodded, thinking the two were worlds apart, just like our governments were at the time.

"This group was like your Cub Scouts. I moved up to the *Hitler-Jugend*, or HJ as we called it, when I was thirteen; this was more like your Boy Scouts. We did things like marching, trench digging, map reading, target shooting, camping, and other outdoor activities. Of course, we were also indoctrinated into our country's National Socialist beliefs. I imagine yours did the same?"

I smiled and chuckled. "Yeah, all that sounds familiar. We had uniforms, and we learned survival skills. We went camping. We shot at targets with our BB guns and, later, with .22 caliber rifles. We saluted the flag and said the Pledge of Allegiance before each meeting. We were indoctrinated just like you were, except we learned about the virtues of democracy, the pioneering spirit, Yankee know-how, and all that other good stuff that made America special."

Johann nodded. "And when you were growing up, I assume you read war comics and saw all the war movies glorifying American soldiers?"

"I sure did." I cracked a grin, remembering all the World War II comics I used to read: *Sgt. Rock and Easy Company; Sgt. Nick Fury and his Howling Commandos; Gunner and Sarge;* and *The Haunted Tank* with Jeb Stuart. I watched *The Sands of Iwo Jima, The Battle of the Bulge,* and *The Longest Day* several times.

"And you played war games with toy rifles? And had toy soldiers, too?"

"Sure."

"So did I! Then you learned about honor, courage, loyalty, and sacrifice as I did. Now, let's compare our two countries when I was growing up."

I voiced a reluctant "Okay."

"Well, once the Second Industrial Revolution got underway, both our countries had to reorient their boys. They were brought up working alone as individual farmers or tradesmen. Now, they had to learn to work together in large factories or on other large-scale projects. Both of our countries tried to instill in their children a national *Weltanschauung*, or what you would call a worldview. They wanted us boys to think alike, work together toward a common goal, and forget about our individual needs." He paused here to check my interest.

"I understand." But I wasn't sure I agreed with him or where he might be headed with this.

"*Gut!*" He nodded and paused a moment before proceeding. "Tell me, Willi, how did you feel about Communism growing up? I remember shortly after I came to America in 1956 that all the schoolchildren were ducking under their desks for air raid drills. I read about the McCarthy hearings, the arms race, and the Domino Theory. Did all those things scare you?"

"Sure. We were terrified."

"As we were back in the Thirties." His head drooped slightly. I could see he was beginning to tire. My discomfort was also returning. I decided now might be a good time to leave. This conversation was going nowhere.

"Listen, Johann. I have a long drive back. My wife expected me to be here only an hour or so."

"Okay, Willi. But you will come back, won't you?" His eyes were imploring. "I have a few more points to share with you. And we already have so much in common! There's still more to explore, isn't there?"

Our commonality was the last thing I wanted to explore, although he piqued my interest with the promise of a few more points to discuss. We both stood up to say our goodbyes when he reached into his pocket, pulled out a card, and offered it to me. It was a business card showing his name, address, phone number, and email address. This old guy was full of surprises. You could have knocked me over with a feather.

"*Auf Wiedersehen*, Willi. That should help us stay in touch. I'll see you again soon, *ja*?"

I couldn't possibly deny the old man's request after that presentation. "I'm impressed, Johann. However, I don't have anything to offer you, but I'll email you all my contact information once I get home."

He nodded, then grunted his acknowledgment as he sat back down and picked up his book. I began walking out when I noticed the old woman in the wheelchair. She was watching me, and I felt obligated to offer my apologies.

"Excuse me, ma'am. I hope our conversation didn't bother you too much."

She laid the book in her lap and took off her reading glasses. "The two of you were a little loud. And, yes, it made it hard to concentrate on my reading, especially when that old man raised his voice. And then I saw his book with that awful picture on the cover."

Her stern voice matched her expression. "You might want to think of others the next time you get into a conversation with him." She had what sounded like a slight Eastern European accent. It reminded me of wife's grandmother, who emigrated from Poland.

If she was Polish, then her reaction to Johann was understandable. The Poles have no great love for Germans, and

Hitler's picture wouldn't have helped. She must have heard Johann ranting about the war as well. I figured I better leave quickly and, hopefully, on a good note.

"We'll be more thoughtful next time, ma'am, and again, I'm sorry if we disturbed you. I was visiting a relative for the first time, and we might have become a little too excited."

"That's some relative you have." She broke off eye contact and picked up her book.

I took the hint. "Well, goodbye then."

She muttered, "*Zay gezunt,*" without looking up. It sounded like *Gesundheit.* I wondered if I mistook her for being Polish. I made a mental note to write that phrase down when I got in the car but forgot about it once other thoughts grabbed my attention.

~ AT HOME ~

CHAPTER 4: INSIGHTS

I got into my car, stunned by everything I had heard. This man and I not only shared the same bloodline but, as he pointed out, shared similar childhood experiences that led to our fighting for two different countries, both of which committed serious war crimes. I looked out at the parking lot and recalled Johann's reference to good and evil.

It brought back memories, and a Bible verse suddenly sprang to mind: *God may perhaps grant them repentance leading to the knowledge of the truth, and they may come to their senses and escape from the snare of the devil…*

I had a major stroke seventeen years ago. It was the culmination of a life spent in fear and vindictiveness. It finally freed me from the snare of the beast and left me repentant, but I was left senseless afterward. As I recovered, I spent every year afterward seeking knowledge of the truth. I kept wondering, how did I get entangled in that snare in the first place? If I gained that knowledge, then I could avoid getting trapped again and find some sort of redemption for my past.

I glanced in my rear-view mirror and winced at my reflection. I had hoped to answer that question after retirement, but now this trip had set me back.

Learning my relation was an ex-SS trooper was a bitter pill to swallow. But the real shocker came when the old man gleefully found commonalities between our two childhoods. He had opened new vistas for me. And, suddenly, the urgency of answering that question became paramount.

The traffic on I-81 was light as I headed home. The trees flashed by, painting a lush green border under an expansive blue sky. The contrast in colors reflected my feelings about Johann. He was pretty coherent, given his advanced age, and he had some interesting insights, but there was something sinister about him. It seemed he was driving me toward some hidden and unsettling destination.

A truck roared by on my left, interrupting my thoughts. I watched as it disappeared over the horizon. I went back to thinking about Johann. It was true that we were both raised in a similar manner, which led to our enlisting. But things must have changed after that.

He appeared to come out of his war well-grounded and firm in his convictions. On the other hand, I came out of my war detached from the world. I had lost most of my beliefs.

I looked out the window and saw the scenery flash by as quickly as the years of my life. I squirmed in my seat and questioned the wisdom of a return visit. The idea of learning more about his past was frankly unsettling. After hearing he was in the SS, no one could blame me for not returning. But they could question my judgment if I did. However, I was always interested in history, and he said there was more to come. Besides, his eyes practically begged me to return.

My exit sign appeared, and a sense of relief washed over me as the past receded. It was only a few minutes more until I pulled into my garage, turned off the engine, and gazed into the rearview mirror. Nothing was moving outside. The light from the overhead garage door opener timed out. I was left alone in the dark, wondering how I would explain this visit to my wife, Cynthia.

When I finally entered the house, she greeted me with a hug and a kiss. I felt the day's weight slough off me like a snake shedding its skin. She still carried her beauty effortlessly as she walked down the hall ahead of me. Her silvery-white hair swayed just above her shoulders as she padded down the hall.

She still had a slight limp from an ankle injury incurred years ago. We were working on our first home when she slipped on the floor joists. I smiled at the memory and thought of our decision not to have children. It turned out to be a good one. We were both too busy with our careers.

We recently celebrated our thirtieth anniversary, and I was reminded of the old saying that God sends you the right people when you need them. Cynthia was living proof of that.

I turned her around and pulled her close. "I love you, pure and simple."

"I know, Will. I love you too."

After we entered the kitchen, I pulled a bottle of wine from the refrigerator and opened it. She poured it into two glasses and led the way into the family room. "I missed you today. How did your visit go?"

"It wasn't what I expected, that's for sure." I was hesitant to go any further, as she had been less than thrilled when I first told her about Johann.

Although she initially encouraged me to research my mother's family, she grew skeptical after learning they came from Germany. Cynthia was raised a Catholic and had a clear sense of right and wrong. The klaxons went off after she heard Johann grew up in Nazi Germany and lived nearby.

I learned two things about her then: first, she felt Nazi Germany was the epitome of all evil; and second, she didn't have the slightest interest in history. When I started watching documentaries on Nazi Germany, she asked how I could watch "such garbage" and left the room as if it would permanently mar her sensibilities.

We sat on the couch, and she straightened up as if to make a major pronouncement. "Well, I hope you got everything you needed today so you never have to go up there again."

It was her way of telling me to end it. I knew she wouldn't like what I was going to say next. "Well," I answered hesitantly, "not exactly. I do plan on going up there again. He's a lonely, old guy, and we still have more ground to cover."

"What ground to cover?" she asked incredulously. "What could possibly require you to make a second trip? I thought you would ask a few simple questions about the family, and that would be it."

A familiar twinge signaled rocky shoals ahead. This discussion wasn't going to get any easier. "He had some interesting insights about Germany I had never heard before."

I was reluctant to tell her about the SS, but I have learned that it's best to be honest and direct with her since the day she uncovered the beast. She has an unmatched bullshit detector, and her ability to ferret out the truth was even stronger. "He fought for the Germans during the war; he was in the SS."

"The SS? *Are you kidding me?* You mean he actually was a *Nazi?*" She practically jumped away from me. I was surprised at her reaction and the bitterness in her tone.

Johann didn't seem like your typical Nazi, so I went out on a limb for him. "He never said he was a Nazi, but I guess he must have been since he was in the SS. He seemed like an average guy to me, just another veteran."

She stared at me, contemplating her next response. "Do you know what the SS did?"

"I know, and he knows it, too. We talked a bit about that, but that's exactly why I want to return, Cynthia. I need to hear his side of the story, why they did what they did."

She looked at me askance as if expecting more. But I paused. What was I about to get myself into? Would making more visits drive a wedge between us?

"What's wrong, Will? You look like you've seen a ghost."

She snapped me back to reality. "Oh, I was just thinking about what he said today. He told me Germany faced big problems after the First World War and had to find a way out. It was a different and interesting perspective." Something just occurred to me. "You know, Cynthia, I studied Japan's point-of-view before World War II in college, and it was similar to what I heard from Johann today. Both of them felt threatened by the West. I learned a few new things about Japan then, and I might be able to learn some new things about Germany now."

"So, you're planning on going up there again?"

"Yes, if you're okay with it."

"Will," she paused to let out a sigh of exasperation. "We both know you'll do what you want regardless of what I say."

It struck me then that there was another reason to return. I cocked my head as I put my finger on it. Johann and I started to bond. He assumed the role of a father figure as he shared his thoughts with me, asked thoughtful questions, and listened with interest. I never had that experience with my father.

Cynthia broke into my thoughts. "Will, I don't think it's a good idea for you to go back there," she said firmly, placing her gaze squarely on me. "You should stop seeing him for your own good. You'll get pulled into something bad that can't be undone. And then what?" She glared at me, growing impatient as I pondered my latest revelation. "And why would you want to make more visits, Will? What's the point?"

Cynthia has an unerring sense of intuition. She knew my stroke had left me somewhat impressionable, and she was undoubtedly worried about what would happen if I spent too much time with an ex-Nazi.

I kept my eyes locked onto hers as I searched for a response, but nothing came. I couldn't articulate any good reason for returning except to plunge further into his background. It seemed as if God had granted Johann repentance. It also seemed that Johann, through all his research, had gained knowledge of some sort of truth. I felt I had to go back. Perhaps he could provide some insight into how and why I wound up in the beast's snare and a way out to find redemption. But I couldn't tell that to Cynthia. Not yet.

CHAPTER 5: A MATTER OF TERMS

Cynthia and I closed out the day watching inane TV shows. Before joining her in bed, I went to my study to check my email and saw several unread messages in my Inbox, including one from the History Channel. The subject line read: Daily Headlines from History. The preview pane showed September 26, 1944: Allies Slaughtered by Germans in Arnhem.

I was curious and decided to open the message. It was about Operation Market Garden, the basis for the movie *A Bridge Too Far*. The article relayed how German soldiers shot Allied parachutists, armed to the teeth, as they descended to kill as many Germans as possible.

Why did the message say *slaughtered* instead of "shot" or "killed?" The Germans were only defending themselves. This headline was misleading. It reminded me of what Johann said about the American media, which, in turn, reminded me to send Johann my contact information before retiring for the night.

When I entered the bedroom, Cynthia was already sleeping. The news was playing on TV, and I turned it off. I took off my clothes, crawled into bed, and began wondering how my mother's family was treated during the two wars. She never spoke about it, and now I started to understand why.

I grew up watching *Looney Tunes* cartoons and *The Three Stooges.* Both shows satirized, demonized, and denigrated the Germans. They were portrayed as cruel, sadistic bastards, just as they were in the *History Channel's* email.

My mother was two generations removed from German soil; her great-grandparents came to America in 1870. Her parents were undoubtedly still assimilating when the First World War broke out, and then she came of age during the Second. It must have been difficult having German roots during those times. They must have felt a lot of humiliation, if not outright discrimination and persecution, from all the negative media coverage and propaganda. And it didn't stop at the war's end.

The next morning, Doris and Daisy, our Norwich terriers, trotted to my side of the bed and began whining until I got up. They are siblings and thick as thieves in taking me through their morning drill, which usually begins at four in the morning. First, they whine until I take them outside. When we come back in, they run around and nip at my heels until I feed them.

After they finish, I have breakfast on the couch and watch the news while they lie beside me. After my first cup of coffee is finished, I leave for my daily walk while they nap. When I return, they wake up and insist on taking their own walk. When we return, Cynthia is usually up and having breakfast.

I went through the complete drill this morning and then sat with Cynthia to watch the news. As soon as it was over, I brewed a second cup of coffee and returned to my study. I was eager to begin fact-checking my notes from yesterday's visit. I sat at my desk, opened my notebook, and started reading.

Johann said he was part of the 12th SS *Hitlerjugend* Division. I searched on the PC and found it was formed in mid-1943. Germany needed manpower to replace the massive losses incurred in Russia, and this division was recruited from HJ groups around the country.

Enlistment was limited to those born in 1926. The 12th was part of the *Waffen-SS*, which was, in fact, the military component of the SS that fought on the front lines. The *Totenkopfverbände-SS* oversaw the camps. Both organizations reported to Himmler. So far, he was correct.

The boys were sent to France in March 1944 after six months of training that was hindered by shortages of fuel, ammunition, and even training staff. They were sent to defend against the anticipated Allied invasion of France, which came three months later in Normandy.

A massive number of Allied troops landed on June 6th. A large and unchallenged navy and air force supported them. Both their offshore and aerial forces bombed the Germans at will. They were able to keep the Allied supply lines open to replenish their troops with supplies and ammunition as the battle wore on. The Germans, however, were pinned down and mostly cut off from any resupply efforts.

The 12th was deployed around Caen, not too far from the invasion site. The Allies planned to secure that city by June 7th, the day after D-Day, but the 12th didn't withdraw until two months later, on August 6th.

The Allies dropped 2,660 bombs in and around Caen during that period, but these boys held on despite being outnumbered, short of supplies, and most importantly, lacking any air support. I read accounts where Allies shot unarmed Germans if they saw SS markings on their uniforms. I immediately thought of my namesake.

By the end of August, the Allied armies were close to surrounding the German forces in Normandy. The 12th was ordered to keep the Falaise Gap open long enough for the remaining German divisions to escape from Normandy before the encirclement was completed. The 12ᵗʰ was one of the last units to make it out.

The 12ᵗʰ started the campaign with 20,540 men and a combined total of 229 tanks and assault guns. After their withdrawal, Army Group B reported that the 12ᵗʰ was left with only 300 men, ten tanks, and no artillery. Other sources report that the survivors ranged from 1,500-10,000. Their losses were terrible, but Johann had made it out.

The 12ᵗʰ was ordered back to Germany to retool for the final offensive on the Western Front, known in America as the Battle of the Bulge. After that offensive fell apart in January 1945, they were pulled back to Germany for refitting.

The following month, they were deployed to the Eastern Front to relieve the besieged German troops in Budapest. After that offensive failed, they fought the Russians in one holding action after another as they retreated westward. They were fortunate enough to reach American lines and surrender to them at the war's end on May 8, 1945.

I stopped reading and shook my head in amazement. What kept these men fighting when they lost one battle after another and against such overwhelming odds? They were chronically short of food, fuel, equipment, and ammunition while their cities back home were being reduced to rubble. One British military historian explained:

The primary difference between the 12ᵗʰ SS and other German formations lay in the singular spirit of self-sacrifice these youngsters espoused in the name of Adolf Hitler and National Socialism…A letter found on the body of a young grenadier killed in the fighting expressed the attitude of many of the division's young men: 'I write during one of the momentous hours before we attack, full of excitement and expectation of what the next days will bring.…Some believe in living but life is not everything! It is enough to know that we attack and will throw the enemy from our homeland. It is a holy task.' [1]

As I read this, I remembered my feelings when I enlisted in 1970. The war in Vietnam was winding down, but I believed it was still possible to save the world and these people from Communism. By the time I arrived in 1972, America had already given up on South Vietnam. None of us wanted to be the last casualty for a lost cause.

Peace with honor was a standing joke as the media ridiculed and satirized every traditional aspect of American society. As the *National Lampoon* inquired on the cover of its January 1972 issue: *Is Nothing Sacred?* The only thing that mattered to me anymore was just getting my ass back home in one piece.

The young grenadier in the 12th had it far worse than I ever did, but he never abandoned his beliefs. He was willing to die for them. Even though his war seemed lost, he didn't worry about saving himself. He was on "a holy task" to save his people and homeland.

I stared at the computer screen and felt overwhelmed by this boy's sense of purpose and self-sacrifice for the good of others. How had he kept his beliefs while I had lost mine?

I looked at the clock and saw it was getting late. Answering that question would have to wait for another day.

CHAPTER 6: THE BEAST

The next morning, Cynthia and I sat down with our morning coffee to watch the news. This had become a welcome routine since I retired. We could never do this when I was working; either I left early for work, or I was away on business. I terribly missed her back then, but I sucked it up and did what needed to be done. It was a lesson I learned early in life.

I sat by her side, sipped my coffee, and felt comforted by her presence. I never knew that feeling as a child. Although I sought my parents' love and attention, neither was forthcoming. My childhood was mostly spent alone in my room, playing with toy soldiers, or reading books for hours.

I gazed over at Cynthia and smiled.

"What are you thinking, Will?"

"What a pleasure it is to be with you."

"You are so full of shit." She returned my smile with her eyes glowing.

"No, I mean it. I spent so many years away when I was working, and now the last two days were spent with Johann and researching my notes. I'm sorry, honey. I missed you."

"Well, don't go overboard with this, Will. I don't want you to get all obsessed to the point where nothing else matters. You were like that with your work and any other project you did around the house. It was almost like you were possessed."

"You're right. In a way, I was." I looked straight into her eyes. "It was my father; he criticized everything I did and made me feel worthless." I looked down at the floor, weighed down by the memories. "So, I worked hard and obsessed over everything I ever did, hoping to be better than everybody else, to prove him wrong." I kept looking down as I remembered all the hurt and all my struggles to overcome it. "He never let up on me and his criticism just burned into me. So I just kept at something until I succeeded."

She looked surprised at my sudden confession. "Well, he's gone now." Her expression softened, possibly because she was thinking of her deceased father, who was very close to her. "But don't you ever miss him? Not even a little?"

I felt like I was going to laugh but held it back. "I don't miss him one bit, and I'll never forget how badly my parents treated you as well."

"I know," she sighed. "I still can't believe how they ignored me when they visited you after the stroke. It was like I wasn't there at all."

"Well, like I said back then, welcome to the club."

That visit was the last straw for me. I cut all ties after that and never saw them again. My father died five years later, and my mother passed on several years after him. I didn't attend either funeral.

We finished our coffee, and I returned to my study, lost in thought about my childhood. I tried everything to be a good son, hoping to gain some praise or affection from my father, but I couldn't remember a single occasion when that ever happened.

Something as simple as playing a game of catch with him would turn into a nightmare of intimidation. When I dropped a catch or missed a throw, he would express disappointment in me. When I did it a second time, he would sneer contemptuously and make a cutting remark about my abilities. When I became self-conscious, and it happened a third time, he would throw his glove down, glaring at me for a second, and then head back into the house. He left me there feeling ashamed of my performance and angry at his. After several more disappointments, I went out of my way to avoid him.

When I was ten years old, I discovered a box tucked away in our garage. It contained my father's Army uniform, an insignia taken from a German uniform, and a book on his division's history. He was a paratrooper in the 17th Airborne Division. I recalled paging through that book and seeing pictures of the men in training, fighting in the Battle of the Bulge, and later crossing the Rhine.

The show *Combat!* premiered on television that year, and I tried to get him to watch it with me, but he snapped at me, saying he had had enough of that "crap." After that reaction, I was afraid to say or ask anything about what I found in the garage.

He never spoke about his experiences in the war, even after I joined the Marines. But, then again, he never told me much of anything. He never offered any explanations for how or why the world worked the way that it did. I had to figure most things out by myself.

My mother, however, did her best to raise an accomplished and cultured son. She pushed me to learn the piano, read as many books as possible, join the Cub Scouts, Boy Scouts, and church youth group, and get good marks in school. She had me take on a paper route to learn responsibility and encouraged me to become a minister. I would read the Bible with her and repeat passages from memory to impress her. She would listen and tell me what a good boy I was but never explained the verses or asked what I thought they meant. I had to figure them out for myself, and they served me well during some rough patches later in life.

My mother loved to talk about her sons to impress others. She was proud of what she had produced but never challenged or questioned my father's rage against her or against us. She took his abuse like a good Prussian. I did as well until I turned eighteen and left the house to join the Marines. The abuse he heaped on me reminded me of being in the beast's snare. I writhed in shame and anger until the stroke freed me from it.

I reclined in my study chair and tried to remember the first time I became aware of being trapped by it. I was twelve years old. It happened on my paper route. Every day, I had to get up at 5 a.m. to deliver the papers in all sorts of weather. Every two weeks, I had to collect money from my customers. Most were pleasant and paid on time, but a few were chronically delinquent.

I had to pay for those scofflaws out of my own pocket and then make several trips back and forth until they finally reimbursed me. As I lugged the heavy bag of papers each morning, I began to resent these people for cheating, humiliating, and inconveniencing me.

An unaccustomed urge arose to get even with them. It goaded me each morning to square accounts. My conscience, however, always pushed back, reminding me that they always paid sooner or later. But the urge persisted. I finally gave in one morning. Instead of placing a paper on their front porch, I grabbed it and threw it into their bushes or, if it was raining, into a puddle.

When they remained chronically delinquent, I'd up the ante. I'd spit on their paper. It felt good to mete out justice. It was only a matter of time before someone saw me and complained to my parents. My father came home after work and bellowed his favorite complaint: "What's wrong with you?" My mother stood by his side, put her hand on her face, and said she was embarrassed and ashamed.

I stood there and sucked up my punishment. By this time, I learned my father would criticize anything I did. My mother never questioned him but just stood by. They didn't ask why I did it or how I felt. However, I no longer cared how they treated me by this time. I gave up the paper route soon after that.

My next memory of being entangled in the beast's snare came several months later. I was at Boy Scout summer camp. Our troop was lined up for dinner outside the mess hall. A boy grabbed my Scout hat and wouldn't give it back. He enjoyed watching me trying to retrieve it while the other boys laughed.

The Scout leader finally intervened and blamed both of us for starting trouble. He made him give it back to me, and I was satisfied with that. But the other boys weren't. They heckled me during dinner because I couldn't retrieve the hat on my own and said I should fight him to get even. The boy who took my hat sat there sporting a smug grin.

Although I was prepared to forget the whole thing, the boy kept grinning and making faces at me while the others continued mocking me. Once again, my conscience said to wait it out, and it would all go away, but the beast replied that I would be labeled a coward for life unless I took the fight. My stomach was churning because I knew fighting was wrong, and, frankly, I didn't want to get hurt. But I finally gave in and agreed to a fight after we returned home.

When our camping trip was over, everyone got together after our next troop meeting and clamored for a fight. They egged us on as we squared off and began throwing punches. I had no desire to hit the kid or get hit, so I danced around until a glancing blow landed on my cheek. It hurt, and then I saw the smirk returning on his face. A blind rage came over me. I threw a punch so hard it broke my hand as it landed on his face.

His nose began bleeding while my hand blew up, turning an ugly shade of black and blue. The fight ended in silence as we separated to tend to our wounds while the hyenas backed off in silence.

I trudged home, knowing I had to face my parents. My father blew up. He looked at my hand and blamed me for getting into a fight. He bellowed out his usual complaint, asking what the heck was wrong with me. He didn't wait for an answer. He stormed off to get his keys to drive us to the hospital while my mother looked on helplessly.

We all sat silently during the drive. My hand was broken, but I felt vindicated. I learned how anger and a quick blow could get me redress. Once again, I felt satisfied that justice had been served.

I looked up at my study's ceiling and wondered, was it my father's abuse that drove me to seek revenge and justice? Before I could answer, another question came to mind. What made him so abusive towards his son?

CHAPTER 7: PRELUDE

About ten years ago, my father died. I didn't learn about it until my brother sent me a package. It contained copies of letters written by my father to his mother during the war. He also included a printed email sent by my father to his grandchildren shortly before he died. My brother said the email was written like an epitaph, recounting events from my father's life, including his time in the war. My brother thought I might be interested in reading them, but I wasn't. I filed them away unread. But now, I was curious.

I swiveled in my chair, opened a drawer in the file cabinet, and began searching, While rifling through the files, I wondered if my father's problems stemmed from the war. He was only eighteen when he enlisted, just like Johann and me.

I found the letters and email. I piled them on my desk and opened the email first. I began skimming through it until I found a reference to his time in the war. He wrote his division was rushed out of England shortly before Christmas 1944 to counter the German offensive in the Battle of the Bulge. He wrote it was one of the worst winters in European history. After landing in northern France, they slogged through snow and bitter cold for two weeks before they reached the front.

I decided to go online to verify what he had written. Research showed his division arrived in France on Christmas Day and finally reached the front in Belgium on January 7th, 1945. It was one of the worst winters on record. So far, so good. He wrote it was early that day when they were first ordered into combat. They were gathered at the edge of a large, open field that was covered with nearly two feet of snow. Their orders were to assault the German positions in the woods on the other side of that field. They discarded their winter gear to move quickly through the open terrain.

I pictured the scene and had a flashback to my first deer hunt. I was twelve years old and was standing on the edge of a similar, snow-covered field at the break of dawn. I was straining to see if there were any deer in the thick woods on the other side of the field. I remember being just as scared as my father must have been, but for different reasons. I feared the prospect of killing something, whereas he faced the prospect of being killed.

My father never went deer hunting after the war. He said my uncle would have to take me if I wanted to go. Deer hunting was a Barnes' family tradition, so I reached out to him. He helped me get ready and told me glorified tales of previous hunts as we drove up to my other uncle's farm.

I remember pausing before crossing that field. My conscience whispered it was wrong to kill, and the memory would haunt me if I did. But the beast whispered that this was a necessary rite of passage. If I returned to the farmhouse, I would be stamped a failure by the rest of the extended family.

The thought of failing made me angry. I pushed aside any reservations and crossed the field. I stopped at the wood's edge and quickly pulled off one glove to load my rifle. The cold gripped my fingers as I pulled the first bullet from my jacket. I looked at the lead tip of the bullet and scraped my fingernail across it, leaving a mark.

My uncle said the soft tip would burst on impact, and the fragments would rip through the deer's insides. There was no question that if I hit anywhere on the deer, it would be seriously disabled. I kept that thought in mind as I grimly pushed each bullet into the rifle with a resounding click.

I took my position in a cluster of trees and waited. The sun had yet to rise above the horizon, and I was told that the deer usually came out slightly before dawn to feed. After a few minutes, there was a slight rustling sound at my side. Several does gingerly stepped out of the woods to graze in the field, followed by a buck.

I slowly took the rifle off safety, raised it to my shoulder, looked down through the iron sights and followed my uncle's advice: "Aim for the heart, right behind the shoulder and slowly squeeze the trigger." As the bullet exploded, the buck jumped and ran back into the woods. The does followed close behind, their tails waving like white flags. I was dumbfounded. The resounding boom had momentarily shocked me, but I knew the deer was hit. I lowered my rifle and trotted over to where the buck had jumped.

A bright red spray covered the snow, and a blood trail led into the forest. My heart was racing. Any reluctance about killing was gone. All I could think about was claiming my trophy and winning accolades from my relatives. However, my uncle said the first thing to do after shooting a deer was to wait a few minutes. You didn't want to follow too soon, or you might spook it, and it would keep running. Instead, you wanted it to tire, lie down, and bleed to death.

After waiting a few minutes, I started tracking, and it wasn't long before I saw something lying on the ground ahead. It was the deer. There was a huge, gaping wound in its rib cage with a piece of lung protruding from it. The mass of lung was covered with foaming, oxygenated blood that was coated with white particles of splintered bone.

Its tongue hung out of its mouth, and its eyes were open but lifeless. I walked behind it, as I was taught, avoiding the sharp hooves if it suddenly kicked. I prodded its head with the business end of my rifle. It was dead.

I had never seen such gore before. A wave of remorse washed over me. No one ever told me what it was like to kill your first deer; either they forgot or didn't care or, like me, kept it inside and lived quietly with the guilt.

My older cousin was close enough to hear the shot, and he came over. I was kneeling over the deer with a knife in my hand. I didn't know how to gut it, so he stepped me through the process.

To this day, I can still see him slicing off the deer's genitals and throwing them away like so much garbage. He slit open the abdomen, and a huge pile of steaming, purple guts came streaming out. He cut through the membranes that held them to the body, letting them slide out onto the frozen ground in a steaming pile. He left them there for the scavengers. The sight of blood or a corpse never bothered me after that experience. I tied the hind legs together and dragged the carcass back down the mountain.

Despite all the bragging and backslapping that night in the farmhouse, I never felt happy or proud about what I did that day. I only felt shame and a simmering resentment for betraying my conscience. I was initiated into the world of men, but the death of that deer still weighs on me.

CHAPTER 8: REVELATIONS

I shook off memories of my past and returned to reading my father's email. His unit, Easy Company, began their assault around 8 a.m. There was little visibility as they advanced through a heavy, low-hanging fog across the open field. They almost made it to the other side when German mortars and MG42 machine guns opened fire.

I looked up the German MG42. It was capable of firing 1300 rounds per minute, which is roughly 21 rounds a second. There was nothing like it at the time. Its rapid rate of fire made a unique tearing sound. American soldiers called it "Hitler's Buzzsaw." The Soviets called it "the linoleum ripper." The German soldiers called it *Hitlersäge* (Hitler's saw) or *Singende Säge* (Bone Saw).

I paused when I read this and imagined running across an open field covered in two feet of snow while a hail of bullets came flying at me through a thick fog. Their baptism into combat must have been terrifying. My father wrote they did not go to ground since there was nowhere to hide. They scrambled the last remaining yards until they reached the woods and took cover. They had several casualties before firing a shot.

He wrote that their captain radioed the battalion commander for help. *We're getting heavy fire,* he quoted the captain. *My right platoon is practically wiped out.* Easy Company had already lost between 20 and 30 men. The battalion commander asked where they were, but the captain couldn't get a fix on his position.

I went back online and found the Regimental records for that day. They showed at 09:38, *2d Bn still on phase line A – cannot advance due to MG fire.* Easy Company was part of the Second Battalion.

The shaken captain and his men were pinned down. German machine gun fire was chewing up the trees overhead, and large splinters flew down, wounding his men. They couldn't move, and their nightmare kept getting worse as the fog began to lift. It would have been suicide to retreat across that open field.

The Regimental records had an entry made at 10:15 a.m. that stated: *E Company 100 yards from phase line b, struck by heavy automatic fire and mortar fire.* My father wrote it was about 10:30 when the captain told him to run along the edge of the woods to find help. My father started running but quickly hit the ground once the machine guns started tracking his steps.

He crawled through the woods until he found another squad. Their situation was just as bad, and they could not help anyone. He wrote, *Things were pretty confusing from this point on as I tried to play catch-up with my squad.* I stopped reading at this point because his statement didn't make any sense. Why did things get *pretty confusing from this point on?* He had only left his squad a few minutes earlier. They were pinned down and weren't going anywhere.

Why did he have to *play catch up* with them? Understandably, he was probably confused. He was pinned down in a strange location under enemy fire. But all he had to do was retrace his steps in the snow to return to his unit.

I continued to read the email and noticed his style of writing changed. It began to read as if it came from a narrative of the battle from another book. There were no personal observations or feelings on the rest of the day's events, and I wondered why.

However, his writing changed back to a first-person narrative as he wrote about events later that day when Easy Company began its withdrawal at dusk. *Somewhere during this withdrawal, I was still trying to get to my squad and came to the clearing where the tank was located. I got out into the clearing when I looked to my left and saw the tank. I thought at that point that it all was over. I ran to the edge of the woods, where a GI was lying and hit the ground next to him. I started talking to him and, getting no response, realized he was dead.*

This really hit me because he didn't look as if he had a wound. Off to my right, I could see our guys retreating, and at that particular moment, the artillery came in as heavy as I had ever experienced. I just lay there and was really shaken up. I tried to get a cigarette out of my pocket but was shaking so badly that I just couldn't do it. When the artillery let up, I took off running in the direction of the retreating group.

I went back online to review the Regimental records and saw an entry was made at 16:20 (4:20 pm): *Chalk White withdrawing. Arty and Mortar fire extremely heavy.* Chalk White was the code name for the 2nd Battalion, my father's unit. I stared at the computer screen and suddenly realized why my father hadn't written any first-hand accounts between 10:30, when he was trying to play *catch-up with my squad,* and 16:20, when he wrote, *during this withdrawal, I was still trying to get to my squad.*

During that six-hour gap, he must have squirreled himself away in the woods, more concerned with saving his own life than with risking a return to help his squad. Easy Company was no further away than the distance he had just crawled.

I was stunned by this discovery and went back to the Internet to research further. I found a website dedicated to the 50th reunion of the 17th Airborne Division. The website posted several interviews with the veterans, including my father, who told the interviewer about the dead GI. The interviewer remarked that this incident *"deeply marked"* my father's life, *and since then, he has kept these facts in his memory as one of the most terrible of his life.*

The interviewer's comment made me pause. Did those *terrible* memories account for his terrible behavior later in life? Did the sight of that dead GI's face linger to condemn him for not returning to help his squad? Whatever the reason, the experience must have unnerved him, for he failed to take one of the dead soldier's dog tags. This was a fundamental duty of any soldier as it would help identify and recover the body later. He was only thinking of himself.

I turned away from the computer and read the rest of my father's email: *The Colonel saw me the next morning trying to get up with my rifle as a prop and said, and I remember this clearly, 'Son, you're not going anywhere' and had the litter bearers carry me to the aid station. I was told when I got to the second aid station further back that the first aid station had been blown up soon after I was evacuated.*

The rest of my career was spent in the hospital, and I was most fortunate in not losing my feet. When they cut the boots off me, they were completely black. I did get a medical discharge, and I sure consider myself as a 20-year-old kid very lucky to have survived.

I put down his email and rifled through the other letters. There was one written from boot camp to his mother. He sounded full of piss and vinegar, ready to kill some Germans. It reminded me of a loudmouth named Davis, who was in boot camp with me. He was yapping on the bus ride to Parris Island about how he couldn't wait to get to Vietnam so he could kill some VC.

A couple of weeks later, Davis dropped out of a run. A cluster of DIs swarmed around him, screaming at him to get up. But he didn't. The next day, he was sent to the Motivation Platoon. This was a one-day assignment where recruits were subjected to grueling punishment to remind them that quitting was not an option. He returned to the barracks at the end of the day, covered in mud. He was dragging his rifle behind him all the way down the squad bay to his bunk. He undressed, went into the showers, and cut his wrists. Davis's false bravado vanished that day, much as my father did in the Ardennes.

After that day in the Ardennes, he was sent to the rear to be treated, carrying all the shame that stayed with him for the rest of his life. No wonder he was angry. No wonder he couldn't show love to his wife or children. He was too wrapped up in himself to think about others. He was consumed with hiding the truth of what happened that day.

I stretched back in my desk chair and had a revelation. It came from a verse by Saint Matthew: *For whoever wishes to save his life will lose it; but whoever loses his life for My sake will find it.*

By focusing on his survival rather than on the lives of others, he condemned himself to a lifetime of shame, fear, and anger. He was ashamed of his behavior and feared others would discover what had happened that day. And he was angry because it never left him. As far as I know, he went to his grave that way.

I put down the email and realized that remembering that verse was the first positive thing that ever came from my father. And then another verse sprang to mind: *For I, the Lord, your God, am a jealous God, punishing the children for the sin of their fathers to the third and fourth generation of those who hate me...* I didn't know how my father felt about God, but I can bet that he cursed Him out plenty that day and each day thereafter.

January 7, 1945 was my family's day of infamy. Each of us was punished for the sins he committed that day.

He force-fed me all his fear, shame, and anger while I was growing up. I hated how it tasted, how it went down, and how it never left me until my stroke. I looked down at the letters and saw the wisdom of an old adage: what you hate in others is what you hate most in yourself.

I swept all the letters back into the folder, threw the folder into the drawer, and slammed it shut. I regretted ever opening it. I don't know why, but I suddenly felt the need to reconnect with Johann. I called, and we agreed to meet tomorrow.

I hung up the phone and looked at the clock. It was time for dinner. I still hadn't reviewed all my notes and wondered about FDR and his financial dealings in Germany. However, I was emotionally exhausted and called it a day.

~ 2ND VISIT ~

CHAPTER 9: JOHANN'S FIRST POINT

I left early the next morning to visit Johann. I was not as positive as I had been last night about seeing him. Cynthia's concerns about him were still resonating with me.

I entered the Garden Room and found Johann sitting in the same space as last time. He was reading the same book with the same coffee cup by his side. The old woman in the wheelchair was sitting on the other side of the room, reading a book as well. I glanced over and saw the title, *The Last of the Just.* I made a mental note of it.

When I left the last time, she said something in a foreign language. I forgot to write it down, but now I couldn't even remember what it was. It didn't sound too friendly at the time, so I quickly walked past her. Fortunately, she didn't look up.

Johann seemed pleased to see me. He smiled and stood up to greet me. After we sat down, I asked him to wait a moment while I wrote something down. It was the title of that woman's book. He was watching me and seemed a bit miffed.

"What are you writing, Willi?"

"Oh, just the name of the book that woman is reading."

"Do you know her? You said something to her as you left the last time."

I grinned because I didn't think he noticed. "No, I don't know her. I just stopped to apologize to her since I thought we were probably too loud and might have disturbed her."

Johann looked at her and frowned. "She came here last month. She keeps mostly to herself and doesn't mix much. She doesn't look well if you ask me."

I shrugged and decided to start right in. "Listen, Johann, when I left the last time, you said you wanted to share a few more things with me. What were they?"

He sipped his coffee and then leaned forward in his chair. "Yes, I did. When you said you wanted to hear my story to learn more about your mother's roots, I decided to share a few points with you that I developed after years of research. We'll discuss them one at a time since they build on each other. I hope that's all right with you."

That sounded like a good excuse to keep me on the hook, but I was willing to listen. "Sure, that's why I'm here."

"*Gut*! Let's get started, then. You'll just have to stop me if I get too boring." He smiled, sat back, and grabbed his cup to take another sip while I prepared to take some notes. "Well, Willi, the first point is this: evil begets evil."

He kept staring at me as I looked up from my notebook and held his gaze. "Well, that's nothing new, Johann. Everyone knows that the man on the cover of your book was the evilest person in history. He started the war and the Holocaust."

"I am talking about the evil that brought him into power, Willi." He stopped to let his statement sink in and fixed his eyes on me, waiting for a response.

"As best as I can recall, Johann, the evil that drove him to power was the Nazis' hatred toward the Jews and their anger over the Treaty of Versailles."

He smiled. "Well, you seem to be a well-informed young man, Willi. What sort of work did you use to do?"

"I was a consultant."

"Always asking questions, always thinking. Am I right?"

"That was my job. Also reaching conclusions and making recommendations."

"Well, there are still a lot of things for you to learn, Willi. Our hatred and anger were actually directed toward an evil that preceded those two issues. You'll see what they were after I finish today."

Uh oh. Now I stepped into it. I knew I shouldn't have come back for a second visit. This conversation was already headed south. "What are you talking about, Johann?"

He ignored my question as he looked down and began scrolling through his iPad. "This little thing is so handy. Before, I had to sift through mounds of paper to find anything. Now, everything is at my fingertips." He paused to look up and smile at me. "I'll tell you what I'm talking about. When I was growing up, my parents used to talk a lot about history and politics over the dinner table, and I learned a lot from their discussions; it formed my *Weltanschauung*. Do you know what that means, Willi?"

"Worldview. You mentioned that the last time I was here. I studied Hegel in college."

"Very good. You are a bright boy! Your mother must be proud."

"She's passed, Johann." I let it go since I didn't want to pursue it any further. He must have sensed my reluctance as he turned his attention back to the iPad.

"I am sorry to hear that, Willi. Shall I continue?"

"Yes, please do."

He paused to resume scrolling through his iPad while I thought about my dinner times as a child. There were never such discussions around our dinner table. My father was an intimidating presence to all of us. Anything I learned growing up came from books, movies, television, or on the street.

"My father was in the Army during the First World War. He often mentioned that the war was strictly a European affair, and that America should never have been involved. America entered the war to tilt the scales in the Allies' favor. But when President Wilson announced his Fourteen Points to end the war, my father said everyone was hopeful that they would be adopted and the fighting would finally end.

"Wilson's points were radical at the time since they didn't include any reparations, plunder, or lands gained during the war. Both sides would just stop shooting and return to where they were before the war. The Allies printed those Fourteen Points and then airdropped them on our soldiers and citizens. They hoped that would convince the Kaiser to end the war as soon as possible."

I had several courses on American history in high school and college but only a vague recollection of this turn of events. "I knew Wilson championed the League of Nations, but I don't remember much more than that, Johann. What exactly were those Fourteen Points?"

He nodded. "I'm surprised you remembered one of them, Willi. There's a good reason why: history has mostly forgotten them. Wilson outlined his Fourteen Points for Peace to Congress on January 8, 1918. The major points were self-determination for all nations, mutual disarmament of all parties, no spoils of war and the return of any captured territories to their pre-war borders. He also called for forming a League of Nations, as you correctly remembered. This organization would settle any disputes regarding how these goals would be achieved."

As he finished this last sentence, his expression became harsh, and his next words spewed out like bullets. "Based on these principles and other conditions, Germany agreed to an Armistice on November 11th of that year. Germany then complied with the Armistice and disarmed while the Allies went off to draft the Peace Treaty of Versailles.

"The Allies presented the final draft to Germany on May 7th, 1919, and none of those fourteen points were included except for the League of Nations; the other thirteen were replaced with harsh terms that severely punished us and strengthened the Allies' position in Europe." He paused to look back down and find his place on the iPad. I didn't say anything out of fear of riling him up further.

"When Germany reviewed those draft terms, they were shocked and quickly submitted a revised version on May 29th. The Allies promptly rejected it. Then, on June 17th, the Allies told Germany they had five days to sign the treaty as-is, or they would invade and occupy Germany, a simple feat now that Germany had disarmed and was still suffering from the blockade."

I stopped taking notes and looked up. "What blockade are you talking about, Johann?"

"In 1915, Britain placed a naval blockade around Germany even though it violated international law at the time. It was never removed, even after the Armistice was signed. Conditions became so desperate inside Germany that people began dying of starvation and disease."

He paused to scroll through his iPad. "Listen to this, Willi. In December 1918, the National Health Office in Berlin estimated that seven-hundred and sixty-three thousand civilians died from that blockade. Churchill, the Secretary of the British Navy at the time, called the blockade his *"starvation policy."* He wanted to, and I quote, *"starve the whole population – men, women, and children, old and young, wounded and sound – into submission"* until Germany signed the Versailles treaty."[1]

Why had I never heard about this before? I shook my head as I wrote "Wilson and fourteen points; Churchill and blockade" and underlined both for emphasis. If all this checked out, then he might be onto something.

"My father was very angry that we were strong-armed into signing that Treaty; it tore his heart to see our territory stripped away from us, especially those lands that were used to create Poland. Those lands were only a few kilometers east of Breslau, our home, and still contained our fellow Germans. My parents became especially fearful when the Allies also carved up the Austro-Hungarian Empire to create Yugoslavia and Czechoslovakia, leaving the resident Germans disenfranchised. Those new states would now be beholden to the Allies who had created them."

He closed his iPad, stood up to stretch, and looked down into my eyes. "Those events formed my worldview, Willi. My country was torn apart and victimized by a few powerful men who engineered a deceitful Armistice. They followed that by drafting a rapacious Treaty that we were forced into signing. They legitimatized their appetite for more power and wealth by having that Treaty signed under duress and creating a new international order that would be controlled by the League of Nations."

He placed the iPad on the table, and his face was still flushed as he exclaimed. "And that was the system I grew up in, Willi, and it cried out for justice and retribution!"

His sudden outburst made me sit back. I came here today to gain more insight into his character and our family history, but he blew past that and made me question my worldview. The first visit with him was bad enough when he said we were both raised the same way. Now he was telling me that the foundation of the system I grew up in was flawed, filled with deceit and extortion.

I shook my head, befuddled by this new perspective on world history. That's when I noticed the old woman in the wheelchair was glaring at us. I decided to excuse myself before any trouble began and made a beeline for the men's room. I briskly walked past her without saying a word.

CHAPTER 10: UPROOTED

I felt disoriented leaving the Garden Room. Johann's latest barrage of facts had uprooted me, leaving me dangling and clueless about where all this was taking me. This was not a new experience for me, however. I had been uprooted several times before and none of them had ended well, which made me think the worst was yet to come with Johann.

The first time was when my father moved us from a small, older town in the country to a modern development in the suburbs. Although the move was only five miles away, it might as well have been to another world. I was fourteen at the time.

My hometown was set in a small valley, nestled between two mountains; one of them was entirely forested while the other mountain held half of our town. The other half of town lay in the small valley. A slow-moving river meandered through the valley. A canal ran alongside it. I lived in the valley. There were plenty of exploring opportunities for a young boy.

The town had grown in layers over the years; each one filled with a different group of settlers from different places. The first group to arrive in town were several local farmers. They had decided in the late 1700s to build a milling business.

The next layer came on the heels of the First Industrial Revolution in the early 1800s. Farmers came to our town to work in the growing steel mill. They preferred the security of steady pay in the mill to the vagaries of agriculture. In the mid-to-late 1800s, European immigrants began to arrive. They sought new opportunities in our country as their continent experienced one war after another.

I grew up in the '50s when the town still had locally owned stores. They were good places to meet people and socialize with them. Memorial Day was a big event for us. The American Legion planted small flags over veterans' tombstones each year to honor their memory. One year, I was chosen to read the *Gettysburg Address* at the service held in the cemetery. The next year, I was chosen again to read the poem *In Flanders Fields*. I still remember one line from that poem: *We are the dead.* It gave me a terrible sense of foreboding when I read it over the microphone into a pervasive silence.

Getting uprooted from that environment and planted into a 60's suburb was traumatic. The old town's character and diversity were displaced by the uniform sprawl of newly constructed homes designed by a single developer. There was no break in the choking monotony. There were no mountains, canals, or rivers to play in, and no local shops to visit and socialize. There was only a monolithic shopping mall several miles away. The sterile modernity left me feeling totally disoriented.

Life got worse after that move. The tragedy of Vietnam began playing out on the nightly news, along with reports of race riots and political assassinations. The flower-child movement gave way to violent anti-war demonstrations. Sentiments of love and peace were displaced with hate and fear. As I thought about it, the political turbulence and fear of Communism during that time reminded me of what Johann had told me about his childhood.

I walked down the hall toward the men's room while my mind scrolled forward to my senior year in high school. I had been accepted at several colleges, but I was desperate to leave my family and a changing world I no longer wanted to be a part of.

I anxiously awaited turning eighteen because I could enlist in the Marines without my parents' permission. The thought of being killed or wounded didn't faze me because nothing looked good from where I stood. I just wanted to get away from it all.

I joined the day after my eighteenth birthday and told my parents later that evening. My father exploded while my mother stood by in genuine horror. He said I didn't know what I was getting into. He said it was another stupid idea of mine, especially since I was already accepted at several colleges. My mother turned away from both of us. She always became deathly afraid whenever he lost his temper, which was often.

He didn't ask any questions about why I had joined and didn't listen when I tried to explain myself. He just droned on like a broken record, playing the same belittling lyrics over and over again. However, this time, I didn't suck up his abuse. I stood my ground and screamed out that I was sick of his yelling, his criticism, and his lack of support. I was going, and that was that. I angrily ripped my shirt apart in frustration, turned away and stormed upstairs to my room.

The door was shut, so I punched a hole right through its cheap veneer panel. Nobody came to talk to me after that. But the old man was right. I had no idea what I was getting myself into. My second round of being uprooted was about to begin.

CHAPTER 11: THE NEEDS OF WAR

I opened the door to the men's room, still ruminating over my past. Johann had just punched holes into the worldview that channeled my life. Not that I was ever comfortable with it. In fact, my dissatisfaction with it led to my leaving mainstream society to enlist in the Marines.

I went into the Marines as a street-smart kid, who came of age in a blue-collar steel town. I felt tough enough to weather anything, but Parris Island proved to be a totally different universe. The Drill Instructors, or DIs as we called them, were trained killers. They screamed, cursed, and bludgeoned us into meeting *the needs of war* as defined by our National Security Act of 1947. They were determined to stamp out all aspects of our prior lives. They snarled, *God may own your soul, but your ass is mine.*

I arrived on Parris Island in early July. Every day was well into the nineties with a hundred percent humidity. We ran and did more pushups, jumping jacks, and squat thrusts than there were sand fleas on that island. Every workout wrung a pool of sweat from us. We gobbled salt tablets like M&Ms. It was a relentless cycle of pain and abuse.

They ran us around an open track each day for three miles in the blazing sun with our combat boots, PT shorts, T-shirt, and cover. The DIs would chant cadence to keep pace: *Never stop … never quit … PT … good for me …* I was too scared to quit and told myself that if someone ever fell in front of me, I would run right over him to stay in formation.

I never thought of quitting. If that happened, I'd be given a General or Dishonorable Discharge, which would brand me a failure and prove my father right. I felt a desperate need to survive as the DIs tried everything to break us.

A cold, steady rage emerged as I was pushed to my limit, and it hardened my being. This was no temporary fix; it evolved into a permanent, steely-eyed focus that drove me to not only survive but also to excel. No one would ever threaten or humiliate me again. I was determined never to be shamed again. Those feelings never left me until the stroke stripped them away, along with my old *persona*.

I had a strong belief in God and brought along my pocket Bible to boot camp; it was the only thing from my prior life that I was allowed to keep. Church services were held every Sunday, and I went there hoping to find some respite from the hell around me. The interior of the chapel was dark and less than idyllic. There were no stained windows or religious images, only murals of Marines in battle over the years. I couldn't believe my eyes.

Once the sermon started, my astonishment turned to disgust. The chaplain began railing against the evils of communism, saying we would be doing God's work by killing godless Communists. I never went back and wondered what kind of system would train eighteen-year-old kids to become stone-cold killers.

By the end of boot camp, I had lost all faith in humanity. We became no better than fighting dogs, beaten, and prodded into attacking anything that threatened us. We had no second thoughts about killing someone who wanted to kill us and were prepared to face either outcome. I didn't realize it at the time, but the voice of my conscience had waned considerably while that of the beast had waxed in both frequency and volume.

I positioned myself over the urinal, closed my eyes, and let nature take its course. I was thinking about returning to Johann when my father's words rang in my ears: *you have no idea what you're getting into.* I didn't know then and didn't know now. I quickly zipped up and left the men's room reluctantly.

On the walk back, I resumed thinking about my training. While the DIs at boot camp conditioned our minds and bodies for war, the troop handlers at Infantry Training in Camp Lejeune taught us how to wage it. We went on 12-mile force marches with full pack and rifle, simulated combat patrols, and conducted night ambushes. We learned how to deploy from helicopters and how to set and identify booby traps. We fired every infantry weapon in the Marine Corps arsenal.

I reveled in this environment, keeping the same cool rage and focus that allowed me to survive in boot camp. At the end of the training, I earned a meritorious promotion to Private First Class.

We finished training at the end of 1970 when the war was mostly over for American ground troops. I was sent to a duty station in the continental US, but my simmering rage against the Corps never diminished. I hated their system and what it did to us. All the while, the beast kept urging me to not only survive but to excel and beat them at their own game.

A year later, I was awarded a second meritorious promotion to corporal by beating out every other qualified candidate in the 1st Marine Division. Six months later, I was sent to Vietnam with the 1St Marine Airwing, and six months later, our squadron was redeployed to Japan where I was promoted to sergeant.

I paused in front of the Garden Room doors. My troubled feelings about this visit began to resurface, but I sucked them up and passed through the doors. There were still more points to hear from Johann. I wondered if they would be as impactful.

I walked in and touched his shoulder to let him know I was back. I hoped the rest of my time with him wouldn't end as badly as my time did in the Marines.

CHAPTER 12: THINGS LIKE THAT HAPPEN

"Ah, you're back, Willi." He smiled and pointed to two fresh cups of coffee. "Look, I took care of us while you were gone. Are you ready to pick up where we left off?"

"Sure." I sat down and opened my notebook, unsure what topic was coming next.

"Well, as I was saying, after the Treaty was signed, my father and many like him felt angry, humiliated, and powerless. After the Kaiser abdicated, the new Republic proved itself to be ineffective in guarding us from the inroads of the East and West. Once the Depression came, unemployment, poverty, and civil unrest increased. National Socialism came into power only because it had a forceful leader who was tightly focused on our survival and restoring our greatness."

He paused to sit back in his chair while I stopped writing to look up at him. His choice of words eerily mirrored my thoughts during boot camp, survive and then excel. His eyes were fixed on mine as he took a sip of coffee and continued. "You must have heard that Hitler seized power after that and turned Germany into a police state, correct?"

"Yeah, that sounds about right"

"Well, Willi, sharpen your pencil. You'll be taking a lot more notes because that's simply not true."

A cold chill ran over me as I remembered why I had to take a break. He had upset my views on recent history, and now he was about to serve up another helping of the same dish.

"I won't get into all the chaos of the Twenties, Willi. Suffice it to say that the Weimar Republic sputtered along until the 1932 elections. The first one to be held that year was in July with no winning majority party. The second one was held in November with similar results. However, the National Socialists did manage to get the highest percentage of votes in both elections."

Johann looked down at his iPad to check his facts and continued. "Hindenburg was president then, and he had to form a government. Since there was no majority party, he had to pick a chancellor from the party with the highest vote count. Hitler was named chancellor on January 30th, 1933, but the National Socialists didn't have a majority in the Reichstag to pass legislation. However, the Enabling Act was passed on March 23rd. It enabled Hitler's cabinet to enact laws without a Reichstag vote.

"Some people say the Enabling Act was passed because of the Reichstag Fire on February 27th. Hindenburg issued a decree after that event to quell civil unrest. It gave the government control over speech, assembly, privacy, and the free press; it also legalized phone tapping and interception of the mail."

I stopped writing, struck by the similarity to recent events in America. The Homeland Security and Patriot Acts were hurriedly enacted after the 9/11 terrorist attacks. They dramatically expanded the ability of our law enforcement agencies to search for telephone records, e-mail communications, and health records with little oversight.

"After the Reichstag Fire decree was passed, the government arrested some four thousand people, many of whom were Communists, and they were detained indefinitely. Their seats in the

Reichstag were empty, which enabled the Enabling Act to be passed. When Hindenburg died on August 2, 1934, Hitler assumed the title of *Führer und Reichskanzler*, which translates to leader and chancellor. Two weeks later, the government held a referendum on merging these two positions, and ninety percent of the electorate approved. Hitler came into power legally and democratically, Willi. The party did not seize power; it was given to them."

All this was news to me. I avoided acknowledging it by keeping my head down and doodling in my notebook. All this information would have to be validated when I returned home, but for now, I was troubled that a democratic process led up to this.

"I'll wait for you to catch up, Willi."

"Thanks, Johann." I finally got over my shock when a sudden thought arose. "What about that Reichstag fire? Didn't the Nazis set it and blame the Communists?"

Johann dismissed my question with a wave of his hand. "One man was arrested and convicted. He said he acted alone, but no one will ever know what happened, Willi. It's like what happened with the sinking of the Lusitania or the Gulf of Tonkin Incident. Things like that happen, and no one will ever know the truth."

"Well, you may be right about that, Johann. But what about the police state that followed and the persecution of the Jews?"

Johann sat back and looked up at the ceiling. "We'll talk about that second topic later but first let's discuss the other topic."

He paused to reflect a moment before continuing. "Do you remember my saying that we had a lot in common when we grew up?"

"I do, but all that changed after we enlisted. After that, our experiences were very different."

"*Sehr gut!*" he exclaimed, slapping me on the knee. "That's correct! And our two countries grew up in the same fashion as well. Once the war ended, they took off in different directions."

I winced when I heard that. "Well, I'm not so sure about that, Johann. But go ahead, and let's hear what you have to say."

CHAPTER 13: *DAS BIEST*

"Well, let's start by looking into how both countries became police states before the war. When the National Socialists came into power, they blamed the Communists for the fire and all the unrest before and after it. They began arresting them and placing them into concentration camps. This is why they weren't at the Reichstag to vote against the Enabling Act."

He drained his coffee cup and chuckled. "And America did exactly the same thing as Germany a few years before during the Red Scare when the government arrested about ten thousand suspected communists. Most of them were US citizens, but there were five hundred and fifty-six resident aliens who were deported.[1]

"And don't forget what happened during the Forties when America rounded up and imprisoned over a hundred thousand Japanese-Americans, most of whom were American citizens; the government confiscated and sold all their property and then moved them into internment camps. So, you see, Germany was no more of a police state than America; we both put potential troublemakers into jails or concentration camps to survive and thrive as a nation."

I shook my head in disbelief. Why was he continuing to compare our two countries and ourselves? As far as I was concerned, he was comparing apples and oranges to make some kind of connection between the two. I couldn't figure out where he was heading.

"And by the way, Willi, did you know that America was among the first countries to employ concentration camps? Even before Germany?"

"What did you say?" I stopped writing and looked up. "*Among* the first? I thought Germany was the first. When did that happen?" I was surprised by my outburst and half-expected him to get angry and shout back at me, just as my father would have.

He only smiled in return. "Spain first coined the term during the Spanish-American War. They detained Cuban revolutionaries in camps called *reconcentrados*, so you can see how the term concentration camp evolved from that. America actually preceded Spain in this practice, but they used a different term when they rounded up and detained the Native Americans; they called them reservations. However, they used the Spanish term when detaining Filipinos during the Philippine–American War."

I looked at him cynically. "Refresh my memory about the Philippine-American war, Johann." I couldn't wait to hear what he knew about our history.

"Well, like I said, Willi, I researched all of this, and my notes are right here. I told you I did my homework." He paused to scan the iPad. "Here it is. America won the Spanish-American War in 1898 and gained the Philippine islands as war reparations. This was a big feather in America's hat as it gave them a foothold in the Pacific. However, a month after that peace treaty was signed, the Filipinos declared their independence and established their own republic.

"President McKinley ignored their intentions and sent troops to the Philippines to assure their 'benevolent assimilation.' But the First Philippine Republic didn't want America's benevolence and declared war. U.S. troops fought back by herding Filipino civilians into camps by the hundreds of thousands to 'protect' them from the rebels.

"Rampant disease abounded in these crowded, unsanitary camps, and many died. People were tortured to get information about the rebels, and many executions also took place. Supposedly, hundreds of thousands of civilians died during this time. You should be familiar with this tactic, Willi. America did the same to civilians during the Vietnam War with the Strategic Hamlet Program.

"When the U.S. acquired the islands in 1899, they estimated the Philippine population at nine million. By 1908, that estimate dropped to less than eight million. And all of those deaths happened fifty years before the Holocaust, Willi."[2] He put the iPad down and challenged me in a loud and demanding voice. "So, after all this, do you think my country acted any worse than yours did, Willi?"

I couldn't believe his audacity and angrily looked away. The old woman was scowling at us. It looked like she was going to say something, but she only closed her book, placed it on her lap, and wheeled away as far as possible. She stopped by the exit, which meant I'd have to pass by her when I left.

Johann didn't seem to notice either of us as he answered his own rhetorical question. "Well, the history books never noticed it, that's for sure. But I did!" He took a deep breath, closed his eyes, and leaned back to relax.

Once again, I was taken aback by his question and tone. I didn't know how to respond. This guy kept bringing up things I was not aware of. But what really got me was his comments about Nazi Germany's struggle to survive and raise itself above others. It reminded me of my own struggles during boot camp.

"But, Johann, America didn't follow Germany into fascism. Didn't your parents and others understand they were losing their freedom under a police state? Didn't they see their freedoms being eroded?"

He sat back up and chuckled. "We all saw it, Willi, but we all thought it was better than enduring all the chaos and poverty at the time. Most of us were willing to temporarily sacrifice some freedoms so we could survive and build a new Germany that would be accepted, respected, and protected. And once all that was done, then we could return to a normal state of living.

"Say what you will about the book burning, banning questionable art, or the Gestapo's spying, the government did what it had to do to maintain our *Volksgemeinschaft*, to keep our culture and society intact and secure. We all sacrificed something to save our culture and recover our place in the world. He sighed and then dropped his head. "But the war ended all that. After Berlin fell, people scrawled on the bombed-out walls: *Aus der Traum*, which means 'The Dream is Over.'

"What you said earlier about the two of us going in different directions after we enlisted was true. But it also held true about our two countries after the war. Germany lost the war and all its dreams. America won the war and kept its dreams of becoming the world's dominant economic system."

CHAPTER 14: *BIÊN HÒA*

I sat there in silence as I empathized with his notion of lost dreams; mine began disappearing in boot camp and were all but gone after Vietnam. But Johann was right about America. It stayed on course. We chased after our dreams of "free trade" and global expansion, mostly by fighting wars to ensure our dominance.

Despite our humiliating loss in '75, we continued to harbor those dreams. In 1990, we levied shock and awe on Iraq during Operation Desert Storm. In 2001, we launched a full-scale war on global terrorism centered on Afghanistan with Operation Enduring Freedom; that mission was further extended in 2015 with Operation Freedom Sentinel.

Johann suddenly sat up and broke my thoughts. "But that's enough of that! I talked too much already. Now it's my turn to ask you some questions. You already told me you were in the Marines, Willi. What was that like?"

His sudden change in topics surprised me. I chuckled at his ability to quickly shift gears and overtake me. I closed my notebook and slid back into my chair. "Well, it wasn't what I expected, Johann, that's for sure. Even though the war was winding down, I still wanted to join, test myself, and frankly, get out of the house to see the world."

I didn't want to drone on endlessly about those three terrible years, so I paused to organize my thoughts. "I also joined the

Marines to be part of the best. I wanted to find purpose and honor in my life."

He inched forward, interested.

"When I got to the induction center, a bunch of guys were already gathered in a big room waiting to be sworn in. One of the uniformed men in charge began to sort everybody out, beginning with the draftees; they told them to gather in the middle of the room. There was a lot of muttering and whining as they shuffled into a group. I stayed behind with the smaller group of volunteers. We were told to move into one of the four corners assigned to each branch of service. The corners for the Air Force and Navy wound up holding the largest numbers of individuals. The Army held very few, and the Marines still fewer."

Johann was listening intently. I also saw out of the corner of my eye that the old woman was watching us. She had a painful expression, and I couldn't tell if she was straining to hear us or if I was being too loud. I learned later she had a son who was killed in Vietnam.

"One of the men in charge yelled at the draftees, 'Listen up, everybody. Most of you guys are going into the Army.' He counted off a large group and sent them to the Army's corner. The remaining ones in the center were confused and started talking among themselves, unsure of what would happen next. Suddenly, the guy in charge said, 'You other guys, move over there with the Marines.' These guys stood there in shock and said they had never heard that the Marines took draftees, and neither did I. Any visions I ever had of *esprit de corps* went sailing right out the window, as those poor sons-of-bitches shuffled over to join us."

I stopped to gauge his reaction. His eyes were still fixed on mine, waiting for me to continue. "I hated Boot Camp. Our drill instructors punished and degraded us and tried to take away any sense of our personal dignity, but I wouldn't let them. I was determined they wouldn't strip me of my self-identity."

He nodded at me and flashed a knowing look. "So, you were in Vietnam… what was that like?"

I never talked about the war with anyone, not even with Cynthia. However, he had been forthcoming with me so far, and I didn't want to discourage him by clamming up about my own experiences. "I went to Vietnam during the last year of my hitch. The North Vietnamese had just launched their second Tet offensive during the spring of seventy-two, which was known as the Easter Offensive. This was different from the first Tet attack in sixty-eight; this one involved more NVA troops than VC.

"By this time, most of our American ground forces had already left, so the ARVNs had to do all the fighting, and they weren't faring well. The Marines were ordered to send four squadrons back to Vietnam from Japan to provide them with air support. One group, MAG-15, sent two squadrons to Da Nang in April, and MAG-12 sent two more to Biên Hòa in May."

"Were you involved in that?" He asked.

"Several of us were stateside and received orders to go to Japan. I got there and was ordered to go to MAG-12 at Biên Hòa, a few clicks north of Saigon. It was a terrible time to be there – not so much physically but mentally. No one wanted to be the last guy to die over there. Or get wounded. Almost everyone was doing drugs or getting drunk to help the time pass and forget the war.

"When I arrived in May, the base was still taking some harassing fire, but we got hit pretty hard in August; more than one-hundred rockets and lots of mortar fire came in one night. One American was killed, and several others were wounded; the ARVN casualties were much higher.

"Then, in September, VC sappers snuck through the perimeter wire and set off the bomb dump. There were many casualties on

70

both sides, and I saw bodies being carried off the airstrip. It was hard watching all those people die, especially since the war seemed all but over. People were dying for nothing."

I hated talking this long about anything, much less this subject. I stopped, but Johann kept watching me, expecting more. So, I gave it to him. "Our squadron was sent back to Japan in January, and I rotated to the States in June when my three-year hitch was over. We were quarantined on Treasure Island in San Francisco Bay for three or four days of processing. I guess they wanted to check us out before releasing us into the real world.

"They finally handed us our separation papers, and that was it. No fanfare, no ceremony, no parade. We were let go as if we were part of a big mistake nobody wanted to discuss. I was pissed off over the whole process. I hated the government and the Marines for years after that."

He shook his head in sympathy and asked if I ever overcame those feelings.

I shrugged. "Well, yes and no. You have to get over those feelings, or you'll drown in them. But there's another part of you that doesn't want to forget because of those who died over there and also because of what you lost, as well."

I didn't want to discuss the subject further, so I turned the tables and asked about his time during the war.

CHAPTER 15: AN UNCOMFORTABLE SENSE

"My experiences during the war were probably no different than your father's ... or any other soldier that fights for his country. No more, no less. But it sounds like mine was very different from yours, *nicht wahr?*"

I cocked my head, not understanding his last two words but answered anyway. "Well, I thought we would have felt the same way since we were both in similar situations. Our wars were almost over, and it seemed pointless to continue fighting. Didn't you or the others feel that way?"

He shook his head. "No," he said simply and firmly. "None of us ever had those feelings, at least as far as I know, not during the war and not after. While we were fighting, our morale stayed extremely high even to the end. We were fighting for our way of life, our families, and our fatherland."

I remembered reading about his unit as he paused to drink some coffee. His expression started turning from one of pride to sadness.

"We were different from you boys in Vietnam, Willi. All of us in the 12th believed in what we were fighting for, and we stuck together. Even after the war ended, the few of us who survived still got together to sing the *Treuelied*, an old military song. It goes like this: *Wenn alle untreu werden, so bleiben wir doch treu.* This means:

When everyone else is unfaithful, we will remain true." He smiled as he looked up at the ceiling, remembering the distant past.

"I'll tell you, Willi, we were trained very differently from you and our other regular troops at the time. We were treated well. In fact, everyone was genuinely concerned about our age, and they gave us a chocolate ration instead of tobacco." He shook his head and brought his eyes back to mine.

"Let me read you something our Regimental leader, Kurt Meyer, wrote about us." He paused as he scrolled through his iPad. "Here it is. *Many established principles of military training were replaced...there was no obvious superior-subordinate relationship...the relationship between officers, non-commissioned officers, and other ranks was that between older and little more experienced and those who were new. The officers' authority existed in the fact that they were role models and mentors to the young soldiers. They strove to emulate the close relationship of a family inasmuch as that was possible... the soldiers entered the fray animated by the thought that their employment would be decisive for the defense of Germany and for its final victory. They were imbued with the belief in the rightness and justice of the German cause."*[1]

He looked up at me. "During training and even afterward, it wasn't unusual for our officers to come and eat with us and spend time talking with us, discussing conditions and morale. They were like fathers to us."

I was astounded. This was not what I expected to hear from someone in the SS, but it helped to explain some of the differences between us after our enlistment. His experience during training was very different from mine, and I suddenly felt an uncomfortable sense of envy. All during my childhood, from the time my father berated me to the time the DIs tormented me, I felt angry, anxious, and fearful of failing. All my thoughts were focused on surviving their abuse and rising above their scorn. There was no room to worry about others.

My thoughts came to a sudden stop when I realized my thoughts mirrored those of my father in the Ardennes. A phrase suddenly crossed my mind; *An unexamined life is not worth living.* I didn't know where it came from at the time, but I felt its gravity.

Johann yawned and stretched in his chair. I wasn't far behind him. I was mentally and spiritually exhausted. It was about time to leave. "I should be going, Johann. You look tired, and I feel the same way." I got up to leave as he watched me, waiting for the next shoe to drop. I obliged him by asking if I could come back.

Johann smiled, stood up, and patted my shoulder. "Ah, that's the boy! We've only covered one of my points today, and there are more to come. They're all part of our family history." He paused to eye me over and then exclaimed. "Before you leave, do you have any other questions?"

I paused to think. Johann sidestepped my earlier question about the Jews and never said anything about Germany's war crimes. I didn't know if he planned to discuss them later or just didn't have the guts to face them. But I did some sidestepping of my own. Although he mentioned my father, I never said anything about his day in the Ardennes or how it related to my self-centered feelings before the stroke. I didn't know if I could ever admit it. "Actually, I have one question. You made a point earlier about evil begetting evil. Just to be clear, what exactly did you mean?"

Johann's face took on a quizzical appearance. "Hmm. If you're not sure, then I'm glad you asked. What I meant is that we all would have been better off if the Allies had kept their promises to include Wilson's Fourteen Points in the peace treaty. That would have been the right and honorable thing to do. Instead, they strong-armed us to get our signature so they could plunder our lands and people. That one evil act generated all the other evil acts to follow, which included the start of the Second World War and all the evil acts that followed during and after."

"Aren't you giving Nazi Germany a pass on this, Johann? After all, they were the ones that started the war."

"We had our share of evil people back then, just like every other country. But my concern is what brings out the evil in men and how can we stop that from happening again in the future." He turned to sit down again. "But we'll have to take that up later, Willi. I'm tired."

"Well, I'll probably have more questions for you after I go through these notes." My earlier unease had passed. I shook his hand and said goodbye.

I headed toward the exit and saw there was no way for me to avoid the old woman. I caught her looking at me and took a deep breath. She laid her book down and leaned forward to greet me. "Excuse me, sir, will you be coming here often?"

She took me by surprise with that question. "Well, yes, I plan to. Johann, that gentleman over there, is a relative of mine."

"So you said," she nodded. Her hair was dark gray and cut short. Her face was pale and marked with age spots. The years bore heavily on her, but I could imagine her as an attractive young woman.

"My name is Lena. What's yours?"

"I'm Will, short for William."

"I heard that person call you 'Willi.' Where's he from?"

Well, she was polite, but she wasn't shy. "Oh, Johann's originally from Germany."

"I'm from Poland myself." Her face relaxed, but she still didn't smile. She wriggled slightly in her wheelchair as if bothered by some type of underlying pain.

I didn't want to be rude to her, but the last thing I needed here was another playmate. My hands were full dealing with Johann.

"Well, it was nice meeting you, Lena, but I have to be going. By the way, that's a very pretty name."

She ignored the compliment. "I heard you two talking about history and the war." She left an unspoken question hanging in the air, begging for a reply.

Her mention of Poland suddenly hit me. I put two and two together, and suddenly, I was interested. "Yes, we were. He's helping me write our family history." I looked into her eyes and saw how lively they were, like sparkling little chips of freshly broken coal. "The last time I was here, you said something I didn't understand. Was it Polish?"

She looked at me for a while before answering. "It was Yiddish, Will. I just said goodbye."

My face dropped. Oh boy, a Polish Jew on one side and an SS trooper on the other. I really stepped into it.

A slight smile emerged as her voice crackled slightly. "Yes, Will, I'm Jewish."

I didn't know how to respond. "Well, like I said, Lena, I really have to go now, but I'll be back again soon. Perhaps, I can introduce you to Johann then."

She gave me a severe look, but her response was surprisingly cordial. "That would be fine, Will." She paused and then said dryly, "Next time."

Exhaling a sigh of relief, I said goodbye and walked out the door. I called Cynthia to tell her I was leaving. I dreaded telling her that I would be back for a third visit.

~ AT HOME ~

CHAPTER 16: DON'T SCREW WITH US

When I arrived home, Cynthia was in the front yard getting the landscaping ready for winter. After changing my clothes, I went outside to help.

After several hours of trimming and raking, we went inside to prepare a hot cup of tea and then to the backyard patio to relax. As I expected, the first question out of her mouth was about seeing Johann again. Her tone wasn't particularly pleasant.

"You're going to see him *again*?" Her next question was even more challenging: "And what in the world for?"

I silently nodded my head. It's been over seventeen years since she discovered my betrayal of her. She had exposed the beast, and my stroke came hard on the heels of that event. Her pain from that moment still lingers. Whenever she suspects I may be turning from the straight and narrow, the scars on her psyche become inflamed, and she presses to get the truth.

Before that incident, I could bend the truth a bit or even outright lie to Cynthia to get what I wanted; she never held any such inquisitions. She was a good and trusting soul and expected the same from others. But she changed after the betrayal. I did as well.

I vowed to be nothing less than totally honest with her after that. I never want to see her hurt again by my lies and deceit.

I stared at my wine glass, recalling my stroke after that event. She sat patiently by my side as I lay in the hospital bed. It was hours before I regained awareness. I remembered looking at her then and seeing for the first-time what love really meant. In hindsight, I saw now that there was a terrible irony at work. My eyes and heart had finally been opened to see and feel the love the between us. However, the specter of my past would forever taint our love.

I picked up my glass and began swirling the wine as I recalled the first time we met. I was initially attracted to her for the usual reasons; she was beautiful and had an engaging personality. And then I became attached to her as she offered me a safe haven from the beast.

And then, as I raised the glass to take a sip, an idea occurred to me. She may have been initially attracted to me for the same reasons as I was to her, but then she became attached to me for a different reason. She saw a troubled soul that was crying out for help and finally found her mission in life, the saving of a soul.

And in spite of everything that happened, she stayed true to her mission. She never gave up on me. It may have been because the regret of my betrayal hung over me like a shroud. She must have seen my contrition, which sustained her belief in love and goodness.

I watched as she looked away and sipped some wine. Tolerating my silence after a probing question was, by now, a familiar tactic for her. After the stroke, I rarely protested against her suspicions. I had no moral ground to stand on. Her anger was justified. To her credit, she accepted my silence as penance and would mercifully stop her grilling.

After the stroke, she was vigilant in keeping me on track. I didn't begrudge her harshness or anger with me; both came from a place of love. I know this because neither was in her nature; she was sacrificing her own peaceful nature to help me find mine.

I took another sip of wine and looked again at Cynthia. She looked back at me, awaiting a response. However, I was too conflicted to reply. I wanted to see Johann again because he had more points to discuss, but it was obvious she didn't and would get upset if I did. I rubbed my head in consternation and suddenly blurted out feelings that had been dormant for so many years. "I'll tell you something, Cynthia. When I returned from Vietnam, I knew there was something wrong with America and with me. Everything I had learned and believed in was dragged through the mud and left there to die. We trashed most of Southeast Asia, killed or maimed our own people, and in the process, put everything our country stood for in the shitter."

She glared at me; she had never heard me speak in this tone. In addition, she hated profanity. "Sorry, honey, but our country was so hell-bent on beating the Communists that nothing else mattered. I went to college after the Marines to understand what was happening to our country and why winning that war was so damn important. I wanted to learn why we were involved in Asia in the first place. And I thought the best way to get some perspective was to study what happened to drive Japan into a war against America."

I stopped to grab my wine and take a sip. She was watching me closely, waiting for me to continue. "I read where Commodore Perry forcibly opened Japan at gunpoint in the 1850s. They were a peaceful country at that time, but Europe and America pushed around the Asian countries for year before the Japanese finally pushed back and bombed Pearl Harbor. It was like Johann said to me: evil begets evil."

I paused, hoping to rein in my feelings, but it didn't work. "And then we retaliated by bombing the shit out of them, pardon my language, and then we dropped the big one on them – twice – just to make sure they and everyone else in the world got the same message: don't screw with us. And now, Johann is telling me that the same sort of thing happened to Germany before World War II, and I feel the same thing happened with Vietnam, except that Russia and China got involved to keep us in check."

She continued staring at me. "That war is over, Will, and so is yours. Why can't you just leave it alone?"

I looked down at the floor again. This is exactly why I never shared any of this with her before. She didn't get it, and it was unfair of me to think she ever would. It made me think of the title of one of Hemingway's short stories: *A Way You'll Never Be.*

She grabbed my hand to get my attention. "Did you hear what you just said? Does that old man really think America pushed Germany into war? What the Germans did was evil, Will. Did someone else push their tanks into Poland to start that war? No. They did that and a whole lot more besides."

Her voice was strident, and her face set in anger. It wouldn't end well if I pushed her much further. "I'm sorry, Cynthia, but after studying what happened with Japan, then hearing what Johann said about Germany and then seeing what happened in Vietnam, I'm starting to think that something was wrong with our country. All I want to do is learn the truth of what happened."

Her face started to soften with my apology, and I quickly continued. "Cynthia, I used to believe that our country was doing good in the world, but something happened to us. Our government and the media began labeling others in this world as evil and dehumanizing them so we would treat them as faceless objects; that would make it easier for us to exploit or destroy them to get what we want."

"You mean like the Nazis did with the Holocaust?"

"We didn't talk about that yet." I avoided answering her question because, like Johann, I didn't think the time was right. And I deliberately didn't mention Lena.

"What I meant was like what we did in Vietnam. What made us devastate that place? The Pentagon Papers proved the leaders of our government lied to us. Their pride and position must have seemed more important to them than our lives or the Vietnamese. As early as 1967, McNamara said he didn't believe we could win the war. But he never did anything about it, even up to the time he left office in 1968."

She sat back in her chair, perhaps realizing that neither of us would win this one. "Okay, Will, go ahead with this but be careful. There may be some real loonies out there who won't understand what you're trying to do. Or take it the wrong way."

"I'm sure there are." I smiled and reached out for her hand. We sat back and sipped our tea until the sun finally set.

CHAPTER 17: SELF-DECEPTION

It wasn't easy to fall asleep that night. All I could think of was coming home from Vietnam. I went to college feeling bitter and determined to understand exactly what led us into that conflict.

I recalled learning how Commodore Perry "opened" Japan for "free trade" with America. He sailed into Tokyo Bay in 1853 with four gunships to "negotiate" the terms for opening up trade relations between the two countries. Japan was a closed nation then and wanted to keep it that way. They managed to stall Perry by telling him they needed time to consider his "offer."

Perry returned in 1854 with ten gunships and strong-armed the shogun into signing the Treaty of Kanagawa. Japan was aware of how the West had plundered China, and they signed the agreement to keep the foreigners at bay. Unlike China, however, they quickly adopted a Westernization strategy that modernized their industry and military while they pursued their own "trade ambitions."

I heard Daisy and Doris whining by my bedside and opened my eyes to see the clock on the bedstand. It was 3:56 am. We moved through the morning drill and then sat with Cynthia to watch the morning news while she had her breakfast.

Since waking up, I tried recalling the key points in my honor's paper. I wrote it in my senior year of college. It was about Japanese-American relations up to the start of World War II. I felt it was the best way to see how we became involved in Asian affairs. Cynthia could tell I was distracted and got up without saying a word. I followed shortly afterward and brewed a second cup of coffee to take back to my study.

I sat in front of my computer and started to outline what I remembered about Japan, how it modernized itself for the next eighty years until it become a competitive threat to American interests in Asia. By 1941, Japan had established itself in Korea, set up a proxy country in Manchuria and occupied most of Northeast China. It had also negotiated a deal with Vichy France that summer to build airbases in Vietnam, which extended their reach into Southeast Asia. America demanded their withdrawal, or they would close the "open door" on "free" trade with Japan.

Japan stood its ground, and FDR was true to his word; he froze all Japanese assets in the US and enacted a trade embargo against them. As a result, Japan lost three-fourths of its overseas trade, including eighty-eight percent of its imported oil, the lifeblood of any industrialized country.

America had forced Japan into making a "Hobson's choice" for the second time in 90 years: they could either submit to American dominance, or they could challenge that dominance by undertaking a war. They took the first option in 1854 but opted for the second in 1941.

Johann said Germany was faced with the same choice in 1919: They either had to accept Western domination by signing the Versailles Peace Treaty or they could refuse to sign, face the continued blockade and a possible invasion. They submitted to the Allies in 1919 but then sought redress once the Nazis came into power.

I grew up believing that America's involvement in foreign wars was to make the world "free" for trade and "safe" for democracy, but both principles hit a brick wall in Vietnam. We propped up a series of puppet governments there that made a mockery of democracy;

they served our interests more than those of the Vietnamese. The whole notion of free trade was jettisoned once we enacted a slew of embargoes against many Communist countries after the Cold War began.

I recalled that Cordell Hull, our Secretary of State whose policies led us into the Second World War, loudly criticized Japan in 1932 for doing much the same as we did in Vietnam after they set up a puppet government in Manchuria. I shook my head and turned my attention to checking out the notes from my last visit with Johann.

The last entry concerned Johann sidestepping my question about the Jews and his avoiding any discussion over Germany's war crimes. I turned to my computer to check whether Johann's division was involved in any war crimes. They were. There were two different incidents that occurred in France during 1944: one was at Ascq shortly before the Normandy invasion, and the other was at the Ardennes Abbey shortly after D-Day.

The village of Ascq is in France, close to the border with Belgium. It served as a vital hub for routing German trains bound for Normandy, typically filled with soldiers and equipment for the anticipated invasion. The 12th happened to be on one of those trains when an explosion derailed it on April 1, 1944.

German soldiers quickly disembarked and rounded up adult males living on either side of the tracks as partisan suspects. Reports indicated seventy Frenchmen were shot next to the railway, and another sixteen were killed in the village. The convoy commander, SS-*Obersturmführer* Walter Hauck, was put on trial in a French court in 1949 and sentenced to death. He was later released in 1957.

It sounded typical of other SS operations, but I decided to dig deeper and found that as 1944 began, Germany began stepping up their efforts to shore up the Atlantic Wall in preparation for the coming invasion. The offshore Allies were also increasing their efforts to sabotage the German efforts by supplying the French Resistance with men and munitions.

Partisans damaged or destroyed 808 German locomotives during the opening months of 1944. Workers from the German railroad system had to be relocated to France to perform repairs, while soldiers had to be diverted from combat operations to protect themselves and the trains.

We had similar problems in Vietnam. The VC continually performed hit-and-run tactics against our troops and supply lines. Like the VC, the French Resistance disappeared into the local hamlets and blended in with the locals.

The incident at Ascq sounded eerily like the massacre at My Lai. Our Americal Division outdid the 12th that day by rounding up and killing between 347 and 504 Vietnamese civilians. These numbers included women, children, and the elderly, all of which the 12th spared. I read where Telford Taylor, a Nuremberg prosecutor, also cited similar parallels between the two wars in his book *Nuremberg and Vietnam: An American Tragedy*.

The second war crime involving the 12th occurred on June 7th, the day after D-Day, when eleven Canadian POWs were shot in the back of the head at the Ardennes Abbey. The Canadian War Commission found Commander Kurt Meyer, the leader of Johann's regiment, guilty of inciting his troops to commit murder. He, too, was sentenced to death, and, like Hauck, his sentence was commuted to life imprisonment in 1946. He was set free in 1954 when the Canadians sent him back to Germany. I made a note to ask Johann about this incident since he painted Meyer as a caring, fatherly figure.

It's generally known that the battle for Normandy was pivotal for both sides, and the outcome would determine the war's end. Handling prisoners was not a high priority. Out of curiosity, I did a search on whether Allied troops committed similar war crimes during the invasion.

A 2010 article in Der Spiegel appeared, and its headline was *The Horror of D-Day: A New Openness to Discussing Allied War Crimes in World War II*. One section caught my attention: *According to the findings of German historian Peter Lieb, many Canadian and American units were given orders on D-Day to take no prisoners. If true, that might help explain the mystery of how only 66 of the 130 Germans the Americans took prisoner on Omaha Beach made it to collecting points for the captured on the beach.*

It is also conspicuous that the Allies rarely captured members of the Waffen-SS. Was it because the members of this organization…had sworn allegiance to Hitler until death and often fought to the last man? Or did the Allied propaganda about the SS have its desired effect on soldiers? 'Many of them probably deserved to be shot in any case and knew it,' a British XXX Corps report bluntly stated.[1]

The *Der Spiegel* article cited several interviews with Allied veterans who spoke of killing wounded German soldiers left on the battlefield or forcing German PoWs to walk through open fields to draw enemy fire or clear mines.

I also discovered the Biscari massacre on July 14, 1943, where American soldiers executed 73 unarmed Italian and German prisoners in Sicily. This war crime preceded the incident at the Ardennes Abbey and executed more victims, but it was never brought up or considered at Meyer's trial.

I shook my head in dismay. The history I learned not only failed to discuss these Allied war crimes but never addressed the context behind the German ones. A verse from St. John came to me, *If we say that we have no sin, we deceive ourselves, and the truth is not in us.* The verse reminded me of the title of my honors paper, *Self-Deception and Self-Defeat.*

I spent the next few days fact-checking everything Johann said about the Fourteen Points, the Armistice, the blockade, the Versailles Treaty, and Hitler's rise to power. I thought he was playing fast and loose with the truth. But everything he said was true. All of this can be found on the Internet now but wasn't generally known or taught when I was growing up.

However, I couldn't find anything about FDR's record as a financial speculator in the '20s, but there was one promising reference in an out-of-print book on the Internet. I found a book dealer who had it in stock and ordered it.

The last thing to check out was Lena's book: *The Last of the Just*. It was a novel written in 1959 by a Frenchman, André Schwarz-Bart. It won the *Prix Goncourt*, France's equivalent of the Pulitzer Prize, and was about a Jewish family who suffered through the Holocaust.

A critic's review mentioned that the book was based on the old Jewish legend of *The Thirty-Six Just Men* or the *Lamed-Vov*. I had never heard of it, but the critic summed it up rather well by stating, *Adapting the legend to serve as his leading motif, Schwarz-Bart depicts the Lamed-Vov as supporting the world by absorbing all its ills and griefs. 'For the Lamed-Vov are the hearts of the world multiplied, and into them, as into one receptacle, pour all our griefs.' Without them, Schwarz-Bart says, 'humanity would suffocate with a single cry.' With them, life can go on, and God can continue to bear the ordeal of looking on the world.*

The critic's review said it was a long and heart-wrenching story, but the closing words of the review really hit home with me, *Finally it is not the martyrdom of his people that haunts Schwarz-Bart… but the sense of all that life abused, broken, and turned to ashes.*[2]

I lowered my head, saddened by the thought of all the innocent civilians who suffered from all the conflicts over the last century. I remembered the numbing sadness that shadowed my anger after returning home from Vietnam. Both of those feelings increased after reading parts of the Pentagon Papers. I saw how our government had lied and misled its citizens into fighting a war that caused so much suffering. It seemed naïve to ask why they had lied, but the answer came quickly enough, and it was as naïve as the question itself.

Our leaders were merely protecting the system that kept them in power. They either were unabashedly power-hungry or subconsciously transposed their selfish needs into high-flying ideals that catalyzed our citizens into fighting wars that kept their system going.

The phrase *Sin of Transposition* suddenly came to mind. I first came across it while reading a book for my honors paper. I couldn't remember where it came from, but I recall it was related to the Vietnam War. The author used the phrase to infer that our government leaders transposed their vision of national self-interests onto broader, universal ideals in order to justify the war. He surmised that they had deceived themselves into believing that the two were identical, a deception which ultimately led to our defeat.

I didn't agree with the author then and still don't. I think those leaders knew very well what they were doing. They were not deceived by any ideals at all. They pursued their ambitions just as their predecessors did to "open" Japan for "free trade" by using gunboat diplomacy. Shakespeare's famous line from *The Merchant of Venice* came to mind, *Truth will come to light... at the length, truth will out*. I was hopeful that my visits with Johann would do the same.

I was finished with fact-checking and transposing my notes onto the computer. It was time to visit Johann again. I called and asked him about visiting tomorrow. He chuckled and said, "*Bestimmt,* Willi. Why not?"

After we hung up, I remembered my promise to introduce Lena to Johann. I shook my head in trepidation. If Johann felt so strongly about getting redress for Germany, then he might learn a thing or two about that subject from Lena.

CYCLE II: THE WAY OF PRIDE

The Lord detests all the proud of heart.
Be sure of this: They will not go unpunished.
Psalms 16:5

~ 3RD VISIT ~

CHAPTER 18: EXPLORING COMMON GROUND

When I arrived the next morning, there was no sign of Lena. However, Johann was sitting in the Garden Room at his usual spot. His eyes were closed, and wires dangled down from his ears to the iPad. He hadn't graduated to earbuds – yet.

I touched his shoulder and said hello. He opened his eyes and looked up as he tore off the earphones. "Willi! Good to see you. How's the boy today?"

"Fine and yourself, Johann?"

"*Sehr Gut*…just resting and listening to Enya. She has a very relaxing voice."

I had to stop myself from laughing. "Enya?"

"Have you ever listened to her, Willi?"

"I have. I have all her recordings and play them while I'm writing."

"What are you writing, Willi?"

"Our family history, and now, I'm focused on your life and mine as well."

He chuckled. "Well, mine will be more work than yours, my friend. Twenty-five years more!"

"I know. That's why I'm here." I sat down and opened my notebook. "Listen, Johann, I went back and read more about the 12th. I discovered your unit was involved in two big war crimes: one was at Ascq where civilians were rounded up and shot; and the other was at the Ardennes Abbey, where POWs were executed. Were you involved in either of those?"

He raised himself in the chair and leaned forward. "No, I wasn't, but I heard about them. At Ascq, one of our trains was attacked by partisans. The French Resistance fought a vicious guerilla war against us. They weren't trained in wartime conventions or military law. They were savages. You should understand, Willi, you were in Vietnam."

I nodded. We were trained on what to expect in Vietnam. We were told stories of guys who died after swallowing ground glass in Coke bottles, about prostitutes who were infected with the "black" syphilis to take us out of service, and the dangers of being isolated from our units both in and out of combat.

"I understand what you're saying, Johann, but that doesn't excuse your soldiers for grabbing and shooting people."

He gave me a harsh look. I remembered what he said about the fate of my namesake and quickly continued. "I read where your division went around the village gathering up people and then just shot them. Is that true?"

"Let me tell you what I heard about this shortly after it happened. The troop train pulled into the station, and then the explosion went off. Several cars were derailed, and then the partisans began shooting. There had been a similar attack there two days earlier, and guards were stationed to prevent another, but that didn't stop them.

"Hubert Meyer, our division commander, wrote about this after the war, and his words follow what I heard. Our troops were ordered off the train and worked with the local guards and police to detain every male found near the station. They were lined up and searched, but nobody was hurt.

"However, several men broke loose and tried to escape. The guards opened fire, and a panic broke out.[1] After it ended, eighty-six civilians were killed and eight more wounded. And that is what happens when civilians take up arms against the military, Willi. It's impossible to separate the partisans from innocent civilians, and it all becomes very tragic."

He got out of his chair to stretch. His account was more complete than I had read, and it sounded more likely. "You're right, Johann. It is tragic." I wouldn't say anything more because I knew our troops committed similar war crimes in Vietnam.

"I'll tell you, Willi; it doesn't surprise me at all that you only read how our troops lined up those civilians and shot them. The West never had anything good to say about us. They never wrote how hard we worked before the war to expand our social services, to provide parity for our workers, and to rebuild our country. At first, I wondered why that was, but then I realized it's just human nature. We did the same with our propaganda."

He sat back down and then leaned forward. "The fact of the matter is that the crimes we committed during the war were no different than those committed by America, England, France, and Russia for years before the war and years after, as well. But you never read or see movies about that, do you?"

He didn't wait for me to respond. "And this brings up my second point, Willi: at the end of the day, all men are alike. Remember what I told you at our first meeting? This was an ideological war. It started years before any shooting began. The Allies were discrediting National Socialism as soon as the party came into power. The Allied government leaders were never objective about our system. They feared it would be an attractive alternative to their system and cause a revolt during the Depression. So, all the history books and movies painted us as evil while they portrayed themselves as shining knights."

He leaned back into his chair to take a sip of coffee. I stopped writing to think about the truth of what he just said. Somehow, it didn't seem unlikely.

"I see you're thinking, Willi. That's good. And here's something else for you to think about. Did you know that the Allies tortured German prisoners to provide self-incriminating testimony at Nuremberg? Or that the Allies submitted forged German documents and photographs as incriminating evidence to the Tribunal? Tell me, Willi, why do you think they needed to do that?"

The impact of what he said hit me squarely between the eyes. I never heard anything about torture or forgery being used at Nuremberg. I thought of all the photos taken at the death camps and took a hard shot at him.

"You've been saying since our first visit that the two of us are alike, and our two countries are as well, but I think you are way off on this, Johann. What about everything Nazi Germany did to the Jewish people? You can't begin to compare our two countries."

He stared at me with that familiar, focused look in his eyes. "If you feel that way, Willi, then you're not familiar with your own American history or ours." He said this calmly and took another sip of coffee. You won't like what I'm going to say, Willi, but the Western powers invaded North America and then murdered, massacred, and pillaged the native people from the first day they arrived.

"American leaders continued to do the same until they reached the Western shore. After that, they began expanding beyond their shore by entering a questionable war against Spain. Very few historians questioned the morality of this nation-building. Instead, most of them praised America's pioneering spirit, the bravery, and vigor which grew your nation."

My hackles were rising as his voice grew louder. "But not all of us were involved in that, Johann. You can't blame all of us. Most of us were just trying to carve out a life and survive."

"That may be so, Willi. But it was all done at the expense of others. Consciously or not, your people benefitted from the actions of your leaders as they orchestrated all those crimes in the name of civilization. Those leaders provided the land and resources that your people needed to grow and prosper and then they supplied the security to maintain it. Your people benefitted from that genocide and from the forced removal of those people. It was okay for America to do it, but not for Germany. What arrogance!"

CHAPTER 19: WE'RE ONLY HUMAN

"Genocide? What the hell are you talking about, Johann?" I blurted that out, expecting him to counter in kind, but he only went back to his iPad and kept scrolling until he calmly tapped open a document.

"Well, here are some estimates. One source says the population of Native Americans living in North America in 1492 ranged from a low of two million to a high of eighteen million. Don't ask me how they made these estimates, Willi. But by 1900, the U.S. census showed only two-hundred and fifty-thousand left. If you use the midpoint of that population range in 1492, which is ten million, then that means that over nine million were eliminated over five hundred years. That sounds like genocide to me, and this doesn't consider the number of Blacks who died from slavery and its legacy, nor all the Chinese who died building your railroads. There are literally millions of victims who died so you Americans could build your *lebensraum* from shore to shore."

I was uncomfortable with where he was going with this, but I wasn't quick enough to counter him; my brain didn't work as fast as it did before the stroke.

"Willi, your government did the same type of evil things that we did during the war; they removed and executed Native Americans just like we did with the Jews. Our *Einsatzgruppen* did the same thing in Russia that your cavalry did in the 1800s. While one unit was out fighting the braves, another went into the villages and murdered the women, children, and elderly and then burned their villages. You must have heard about the incidents at Sand Creek and Wounded Knee."

I nodded. I read *Bury My Heart at Wounded Knee* after returning home from Vietnam. It left me wondering what sort of people we were after learning our troops were doing the same thing in Vietnam a hundred years later.

"And listen to this. I found this quote from Colonel Chivington, who ordered his troops at Sand Creek to execute over a hundred Cheyenne and Arapaho, most of whom were women, children, and babies: *Damn any man who sympathizes with Indians! I have come to kill Indians, and believe it is right and honorable to use any means under God's heaven to kill Indians ... Kill and scalp all, big and little; nits make lice.* "[1]

Johann continued, "There were no movies or photo magazines on the frontier to document these atrocities for the world. Not that it would have mattered anyway. Nobody ever asked the Indians for their side of the story. They had no advocates. You know the old saying that the only good redskin is a dead redskin. Right?"

He was right. The glory of conquering the West was passed down to us kids through movies and television. Everyone cheered when the Indians were mowed down, and we never thought twice about it while playing Cowboys and Indians.

Johann cooled down after he took a sip of coffee and began speaking in a steady, well-modulated tone. "After I came here and read all your history, it was hard to understand why Germany was so maligned. I knew in my heart that we, in the twelve years under National Socialism, had behaved no better or worse than America did over the last several hundred years. Our cause in building our nation seemed just as righteous to us as yours was to your people."

I looked up from my notebook and saw Lena wheeling into the room. Talk about timing. I turned my head and gave her a brief wave. She acknowledged with a nod.

Johann saw me wave and turned his head in her direction. He nodded to her but quickly turned to continue his lecture, raising his voice to reel me in. "When America's military invaded the West, they had the same problem as we had in invading France and Russia; they not only had to defeat the braves in battle, but they also had to eliminate the others who helped them to fight, including the women, the elderly and young children. With non-uniformed enemies, you never know who to trust or who might shoot you in the back. You lose all humanity in that type of situation." He sat back, scratched his head, and said softly, "We have no monopoly on wartime atrocities, Willi."

He stretched back in his chair, rubbed his eyes, and sighed as if to signal an end to this topic. "*Ach*, but what's the difference? We lost the war. We were punished for what we did. It's all water under the bridge. But America," he said with a rising tone as he sat up in the chair, "was never punished for its crimes. It always had the luxury of winning its wars."

"But we never won in Vietnam!"

"That may be the case, but you didn't lose either; you just picked up your bags and left. No one held you accountable for what you did there. You were never defeated or occupied." He paused for dramatic effect as he let his words sink in. "Or judged."

My thoughts returned to all the devastation we imposed on Vietnam and elsewhere during our many wars. There was a trail of bodies leading all the way back to the pilgrims. Undoubtedly, our system had been good to us, but what about everyone else who lived outside of it or got in our way? Did they have to suffer and bear the burden for our benefit?

Johann must have seen my expression change from anger to pensiveness and quickly seized the opportunity to interject one more thing. "I'm not proud of what my country did out of desperation during the war, but I am proud of all the good we accomplished before the war. What do you think?"

"I don't know what to think, Johann. Maybe, the Allies wanted to make an example out of Germany, so people would focus on their crimes and forget about the past. Maybe, they wanted people to concentrate on the future and the new world order."

"I'm sure they did! Why would they want to do otherwise?" He looked tired and started to rub his eyes. He opened them wide and then said sternly, "But I'm equally sure the people on the losing end haven't forgotten what was done to them. They're probably still waiting for a chance to recover what was lost to the imperial powers."

His tone of voice and choice of words became threatening. He paused for effect, waiting to see how I reacted. "How about you, Willi? Have you ever done anything in your life that you wished could be whitewashed or rationalized away?" He stared at me like a hawk before diving in for the kill. "Wouldn't that be nice?"

I was caught like a deer in headlights. There were a few things that I wished could be erased. They weighed on me like millstones around my neck.

Johann saved me from responding. "Ach, you shouldn't worry about it. As I said, we all make mistakes. After all, we're only human."

This discussion drained me. I no longer knew what to think about him. He was hard as nails one moment and compassionate the next. His insights were compelling but also repelling. If the last two visits had shocked and uprooted me, then this visit had planted me on foreign ground without any bearings.

Something caught my eye. Lena was wheeling over to us. Johann caught my glance and watched her approach with a wary expression.

CHAPTER 20: LENA

Lena was by our side in no time and greeted me warmly. "Hello, Will." I was about to greet her when she abruptly turned her gaze over to Johann. "My name is Lena. You must be Johann. Will told me about you, and I thought I'd introduce myself."

I quickly chimed in to allow Johann some time to respond. "Johann, Lena comes from Poland. I promised to introduce you two, but she beat me to it."

He smiled warmly at her and stood up. "I'm pleased to meet you, Lena. You may have guessed I'm from Germany. My accent gives me away."

She kept her poker face. *"Ja, ich kann sagen.* Will told me."

"Ah! You speak German!"

"Yes, as well as Yiddish."

The smile dropped off Johann's face. After a moment, he regained his composure. "Well, let me welcome you to our community," he said graciously. "I've lived here for seven years. I came after my wife passed. I sold my home since I didn't want to keep it up anymore and didn't want to burden my son and his family. He visits every week, and now Willi comes to see me as well. Do you have any relatives who visit you?"

"No. I'm alone."

"No, you're not… you're here with us now." His smile came back.

She managed a brief smile, which quickly vanished. "So, you were in Germany during the war, Johann? I hear you two talking quite a bit about it."

"Yes, I grew up there but came to America in 1956."

I could sense that some initial sparring had begun between the two. I watched silently from my neutral corner as Lena took an initial jab at Johann.

"Were you in the war?"

"Yes, I was." Johann glanced at me, but I kept a blank face, offering him nothing. He was on his own. "I joined in 1944 when I was eighteen years old. When did you come over here?"

"I came over in 1948. I was also eighteen in 1944." She held out her thin left arm to show several faded blue numbers. "I was in Auschwitz at the time."

Johann stared at her arm, and silence descended on all of us.

It was time for me to jump into the ring and break up the clinch. "Johann grew up in Breslau," I said. "That's where my family came from as well. He's been helping me write my family history," It was a weak effort, but she was gracious enough to let it work.

"I was raised in Lódz, Will. It's midway between Warsaw and Wrocław, which was then Breslau." She swung her head over to face Johann without missing a beat. "Did your family survive the war, Johann?"

His expression changed from surprise to sadness. "No, they did not. Did yours?"

"I lost thirty-two members of my extended family, which is only a small fraction of the Jews who died. I used to wish I hadn't survived as well, but as I got older, I learned that life has a mind of its own."

"Yes, it does," Johann replied. "Those were terrible times, and I often feel guilty about surviving them. I told Willi that, since I retired, I've been trying to understand what led up to the war, and that's what we've been discussing."

I smiled. "I majored in history."

She looked at me with a dubious grin. "I heard. And you were in a war, as well?"

"Yes, ma'am. I was. In Vietnam."

"Hmm." Her brief acknowledgment left us wondering where she would go next.

"What about you, Lena? What's your history?" It just came out of me; the silence was becoming too oppressive.

She ignored me and looked over at Johann. "How about you, Johann? Are you interested in hearing about my history?"

He pulled himself up as straight as possible in his chair as if to defend himself. "I have never spoken to a Jewish person about what happened, but, yes, I would like to hear your story." He relaxed a bit, and so did I.

She asked for a water bottle, and I jumped up to get it. Once we all settled in, she started. "As I said, I was born in 1926 and grew up in Lódz. My father's family left Spain in 1492 after the Alhambra Decree. It was Queen Isabella's way of forcing the Jews to leave Spain or convert to Christianity.

"So, they left for central Europe and settled near Łódź. They lived in a *shtetl* which grew into a vibrant community by the time I was born. I had a happy childhood there, even though there were a great many things that a Jew could not do, but we had strong ties within our community, and I had a loving family. My father was a teacher, a gentle soul, and I went to a girls' school before the war began."

She paused to shift her position, and a look of pain came across her face. Johann asked if she felt all right. She nodded, took a sip of water, and continued.

"All that changed in 1939 when the Nazis invaded. I was standing on the sidewalk when the Germans marched into the city. The occupation started, and my whole world crumbled. First, they removed the intelligentsia. Then they imposed rules for controlling the Poles, but it went worse for us. We were immediately forced to wear an armband, which soon had the Star of David patched on it. By the end of the year, we were all moved into a ghetto. You could only take what you could carry on your back. Everything else was confiscated. We were there for a while, and then they moved us to an even larger ghetto still within Łódź. There were about two hundred thousand of us."

She paused to take another drink and had a faraway look in her eyes. I knew this story never ended for her, and I wasn't about to interrupt her. Neither was Johann.

"I was fourteen when my mother, father, sister, and I were moved into the ghetto. It was surrounded by barbed wire and armed guards. We were gradually separated into two groups: those who could work and those who couldn't.

"I am only here because I was considered strong enough to work along with the rest of my family. We never knew what happened to the others who weren't, but at some point, their clothes returned, and we were made to clean them and check for valuables. Occasionally, we found bullet holes and blood.

"I was lucky. I was young and healthy. The SS wanted to kill us, but the army needed our work, and, for a time, the army won. Don't ever think that we worked willingly; without work, you couldn't get your food ration, and without a ration, you wouldn't survive for more than a day or two.

"One day, we heard rumbling in the distance. Shortly after that, the commander of the ghetto told us the Red Army was coming. He wanted to protect us by moving to another camp, so we were sent to Auschwitz in August 1944. When we arrived, men with shaven heads started yelling at us to get off the trains and pushed us into separate lines of men and women.

"My mother, sister, and I came up to a long table with German soldiers who looked us over and pointed either to the right or left; right meant death, but I didn't know that. All I knew was young women and girls were moved to the left. Crippled people, lame people, and emaciated people were moved to the right. Before I knew it, I stood in front of another table, and an officer asked how old I was. I said, 'Eighteen.' And he said, 'Old enough' and sent me to the left. My mother and sister were sent to the left, too. I don't know what happened to my father; I never saw him again."

She paused, her chest heaving to contain her emotions. She let out a long sigh and went on. "After that, they lined us up each day to examine our bodies. They placed the emaciated ones to the side, and we never saw them again. My mother gave half her rations to my sister and me to keep us going, but one day…"

She stopped as her eyes teared up. Johann and I looked at one another, knowing we had to hear her out. I wondered how he felt about hearing all this, but he only presented a long face that didn't express guilt as much as sadness.

"My sister and I were finally led over to Birkenau. We were sent to the showers, and thankfully, water came out. We were told to sleep on a pile of coal dust. The next day, I looked up at the sun and saw a red circle surrounded by black smoke. Next to me sat a couple of women. I asked them what all that black smoke was. They said, 'they are burning the dead. They die after they go to the showers; instead of water, gas comes out. And then they carry them out and burn them. Consider yourself lucky because you will be working. We wish we could go with you.'

"After that, I was sent along with several thousand others to work in Breslau. I don't know what happened to my sister. I ended up in an underground airplane factory. We worked twelve hours at night in that factory. We were expendable. When someone died, they got a replacement.

"By the start of 1945, we could hear the guns in the distance and knew the Russians were closing in. The guards forced us to leave on foot before they arrived. For food, we had nothing, and for drink, we had snow. For three days, we marched. Whenever we rested and had to perform our necessities, they watched us, both men and women, together. Some would sneak out and escape, not even afraid of the bullets.

"After those three days, we came to a small town and saw a train full of prisoners. They were trying to move everybody into the center of Germany to liquidate us. We were packed into the train like sardines. I was in the last detachment. We got off in the darkest of night and walked several kilometers to a concentration camp. I couldn't read where I was because it was so dark.

"We were given a shower. Again, it was water, not gas. They took some of our clothing, considering us too well-dressed. We were then shoved into an overflowing barracks and left to die. We had a minimum of food and a maximum of lice. Pretty soon, I couldn't get up anymore. There was little compassion left because everybody was in the same boat.

"The miracle happened on April 15, 1945. The British came and freed us. They told us to stay in the barracks, and they would distribute food. They gave us a tin of pork and some biscuits. I was too weak to open the tin of pork. I would have been a goner in a couple of hours if I had eaten it. Our stomach linings were shot by then. Bodies were stacked up two stories high between the barracks. Bulldozers came in to perform the only burial ceremony they would ever have. I learned later that they killed twenty-thousand Jews a day there.

"I don't know where my mother or sister lies. Later, I found my father had died of malnutrition and exhaustion in January of '45. I was finally freed from the camps but not from my memories. I had seen the worst things a person could ever see."[1]

CHAPTER 21: THINGS MAY GET INTERESTING

She wiped her eyes while Johann reached out to touch her shoulder. "Why don't we stop for now and take a rest?" She nodded weakly. "You can join us anytime you'd like, Lena."

I quickly added, "Yes, please join us, Lena. It would be good to have your company."

We both watched as she straightened herself out in the chair. "Thank you, I will. But right now, I have to go back to my room." She turned her wheelchair around to leave when she suddenly swiveled to face Johann. "Were you a member of the party, Johann?"

He knew what she meant. "No. I was only eighteen years old when I joined the *Waffen-SS*. As I told Willi, our division was thrown into battle on the Western Front, and then we were sent to the Eastern Front in 1945 to fight the Russians. I had no part in these camps, Lena."

I could tell by the set of her face that she was pondering a response. "You were part of it, Johann, whether you knew it or not. Your government persecuted Jews for years before the war started, and you can't tell me you weren't aware of it."

Johann's face muscles tightened as he sat up and leaned forward. "I fought for my country and my people, and on this, I stand on my own merits. I sincerely regret what was done to you and your people."

"But don't you realize the German Jews were your people, Johann? I heard you talking about this *Volksgemeinschaft* business and how German culture was so unique and wonderful, but how many German citizens were Jews, and how many contributed to the German culture and fought for Germany in the First World War? How dare you speak that way!"

The old man was flummoxed. She wasn't about to let up on him and inched herself forward to continue. "You said *Volksgemeinschaft* was unique to the German people, and it was like saying the American Way was unique to all Americans. Well, Americans come from many different races and religions, but we all listen and dance to the same songs and celebrate the same national holidays.

"Different groups have unique traditions but still belong to the same country, follow the same laws, and share in the common culture. Can't you see that? You should since you've been living here for the last sixty-plus years."

He was looking down at his iPad. "You're right. I only meant that we had to protect ourselves from outside influences after the First World War and how proud we were after recovering and rebuilding our country during the 1930s."

She inched closer to him while I retreated further back into my chair. "You should have thought more about your fellow citizens and how all those actions impacted them. You should be ashamed of what your government was doing to its Jewish citizens, Johann. And this is not to mention what was done to us during the war."

She turned around to face me. "And you, Will, you said you were also in the service, didn't you?"

"Yes, ma'am, I did. I was also eighteen when I enlisted in the Marines."

"And you fought in Vietnam, correct?"

"Yes, I was there."

"Hmm." She paused to look down into her lap. Johann and I exchanged glances, wondering what she would say next. "Then perhaps all three of us are victims," she said sadly. "Maybe we have a lot to discuss after all, but it must wait. I'm tired and need to excuse myself for now." She turned around and wheeled herself out the door.

"Wow." I didn't know what else to say as I watched her push the handicap button and exit through the automatic door.

Johann looked over at me and raised his eyebrows. "*Ja*. Wow, indeed!" His face broke into a grim smile. "Things may get quite interesting from here on in, *nicht wahr?*" He stood up and grabbed my arm. "Come. Let's go get some lunch."

CHAPTER 22: LEON

Johann and I walked to lunch in silence. Lena certainly derailed our conversation, putting Johann's second point about all men being alike into question. I wondered what he was thinking of when he came up with that piece of sophistry. As far as I was concerned, it sounded like he was trying to get his country and himself off the hook.

Johann suddenly stopped and waved at someone walking toward us down the adjoining hall. Johann introduced us as soon as he joined us. "Willi, I'd like you to meet Leon. He's a good friend."

I extended my hand, and Leon took it with a big smile. "John, is this the new guy you've been telling me about?"

I looked at Johann; he didn't seem to mind being called John.

"*Ja*, he's my long lost relative. He's researching the family tree. Unfortunately, I'm not much help."

Leon looked me over. "Are you from Germany, too?"

"No, but my mother's line came from Germany in the 1800s. I tied her to this tough old nut after a lot of detective work."

"Really?" Leon looked at Johann. "Has he met your boy August yet?"

Johann replied quickly, "No, not yet."

"He's John's kid. He comes by here once a week."

Johann looked at me and then went back to Leon with a smile. "Leon likes getting involved in other people's affairs."

"C'mon, John, let's grab us some lunch. You want to come, Willi?"

"You two go ahead. I better head home."

Leon reached out to grab my arm. "C'mon, we'll keep the old guy company." I gave in, and we headed off to the dining room.

During lunch, the three of us discussed the weather, the food, and retirement. After lunch, we all got some coffee and returned to our table.

"So, John, what were you guys talking about this morning?"

"Oh, we were just talking about our two wars."

Leon looked at me with arched eyebrows. "Which war were you in, Willi? Granada?"

"Vietnam."

"What? You look too young, man. I was over there, too. Drafted! Too poor to go to college and get a deferment. Just like a lot of other brothers. You?"

"Well," I said, "I enlisted. At least you had a good excuse for being there."

"Yeah, I was there with the Americal Division from sixty-nine to seventy."

"I was in the Marines. I was at *Biên Hòa* in '72. You probably got into some nasty stuff back then."

"Oh, you could say that." He broke into a bit of a smile. "But we sure made some history, man. We were the first unit to refuse orders in that fucking war. Let me tell you about it."

I looked at Johann, expecting a strong reaction to Leon's statement. But none came. He sat still, eyeing him closely.

Leon's eyes lit up as he leaned forward. "My company had just humped its way through the Songchang Valley for five days under heavy fire. It was August. Monsoon season Raining like shit. And we had to walk through this fucking elephant grass. Couldn't see a goddamn thing. We were under fire the whole time, and you never knew where it was coming from. They were just picking us off, man." Leon started rubbing his head as if to calm down the memories that still haunted him.

Johann put a protective hand on Leon's shoulder. "You never told me this, Leon. You don't need to talk about it if you don't want to."

Leon reached up and grabbed Johann's hand. "I know, but Willi's the first brother from Nam I've seen in a long time. It just came out. Anyway, after those five days, we were about done. Wet, tired, stinky, and dirty. I had bloodstains on my fatigues from handling the wounded and humping the dead. Our company was down sixty men when we got orders to launch another assault. We all looked at each other. No way, man. We flat-out refused. Our lieutenant got on the horn with HQ in Da Nang and told them we weren't going anywhere, so they sent a first sergeant to get us out of there. And you know what? They didn't do shit to us. No punishment. No court martial."

"I would like to say one thing, Leon, and I hope you won't take offense."

"No problem, John. We're cool."

"Well, there is one thing about America I will never figure out. When I was growing up, Germany was harshly criticized for its race relations, mostly because of the Jews."

"What?" Leon interrupted. "You guys thought Jews and whites were different races?"

"They were considered that way in Germany back then," Johann admitted. "Anyway, I still haven't figured out how America got away with treating their Black citizens the way they did. We had signs saying, 'No Jews.' America did the same only they turned it around by saying, 'Whites Only.' We passed the Nuremberg laws restricting Jews, but America already had laws like that for restricting Blacks. I just wondered how you felt about that since you were fighting for a country that treated you so badly."

"Hey," Leon said, his eyes flashing, "You're not telling me anything new. My father was in the military during World War II, and he said we were segregated and assigned to all the shit details like unloading supplies, driving trucks, digging ditches, or cleaning latrines. That's the way it was for us back then, and it was that way for a long time; it seems like it's still that way for a lot of us, and I know some people who aren't so happy about it." He paused for a moment to look over at Johann. "So, I guess when you were growing up in Germany, the Nazis were running the show, right?"

"Yes, they were." Johann nodded.

"From what I learned, everybody in Germany was doing fine until the Nazis came along and started beating up the Jews, sending them into camps and stuff. That was a pretty shitty thing to do, and then they started invading other countries. No wonder everyone was so pissed off at them."

I could tell Johann wasn't expecting that response. He looked blankly at Leon and nodded slowly. I sat there waiting for another lecture but was taken aback by his deference.

"I see your point, Leon. That's probably true."

Johann's eyes switched over to me. They seemed to hold some unknown sadness. Perhaps Leon's words reminded him of Lena, so I quickly intervened. "So, Leon, how did your father feel about your being drafted?"

Leon put down his cup. "Well, I'll tell you something, Willi. I remember watching the news back then with my dad when Muhammad Ali came on and said, 'I ain't got no quarrel with them Vietcong. No Vietcong ever called me nigger.' My dad said Ali was a coward who didn't want to lose his paycheck. When I got drafted,

114

he said it was a good thing because being in the army was a whole lot safer than being in Newark because of all the riots going on."

Leon chuckled and shook his head. "Then, during the late Eighties, we were watching the news when Ali was diagnosed with Parkinson's. They played that same news clip from the Sixties, and my father said, 'Ali sure had some balls to do that.' He was quiet for a while and then said, 'Ali got it right, though. All of us should have stood up with him then. None of that damn war was right.' "

Leon's smile was gone, and his face turned serious. "The TV showed clips of the war, and my dad said, 'Son, I'm glad you made it home. You know, the government could've used the billions of dollars they wasted on that war to get rid of these damn ghettoes and improve life for Black people rather than bombing the hell out of that country and killing all those yellow folks.'

"Then, my dad choked up and said: 'Ali was right to say what he did. He was a good man, and I respect him for that. I wish I had had his conviction. I wish I had stood up for you back then. But I was just trying to make do for our family and keep us out of trouble.' " Leon was clearly struggling to keep his emotions in check.

"I would like to hear everything Ali said during that press conference," Johann said.

"Let's look it up," I asked Johann to borrow his iPad. I found his remarks and saw why the media never reported everything he said. It was an explosive time. Anything could have happened if it had been reported in its entirety. "Here it is, guys, and he sure didn't pull any punches. Listen. *My conscience won't let me go shoot my brother, or some darker people, or some poor hungry people in the mud for big powerful America. And shoot them for what? They never called me nigger, they never lynched me, they didn't put no dogs on me, they didn't rob me of my nationality, rape and kill my mother and father ... Shoot them for what? How can I shoot them poor people? Just take me to jail.*

I'm not gonna help nobody get something my Negroes don't have. If I'm gonna die, I'll die now right here fighting you, if I'm gonna die. You, my enemy. My enemies are white people, not Viet Congs or Chinese or Japanese. You my opposer when I want freedom. You my opposer when I want justice. You my opposer when I want equality. You won't even stand up for me in America for my religious beliefs and want me to go somewhere and fight, but you won't even stand up for me here at home."[1]

I gave the iPad back to Johann and he set it down on the table. "Listen, Leon, you know me; I read every day. Not too long ago, I read an article in *The Atlantic* magazine that America should be paying reparations to the Blacks ... just like we had to do for the Jews."

CHAPTER 23: REPARATIONS

Leon snorted. "Reparations? Huh! I won't hold my breath waiting for that to happen." He swiveled his head back and forth between Johann and me to check our reactions. "I heard all this shit before. Congress drafted several bills, but none of them ever came up for a vote; there's not enough gold in Fort Knox to pay us back for what they did."

"Money is not the issue, Leon. They're never going to pay any reparations until someone forces them to. No one ever sat in judgment over America like they did with us after the war. We were forced to admit our guilt and pay reparations, and we are still paying them today."

Johann looked over at me. "Willi, you should read that article." He looked down at his iPad. "It was in the June 2014 edition of *The Atlantic* and was called *The Case for Reparations* by Ta-Nehisi Coates. And while you're at it, take the time to read the book *After the Reich*. This book will give you an idea of how we were treated after the war, and you'll see how the Allies came to Nuremberg with unclean hands."

Leon stared at Johann with a puzzled look. "John, wasn't Hitler some kinda crazy racist, a real nut who always screamed and chewed carpets?"

Johann didn't flinch. "I can tell you, Leon, that he personally acknowledged Jesse Owens' victory at the 1936 Olympics and that all the Germans stood up and cheered when he won. There were also several American reporters in Berlin who watched and reported the same thing. Look it up! You'll also see that FDR never invited him to the White House."[1]

This statement really irked me. I never heard of any such thing. I made a note about Jesse Owens and underlined it while Johann continued. "And by the way, Leon, did you ever listen to or read one of Hitler's speeches? People thought he was crazy because they only saw short film clips of him ranting and raving, but Sumner Welles, the Under-Secretary of State, thought otherwise. He met with Hitler in 1940 and reported back to FDR that he was *dignified both in speech and movement... he spoke with clarity and precision, and always in a beautiful German...*"[2]

Leon didn't change his expression but was listening intently.

Johann continued, "When you saw him screaming, he was angry at the Allies for what they did to Germany after World War I, just like the Black Panthers were angry at white America for its legacy of slavery and racism. Those Black Panthers were good socialists who took matters into their own hands and cared for their people and communities. And they, just like us, had to arm and defend themselves against a system that wanted to maintain the status quo and used force and dirty tricks to shut them down. Has anything changed since then, Leon?"

Leon had been quiet for a while as he appeared to be reflecting on his past. "John, right or wrong, I only worried about myself back then. The only time I ever got pissed off about race was when some honky rubbed it in my face. We were all angry back then, and all the riots showed it. But during the war, our unit was pretty tight; we all got along without much trouble. And since then, I don't know. In some ways, things have gotten better, but in other ways, they're still the same."

Leon shrugged and turned around to face me. "Willi, you remember all the Black guys doing the dap back then? There were a lot of Black groups in the Nam, like The Zulu 1200s, De Mau Mau, and The Black Liberation Front. They made a lot of trouble in-country, like the big race riot in LBJ right before I got there."

"Slow down, Leon," Johann interjected. "Dap? LBJ? Do you mean President Johnson?"

Leon laughed at Johann's bemused face. "I forgot, John, you don't talk the talk. That's okay. Dap is a special handshake all the brothers use. D-A-P: Dignity and Pride. And LBJ was the Long Binh Jail – a US Army prison in Vietnam. Blacks made up about sixty percent of the inmates there even though we were only eleven percent of the soldiers in-country. The prisoners rioted in August 1968, and it lasted over a week. They burned the place down, man. Anyway, John, if no one fucked with me, I didn't fuck with them. I just kept my head down and went with the flow."

He paused for a moment to reflect. "I came home from that place all pissed off because all the poor white and Black kids were being drafted and killed because we couldn't afford college like the rich white kids. We were all thrown into the shit to be killed along with the dinks. And we blew the shit out of that place, man. America was like one big bad mother fuckin' jolly green giant stomping all over that country. Sure, I had problems with all that, but I got out and just said fuck it. I got a job, got married, had kids, and settled down. And that's it. I got no axe to grind with anyone anymore, and life's been pretty good ever since."

Leon looked at his watch. "Damn, it's getting late. I gotta go. My afternoon class is starting soon." He broke into a wide grin and looked over at Johann. "And by the way, old timer," he said jokingly as he stood up to leave, "you better lighten up on that Nazi shit. There are some folks here with long memories."

Johann wasn't laughing. "I'm not responsible for what memories they have, Leon, especially when those memories aren't well-informed. I am more than willing to discuss that with anyone anytime."

When he said that, I thought about Lena and wondered what would happen the next time we got together.

CHAPTER 24: WE'RE ALL FLAWED

Johann sat back and stretched out his arms. "You know, Willi, it looks nice outside. Let's finish our coffee here and then go outside to get some fresh air."

"Okay, Johann. So, tell me, what was it like coming to America in 1956?"

He squinted and put on a wry grin. "We Germans have our share of idiots, just like every other country. But after coming here and watching your TV shows and commercials, I became convinced your country was way ahead of everybody in this category."

Johann sipped his coffee, shook his head, and knitted his brows as his face turned serious. "But let me return to my second point, that all men are alike. Did you know that the American government, both before and after the war, conducted medical experiments on humans, just as we did?"

I rolled my eyes in disbelief as he began scrolling down his iPad screen. Here we go again.

"Here it is, Willi. The US Government performed a syphilis study at Tuskegee on Blacks that started in 1932 and didn't end until 1972. US health officials in this experiment pretended to treat six-hundred diseased Black men by giving them placebos. They let these people suffer for years to track the disease's long-term effects."

I remember this being reported in the press but didn't think it compared to anything done by Nazi Germany. "You're going to compare that to Mengele's horrible experiments? What about those twins?"

"Let me continue, Willi. Everyone knows what the Nazis did, but this was only the beginning of what your country did. Project 4.1 took place in 1952 when the American government wanted to test the effects of radiation. They dropped nuclear bombs on islands close to the Marshall Islands, a US protectorate. They never warned the local inhabitants about the explosion or shielded them from the exposure. They wanted to see the effects of long-term radiation poisoning and never treated them afterward. By 1974, almost a third of the exposed islanders had developed tumors.

"And then we come to the Vietnam era, Willi. From 1965 to 1966, the Dow Chemical Company, Johnson & Johnson, and the U.S. Army conducted 'dermatological research' on seventy-five Vietnamese prisoners to assess the effects of Agent Orange on humans. These prisoners were injected with dioxin, a component of Agent Orange, which was about five-hundred times the amount the study originally called for. This caused severe acne eruptions on the face, armpits, and groin, which I expect was quite painful. I read where the effects outlived the experiments, just like when the US Army conducted experiments on their soldiers with LSD, VX, and BZ during the Fifties through the Seventies to increase their aggressiveness in combat.

"Then, there was Project MK/Ultra, sometimes called the CIA's mind control program. These medical experiments were done on unwitting U.S. and Canadian citizens to determine which drugs and procedures would be effective in conducting interrogations. This study began in 1953 and ended in 1973."

I knew something about this experiment. People were slipped LSD unawares and then interrogated under bright lights. I remember that the victims were either from the CIA, the U.S. military, or captured foreign spies. "I'm familiar with that one as well, Johann. I think some people died as a result."

"That's right. You probably heard about Frank Olsen. He threw himself out of the window of his thirteenth-floor room at the Statler Hotel in New York City nine days after the CIA gave him LSD. The agency finally admitted to it in 1975. America was never called to account for these crimes, Willi, but none of this was well publicized. Not too many people were aware of what happened, and who knows what other tests your government did that we don't know about?"

A wry grin crossed his face. "What do you think, Willi? American medical experiments lasted longer and involved more victims than ours did, but your government was never painted as notoriously as ours. I'm not trying to be cynical about this, Willi. But why is Nazi Germany always called pure evil when other countries have been doing the same things for years, both before and even after the war?"

My sense of being thrust into unfamiliar ground returned. I began seeing things in a different light, and it didn't reflect well upon us. It was discomforting.

He must have seen the quizzical look on my face. He paused to shake his head, then leaned forward and softened his tone. "Sometimes, I think the media portrays us this way to sell more papers or movie tickets or to distract people from seeing that their governments commit the same crimes. And that's what worries me most, Willi. I'm afraid the American government has never stopped this behavior, especially since they've never been held accountable for it."

He leaned back and drank from his coffee cup while I tried to muster a response. "But two wrongs don't make a right, Johann. That doesn't excuse what your country did."

"I know, but you're missing the point, Willi. All men are alike. We are all born innocent without bias. But over time, each of us develops a sense of self. And that self comes to see others as different and other systems as different. And that difference usually makes us suspicious of others.

"And most people start planning how to protect themselves from that difference, or they start scheming to take from others to either level or increase that difference. And that is when conflict arises, whenever one's self-interest begins to outweigh everything else. And that is the point when evil begins to emerge."

"Why do you say *most* people? Didn't you say we're all alike?"

The old guy nodded in acknowledgment. "Well, Willi, we're all born alike, but some look outward and consider the needs of others while others choose to look inward and focus on their own needs."

He paused to look outside the cafeteria window. "Remember what I said about evil begetting evil? It does no good for any one system or ideology to label another as criminal or evil. It solves nothing. Nor does it do any good for one system to use deceit or extortion to get what they want from another system. As long as self-interest is involved, there will always be conflict and lingering resentment after that conflict is over."

CHAPTER 25: MAKING DISTINCTIONS

I watched him and began to wonder about his motives. Was he trying to absolve everything the Nazis did? "But what about the whole Master Race idea, Johann? Didn't the Nazis develop that? That theory certainly pitted them against everybody else in the world."

To my surprise, he answered without blinking an eye. "That is an interesting topic, Willi, and I'm glad you asked. However, the whole idea of a Master Race began with eugenics, which was developed first in England and took off in America before it ever came to Germany."

I had heard of eugenics before, but it was always in the context of a distant past. It was a failed science that came to a screeching halt after the fall of Nazi Germany. I chuckled, remembering Captain America, one of my favorite comic book heroes, who fought against the Nazis; he was a classic example of genetic engineering.

"Johann, I don't know much about eugenics. But wasn't it some sort of effort to improve the human race through genetic engineering? That's different from claiming you were the Master Race and superior to everyone else."

Johan furrowed his brows and shook his head in disagreement. "Back then, people felt that race was everything. The world was becoming smaller through the introduction of airplanes, ships, and railroads. People of all different backgrounds were suddenly being brought together and soon began competing for the same resources. Unfortunately, each group looked different, spoke differently, and acted differently than the other. Since these different groups didn't understand each other, they didn't trust each other, and this caused a lot of fear and tension between them.

"But misunderstanding was the real issue, Willi. It caused one group to make distinctions from other groups. The whole notion of developing one's race into a Master Race was a logical extension of that thinking. Everyone was too concerned with securing their group to appreciate that we're all born of God, that we're all one and the same." He paused when he saw me staring into my notebook without writing anything. "What are you thinking about, Willi?"

I was about to suggest that we forget about the whole thing since he kept deflecting everything wrong about Nazi Germany back onto everybody else when I noticed Lena was sitting several tables away. Some people sitting between us must have just left the dining room. She caught my look and held my gaze as she pulled away from the table and approached us. I stood up to greet her while Johann hurriedly followed my lead. Given the subject matter we were just discussing, he appeared surprised and concerned by her arrival. We both stood up as she arrived at our table.

"Good morning, gentlemen. What were you just discussing, Johann?"

Johann said, "Oh, just some history."

"Sit down, you two. I heard you mention something about race, Johann. What exactly was it?"

Johann looked warily at me and then back to Lena. "Oh, it's not that important," he said, waving away her question.

She watched him and then called his bluff. "I shouldn't have interrupted you two. I'll just leave, and you can continue your conversation."

Johann ducked her jab and counter-punched. "No, you don't have to do that, Lena. Willi was just asking about National Socialism's position on race."

"I overheard some of it, Johann," she said matter-of-factly. She moved uncomfortably in her chair and swept her hair back. "I think I'll stay if you don't mind."

Johann nodded and replied. "Well, as I was saying before, Willi, this whole Master Race idea came from eugenics. Britain started it during the early Twentieth Century, and it soon spread to America, where it became very popular. In fact, California passed a eugenics law in 1909. It gave state prisons and mental institutions the right to sterilize anybody they deemed 'unfit' or 'feeble-minded.' Dr. Leo Stanley was the chief surgeon at the San Quentin penitentiary, and he operated on criminals between 1930 and 1959 to prevent them from reproducing. He stated his goal was to, and I quote, *help a new, ideal man emerge*.

"California was, in fact, the third state in the US to pass sterilization laws that would prevent undesirable traits from spreading to future generations. The thought was to purify the race and, over time, decrease the inheritance of criminal tendencies and mental deficiencies. This would reduce the number of inmates and save the state money."

I could see Lena's face tightening and her whole body getting more and tense. Johann didn't seem to notice and continued.

"By 1921, California accounted for eighty percent of all nationwide sterilizations. Between 1909 and 1963, about twenty thousand forced sterilizations were performed in California's state institutions alone. Does any of this sound familiar to you two?"

Lena seemed to be simmering, so I quickly broke in. "I never heard of anything like that happening in the States, Johann. I did hear about it in Germany, though, and I believe it was mostly done in mental institutions during the Thirties before the war."

"And guess where we got that idea? In 1927, your Supreme Court upheld a state's right to sterilize a person considered unfit for procreation. Justice Holmes said: *It is better for all the world if, instead of waiting to execute degenerate offspring for crime, or to let them starve for their imbecility, society can prevent those who are manifestly unfit from continuing their kind.*

"So, you see, all this thinking and all these programs started in the U.S. before they were even considered in Germany. America was trying to engineer its own Master Race before we ever did." Johann paused to look down at his iPad. "Oh, and by the way, Willi, this is from *The New York Times* yesterday, *Argentina Rejects Legalizing Abortion … Argentina is the birthplace of Pope Francis, who recently denounced abortion as the 'white glove' equivalent of the Nazi-era eugenics program."*

He put the iPad down and looked at us with wide-open eyes and an exaggerated grin. "Why didn't he say it was the equivalent of the California eugenics program? After all, California started it before we did and even continued it after the war, and they probably had more victims. It's been almost seventy-five years since the war ended, but we're still being tagged with labels that really belong to others. Do you think this is right, Willi?"

I looked up from my notepad and saw Lena shaking her head and looking like she was about to boil over. Before I could say a word, she quickly answered him. "Just because California did it first, didn't make it right for Germany to do what they did."

Johann leaned forward and assertively answered her. "No, it didn't. And that wasn't my point, and I apologize for making that remark about the Pope. My point, Lena, is that we weren't different than anyone else."

Johann quickly ducked his head to look at his iPad. "Let me find where I left off so we can finish this topic. Here we are. Here are some of the other things that prove I'm right! When Hitler was in Landsberg prison in 1924, he read American books about eugenics. He corresponded with Leon Whitney, president of the American Eugenics Society, and Madison Grant, who wrote *The Passing of the Great Race*. Hitler wrote Grant from Landsberg and said this book served as his 'Bible.' Grant's book outlined the racial history of Europe and was published in 1916. He extolled the Nordic race and bemoaned its corruption by others who lacked blond hair and blue eyes.

"One of Grant's major concerns was American immigration. His views led Congress to pass the 1924 Immigration Act, which barred certain races from entry. The Department of State said the Act would *preserve the ideal of American homogeneity*, which, at that time, was the white majority."

Johann paused to see if Lena or I had any reaction.

CHAPTER 26: A NEW FRIEND

This was familiar ground to me. "I studied that Act while I was in college, Johann. The Japanese were angry about its passage and felt it demonstrated America's racial prejudice; it helped fuel Japanese nationalism and led to a distrust of American foreign policy, especially given America's recent record in the Philippines."

Lena looked over at me and asked what my major was in college. I told her English and history. "I graduated with honors in history, and my paper concerned Japanese-American relations before the war. The title was *Self Deception & Self Defeat* because both countries deceived themselves into believing their national interests in Asia aligned with the more universal ideals of peace and justice, but both countries suffered defeat. Japan's defeat was military while America's was moral when we dropped the atom bomb."

"You seem proud of your work."

"I was at the time. I worked hard for it."

"Was that before or after your time in the war?"

"It was after. The Marines taught me how to apply myself. I was only eighteen when I enlisted. I went to boot camp and survived it by learning to apply myself. I developed a drive that wouldn't let me quit. That drive pushed me through college and building a career..." I stopped, realizing that I was talking to the ultimate survivor. She seemed to be looking right through me. "You must have had that drive to survive as well, Lena."

"No, I didn't have that drive, Will. There was little of that left after we were beaten, starved, and worked to death. My mother lay dying next to me while I was starving, and all I could think of was to share what little I had with her. I never felt I would survive."

She paused to look down at her hands. "It just wasn't that important to me anymore…but my mother was." She looked at me with grief still in her eyes and stretched her hand out to grab mine. "You can drive as hard as you want, Will, but you'll never bull your way through everything in this world. You'll only wind-up ruining things for yourself and others. You have to learn how to live in this world and share it with others. We all need to focus on making the world a more just place for everyone."

My ears perked up when she mentioned making the world a just place. I recalled the review of her book, *The Last of the Just*, and cast my eyes downward, remembering all the shit I put others through by heeding the beast and thinking of my needs. "You're right, Lena. I never saw things like that. Thanks for sharing that." If Johann was becoming a father figure for me, then Lena was becoming the type of caring mother I had always hoped for.

Johann sat quietly doing our exchange but now tried to mend some fences. "Let me say again how sorry I am about your mother and what you had to endure, Lena."

I looked over at Johann. He parroted the same excuses I made to Cynthia when she uncovered the beast. I learned how hollow an apology can be after inflicting so much pain. The only thing one can do after that is to shroud your face and bear your regret in silence. I had no idea how Johann really felt, but I noticed his gaze never left her eyes.

Lena nodded. *"Du bist sehr nachdenklich … Dankeschön."*

I knew *dankeschön* meant "thank you" but had no idea what the preceding words meant. Johann obviously did as he reached out to pat her on the shoulder.

My phone started to vibrate. I pulled it out of my pocket. It was Cynthia. "Will, where are you? I hope you're on the road. We have that wine and cheese thing with our new neighbors at four o'clock."

Oh shit. I always call when I leave, and it's always before Johann's lunch. I forgot to call this time because I went to lunch with Leon, and then Lena came over. I looked at my watch and saw it was almost two. I was surprised she waited this long to call. "I got tied up meeting a couple of new people here, Cynthia. My bad. I'll leave right now, and I should be home soon."

I hung up, and Johann was quick to grab my attention. "Willi, before you leave, I want to apologize for losing my temper with Leon right before he left." He stopped to look over at Lena, who remained silent. Then, he said something that seemed totally out of character. "*Ach*, I should just learn to let things go. My days of fighting and arguing are coming to an end. I read somewhere that the world runs best by letting things take their course, and perhaps that is the best advice."

It was my turn to laugh. Was he turning over a new leaf? "Well, you did get pretty fired up over his last remark, Johann."

Lena stared at him with an arched eyebrow.

"Pardon me, Lena, but I got irritated with my friend earlier. I wasn't angry so much with him as with all the people who twist things around and don't try to understand how we felt during those times. Their distortions led to war, which caused so much pain and suffering for everyone."

I did a double-take. Did he just contradict himself? He sounded like his old self and belied what he said only seconds ago about letting things go. I was about to say as much but had to get going. I did, however, make a mental note to follow up with him later.

I stood up and said my goodbyes. Johann and Lena left the cafeteria with me until Johann branched off to his room while Lena and I continued to the main entrance. Lena stopped me once she saw Johann walk out of sight. "Will, you said you were really proud when you completed your Honor's paper, and your drive helped you build a successful career, but you don't appear that way now. Did something go wrong?"

I really didn't want to discuss my past with her. I was in a hurry to get home, and besides, I was pretty much played out, but somehow, I just blurted out that I had a stroke. "After that stroke, Lena, all my drive and pride just vanished, along with a lot of other things." I was surprised by my admission.

"A stroke! When was that?"

"I was forty-eight then… about eighteen years ago."

"So young… but you seem fine now."

I looked down at her with a weak smile. "Well not so much, but that's a long story, Lena. Maybe we can talk about it some other time. I told my wife I was leaving, and she'll kill me if I was late for this party with our neighbors. I really have to go."

We said our goodbyes, and I walked away feeling like I had just entered into a new relationship. It felt like falling into a fast-moving river, pulling me away to God only knows where.

~ AT HOME ~

CHAPTER 27: RED-HEADED STEPCHILD

I drove home reflecting on what Johann said about America using concentration camps, conducting medical experiments, and running eugenic programs. This visit proved to be even more unsettling than the last two. Could he possibly be exaggerating? I didn't think so because everything he said up to now was true.

The sun was already deep into its descent and blinding me. My visor provided little relief against the bright glare that seeped in underneath. It was almost as harsh as Lena's admonitions about bulling my way through life. I smiled because she was right.

I've always felt you're never too old to learn and, after these last three visits, I've learned that the converse is also true: you're never too old to unlearn. It's just a lot harder.

I looked out the side window. The greenery bordering the highway whizzed by; it brought back memories of passing over treetop canopies in Vietnam as MAG-12 headed back to Japan. The plane was full of exhausted troops, many of them were wasted from drugs. It was a pitiful sight.

It was the same situation when I left Japan when my hitch was almost over. Everyone was wrung out. There was the initial joy of leaving, but that left once we got closer to stateside. We flew into to San Francisco where a number of us were shuttled off to Treasure

Island to be discharged. There was no decompression or re-orientation. No speeches, fanfare, or bands playing. After several days, we were simply dismissed. I angrily tore the sergeant stripes off my blouse and changed into jeans before grabbing the first bus to the airport.

I left the Corps sickened and disgusted by what we had done to South Vietnam. We were an industrial giant employing sophisticated technology and weaponry to destroy a tiny agrarian country. We dislocated their culture by hooking them on to our Western ways. And then, after we were gone, they were left holding the bag.

The returning veterans were also left holding the bag. Civilians treated us like red-headed stepchildren, avoiding us and not offering any consolation. The government provided us with the GI Bill and VA mortgages but otherwise left us alone. We had to fend for ourselves as we tried to return to normal. But normal was lost forever.

After the incident at My Lai, we were called "baby killers" by our peers and cast as deranged sociopaths in movies and TV shows. I couldn't understand a nation that didn't appreciate our service or sacrifices. Our government took no moral accountability for that war, either to us, the South Vietnamese, or the world.

I couldn't accept any of it and went to college trying to understand why that goddamn war ever took place. I also wanted to show all these civilians that I was more than just a red-headed stepchild.

I was driven to excel in college, just like in the Marines. I survived one shitstorm with two meritorious promotions, and now I was bound to do the same in college. I drove hard to earn two degrees in only three years. The GI Bill picked up my college tuition, but I had to work forty-eight hours a week to pay for my books, apartment, car, and other necessities. There was no time for friends or social life, but I didn't feel the need for any.

Things changed during my junior year. South Vietnam fell, and our economy went into the shitter. The North Vietnamese, the Khmer Rouge, and the Pathet Lao surged in our wake, spreading death and destruction throughout the parrot's beak of Southeast Asia.

None of this improved my disposition. I watched the Americans and South Vietnamese flee from our embassy in Saigon like escaping criminals. They ran up to the rooftop and scrambled into helicopters. People were jumping onto the helicopter skids, and their belongings fell off them like so much discarded loot. It was a pathetic scene.

I watched those same helicopters landed on our ships, disgorged their passengers, and were jettisoned into the sea like so much trash. The sailors had to make room for the incoming boatloads of refugees, and there was nowhere else to put them. It was like watching a Marx Brothers movie, but nobody was laughing. Leon's father was right: all the billions wasted on that war should have been spent helping the poor at home.

After watching that debacle on the news, I walked around campus with a permanent scowl on my face. My beard, long hair, and faded field jacket didn't help matters. They all communicated menace. No one came close to me, and I can't say I blamed them.

CHAPTER 28: ALICIA

It was around that time that I met Alicia. She sat next to me in philosophy class. She was introduced to the class as a student from Mexico who came on a government scholarship.

One day, our professor was discussing Heidegger and phenomenology. She leaned over and desperately asked me to explain what he was talking about. She surprised me as I had never seen her speaking to anyone in class.

I was listening intently to the professor, but her question made me glance over and silently acknowledge her. Her eyes connected with mine and conveyed loneliness; she seemed more interested in connecting with me rather than my answering her question. She struck me as an 18-year-old innocent. I felt a pang of remorse for her as she seemed as lost and out of place as me.

I waited for the professor to pause for a moment and then whispered to wait until class was over. Afterward, we decided to go to the local coffee shop to talk about Heidegger. We sat down, but she started talking about her family instead. She was obviously homesick. She told me her father had left home to work while her mother raised her and her brother. She said she really didn't know her father. As she spoke, I began to sense a dark side to her. I looked across the table and saw some ill-defined sorrow in her eyes. I felt as if I were witnessing another tragedy, another case of life stunted before it ever bloomed.

There was a flip side to my anger after the war. It was sorrow. I was angry at all the bastards who started the war, but I felt sorrow for all those who suffered as a result. I felt a common bond with her almost instantly.

Our coffee sessions after class soon became an afternoon ritual. We met twice a week to commiserate. We did not so much fall in love as we held one another up and let the rest of the world go its own way. I never expected anything from her. I spent time with her only because she needed help, and frankly, I needed a touch of humanity myself.

I'll never forget one afternoon that came several weeks later. It was snowing lightly with only the slightest touch of a breeze. The trees' bare branches held a blanket of fresh snow, and the air was crisp and clean. We sat on a bench for a moment to watch Nature paint an aesthetically pleasing picture.

She had something to tell me that afternoon. She was abused by a high school teacher and tried to commit suicide afterward. I couldn't determine whether the drops on her face came from tears or melting snow.

I invited her to my apartment to discuss it privately rather than in the crowded coffee shop. We sat on the couch and talked about it for a while until I had to get ready to work my evening shift. I went to the bathroom to shave, and when I returned, she wasn't there. I wasn't quite sure what happened until I found her in my bed. She said nothing. She just watched me, with the sheets pulled to her chin, waiting for a response.

I couldn't handle rejecting her and crawled into bed with her. To this day, I don't know if she really wanted me or was just reaching out to the first person who showed any interest.

Regardless, after that night, we became two lost souls bound together by tragedy.

The next morning, I woke up before she did. She was lying in bed, and her long, black hair made me think of all the Vietnamese who were either blown up, burned up, or left twisting in the wind. She took on the guise of a lost war orphan, and I was hooked.

After that, I waited a few more weeks before asking her to move in with me, and she agreed. There didn't seem to be any other alternative without further damaging her fragile state. In any event, it didn't matter to me; my life felt like it was trashed anyway. The damage done by my father and the war seemed irreversible, but perhaps my helping her would be a shot at redemption for both of us.

After a few months, our daily lives became routine until her father died. Her mother begged her to come home. I knew if she went back to Mexico, she wouldn't return. Besides, I wasn't ready for her to leave. It was a dilemma, and the only solution seemed to be marriage, so I asked.

She didn't seem surprised by my proposal but put the onus back on me. She asked if I really wanted to, and I suddenly realized that I no longer wanted to be alone anymore. We were married soon after and she became pregnant a month later.

Life seemed to improve with the promise of a child. The mid-1970s was a bleak period, shrouded in misery. Nixon and Vietnam both fell in disgrace. Gas rationing hit and then the rise of inflation all led toward a grim future. Her pregnancy, however, brought a sliver of light into our lives. But it didn't last. When Alicia was seven and a half months pregnant, her water broke.

Our daughter's lungs weren't fully developed, and she had to be placed in an incubator. We watched helplessly for a day and a half as she labored at breathing. She passed away without ever being held by her parents.

My devastation was bottomless. I tried praying while she lived, but things went black after that. I couldn't believe her life could be snatched away so quickly or that God would deliver yet another crippling blow to my joyless life.

I tried to find comfort in my pocket bible, but none ever came. The beast repeatedly whispered to stop grieving and focus on school and my job. I sucked up the grief and went back to both in an almost catatonic state.

Alicia numbly absorbed the tragedy. She dropped out of college to work and had no words of recrimination toward God, me, or anyone else. I wasn't sure about her state of mind as the days slipped by. We only exchanged blank expressions with each other as the days passed and never mentioned our baby's passing. After several months, the sadness became part of our daily lives.

I stopped reliving the past when a phrase from the review of Lena's book sprang to mind: *the sense of all that life abused, broken, and turned to ashes*. It perfectly described my state of mind then and now.

The exit sign for my town appeared and pulled me back to the present. It was a relief to flip on the turn signal; it indicated that I was almost home. The rhythmic clicking washed away all thoughts of the past.

CHAPTER 29: LARRY THE LAWYER

I made it home with half an hour to spare. I pulled into the garage, stopped the car, and sat in silence. A phrase began resounding in my head: *Action without knowledge is not action and knowledge without action is not knowledge.* It sounded profound the first time I heard it, but it had no relevance for me at the time. Now it does.

The first part of that phrase fit my life before the stroke; the second part fit my life after. Before the stroke, I was driven to act without thinking about the impact on myself or others. After the stroke, I knew I had acted wrongly but I was stuck there, without any purpose to drive my actions.

I quickly shook off my thoughts, got out of the car, and went inside. Cynthia was sitting in the family room watching TV. She didn't get up. "Sorry, I forgot about the time, Cynthia. We really got bogged down today."

"So why didn't you call me and tell me you would be late?" Her tone was challenging. She never forgave me or forgot the day she uncovered the beast. And neither did I.

"I'm sorry. I should have called."

"You should have." Her voice rose, and she still hadn't turned around to face me. "You always get locked up in your own world and lose sight of everything else. You may think you have changed,

141

but you really haven't." She turned around and looked directly at me.

"You're right. I'm sorry."

"I'm getting tired of hearing you say you're sorry. You know I worry about you. What if something happened and I'm just left waiting on your call?"

"I just got too wrapped up. I left as soon as you called."

"Well," she relented and gave me a half-smile, "was your visit worth it?"

I rolled my eyes and sat down. "Jeez Louise, you wouldn't believe my day. It was interesting, all right. I have to research everything he said today to see if it's really true or not."

"Does it really matter?" She looked askance at my excitement.

"Well, it does to me. I need to see whether he's exaggerating, misleading, or telling me the truth. I also wound-up meeting two other people. One was a guy who served in Vietnam, and the other was a woman who survived Auschwitz. What are the odds of that happening? I'll probably go for a couple more visits and that should end it."

"Will, I meant what I said. I really don't like you going there. You're the one who said you wanted to put the past behind you. I think you're getting obsessed with this whole thing. And now, these new people?" She glared at me and didn't wait for an answer. "What the heck are you getting into, Will? What will that woman think about your talking to a Nazi? What if other people find out?

"I don't think it's good for you. I told you before that you'll probably hear things from him that you shouldn't, and they'll affect you. And now you're involving that poor, old woman?" She looked away for a moment, and then her eyes shot back to me. "What are you trying to get out of all this, Will? What's the point? You know what they did was terrible, and there's no point in rehashing it or justifying any part of it."

"I know what they did was terrible, but I want to know why they did it. What drove them into doing what they did?" I looked back at her cold stare and stopped speaking. I didn't want to tell her that I was also speaking for myself, that I wanted to find something that would explain why I did the terrible things that I did.

She wrinkled her nose at my response and got up. "Okay, it's getting late. Take a quick shower and then let's get over to the neighbors. I don't want to be late. And please don't say anything embarrassing!"

I smiled and kissed her. "I'll be careful, honey. I promise." I set off for the bathroom before she had the chance to give me another earful.

We left for the party at the appointed time. I had briefly met the husband, Larry, a few days earlier but didn't have a chance to meet his wife. When we arrived and made introductions, I learned his wife's name was Adriana, and his last name was Gallagher. I thought mixing an Irish Gallagher with a half-English Barnes was probably not a good idea. And then I saw that our wives were equally mismatched. Adriana was a Latina with long jet-black hair and deep brown eyes, while Cynthia was Polish with blond hair and green eyes. I hoped all our differences weren't an omen for the evening ahead.

We walked through the house, stepped outdoors onto the patio, and sat down. After a bit of small talk, I commented that Adriana was a lovely name but one you hardly ever hear. I asked about her family name, and she said it was *Obregón*. I asked about her roots since that name didn't sound familiar either.

She put her glass down and looked at me matter-of-factly. "My last name came from an Irishman who married a Mexican woman; *Obregón* came out when anyone in Mexico tried to pronounce his last name, O'Brien. He fought in the San Patricio Battalion against the Americans back in the 1840s."

"How about that," I said, putting down my glass. "I was a Marine. The Marine's Hymn has a line about the Halls of Montezuma from that war, that's the name of the castle that they stormed during the Battle of Chapultepec."

I was pleased with myself and sported a wide grin until I saw Cynthia's eyes glaring at me. She knows I invariably get into trouble whenever I try to be the center of attention. Larry's eyes rolled back at the comment as well. This didn't bode well for me.

Adriana stared at me without smiling. She said the San Patricio Battalion was formed by immigrant Irish Catholics who deserted the American Army. They left because of the physical abuse and poor treatment they received from higher-ranking, native-born Protestants. They also left because their Catholic brethren in the Mexican Army promised them better treatment and land grants if they joined.

I felt like I was being lectured to. Nobody interrupted her as she continued. "They fought at Chapultepec. And then there was another battle against the Americans at Churubusco. The San Patricios fought until their ammunition ran out. The end of the battle was not pretty." She glared at me as she sipped her wine. She finished with a bitter tone. "It was the end of the war."

Larry quickly interceded. It was obvious he wanted to give Adriana a moment to cool down. "After Adriana and I had been dating for a while, she told me the whole story. You wouldn't believe what happened to those guys after they surrendered. The U.S. Army didn't take kindly to deserters who joined enemy forces."

They all turned to look at me, clearly expecting a response from a veteran. "Well, I guess whatever the army did to them was pretty bad, considering they deserted in the first place because of bad treatment ..." I just let my voice trail off before I said anything else that might get me into trouble.

Larry sipped his wine glass and prepared to take center stage. "Listen, I was really interested in this because I'm a lawyer. I wanted to see how the army handled this as it involved deserters who became enemy combatants."

Cynthia perked up and saw an opportunity to derail the conversation. "What area of law are you practicing now, Larry?"

"Oh, I'm a litigator. I try the big cases for corporations, but I'm also a bit of a legal historian. I won an award in law school for a paper I wrote about the Nuremberg Tribunals. I understand the military mindset all too well from that."

Cynthia stared at me with a don't-you-dare look. I leaned back and brought a glass of wine to my mouth.

Adriana leaned forward and urged her husband. "Go ahead, Larry, tell them what happened."

"Well, after the battle, the American Army immediately convened two separate court martials for the battalion survivors. At neither proceeding did the men have any advocates, nor were there any transcripts. The verdict came as no surprise; they were all sentenced to death. However, the method of executing them did not comply with existing military regulations. All of them were hanged."

He looked over at his wife. She shrugged and turned her head away from us. Larry also shrugged and continued to relay the rest of the story in his best courtroom manner. "Execution by hanging was a violation of the Articles of War at the time. Death sentences for uniformed soldiers were to be carried out by a firing squad; hanging was reserved for spies or soldiers who committed atrocities against civilians. In all, fifty men were hanged. It was the largest mass execution in U.S. history."

Adriana turned to face the group and fixed a steely glare at me. "There were three separate hanging events; in one of them, thirty men were hung on the battlefield of Chapultepec."

Larry jumped in again to keep Adriana at bay. "You're absolutely correct, Adriana. General Winfield Scott mustered both armies to watch the hanging at Chapultepec. A Colonel Harney oversaw the execution and ordered the bodies to remain hanging from the gallows. He said: *I was ordered to have them hanged and have no orders to unhang them.* I can't remember the writer who covered the event, but he said it was *a refinement of cruelty and... fiendish.*"[1]

Adriana turned her eyes away from me and swept her long hair aside. She took advantage of Larry's pause to resume her story. "Some of them managed to escape and found work at the Mexican arsenal in Guadalajara; others took advantage of the land grants promised by the Mexican government; one of them was Peter O'Brien, my ancestor."

Cynthia seamlessly changed the subject by asking Adriana if she was born in Mexico. She nodded. "I was, but I came here to get my law degree at UPenn, where I met Larry."

Although I was tempted to explore the San Patricios further, I thought the better of it and let Cynthia carry on the rest of the evening's conversation. It ended amicably enough, and we all promised to do it again soon.

CHAPTER 30: LULU

After we came home, I looked up the San Patricios and came across George Ballentine; he was an Englishman who recorded his experiences with the American Army during the war. He wrote, *There was a portion of truth* to the San Patricio members deserting the American Army because of their Catholic faith and poor treatment. He described their punishments for *trivial offensives* to be both *revolting and disgusting.*[1]

Mexico enticed American Catholic troopers to desert by distributing handbills that appealed to their shared faith, stating, *You must not fight against a religious people, nor should you be seen in the ranks of those who proclaim slavery of mankind as a constitutive principle ... liberty is not on the part of those who desire to be lords of the world, robbing properties and territories, which do not belong to them and shedding so much blood in order to accomplish their views, views in open war to the principles of our holy religion.*[2]

The Mexicans had a point. Slavery was still legal in the U.S., and the Americans were anxious to grab their land. A victory over Mexico would provide them with the ports of San Francisco and San Diego, as well as the trade routes running through New Mexico and the rich mineral resources of the Nevada territory.

It reminded me of Johann's remark about American *lebensraum.* After all the history lessons today, I was left despondent and went to join Cynthia in bed. She was already asleep when I entered the darkened bedroom. I slid gently beneath the sheets and thought about tonight's get-together. Adriana's long, jet-black hair and cutting remarks reminded me of Lulu.

I met Lulu during my R&R in Taipei, Taiwan. I went there after a couple months of months in Vietnam. We arrived at CCK airbase the day before Christmas in '72. A U.S. government bus was waiting to drive us into Taipei. The ride was long and uncomfortable.

When we finally got to the hotel, several people stood outside the front door. A middle-aged man emerged to greet us and, without wasting too much time, told us we could pick any of the women behind him. Looking at the faces before me, I was struck by one whose eyes locked onto mine. If eyes are the window to the soul, then hers were shining brightly like a beacon. I quickly picked her out.

I stood by the window in my hotel room that night and watched the twinkling lights of the city. It dawned on me that it was Christmas Eve, and the only person I had to spend it with was a prostitute. I had no illusions about our arrangement. There was no room for feelings in her trade or mine. Regardless, the next three days with her were restful and relaxing. She couldn't have been more gracious and considerate as she showed me around the island and introduced me to Chinese food and customs.

While lying next to Cynthia, I realized I never did anything special for Lulu. I was so glad to be away from the war that I only thought of myself. I don't think I gave her half the attention she gave me. Johann asked me earlier today if there was anything in my past that I wish could be whitewashed away. He didn't give me time to answer, but I wish I had a do-over with this woman.

Our last night together was spent quietly. I was packing my clothes and glancing now and then at her as she looked out the window. She was in her robe, with her figure outlined by the city lights. The thought of going back to *Biên Hòa* tomorrow depressed me. I walked over to the window, touched her on the shoulder, and said as compassionately as I could, "How can you live like this, Lulu?"

I expected her to turn around and hug me, but she abruptly spun around and glared at me. "How can you judge *my* life, Will?" She emphasized her point with a poke to my chest. "How do you know how *I* live? How *I* feel?" She continued staring at me with a cold detachment.

I was stunned. "I don't, Lulu. But I've come to care about you. I came here not caring about anybody or anything, and you helped me feel good about myself and life for a change. I thought maybe I could say or do something good for you."

"Just like all the good you're doing in Vietnam?"

We had never discussed the war. They were probably told to avoid the subject. "The war has nothing to do with this. This is just you and me. This is not politics." I became adamant. "This is no bullshit, Lulu. You can't keep on doing this. Some of the guys that come over here can be real pigs, and some can be very mean. Something might happen."

"I don't worry about the future, Will, so don't care about me. You Americans are such busybodies! You come over here, upset everything. You think you doing good, but you upset the balance of everything and make things worse."

She sounded ungrateful like she wanted to get rid of me. I became angry and defensive. "I know when something's not right and when to do something about it."

"You know nothing. You stick your nose into everybody's business," she asserted evenly. "It's like you're dropping a stone into a pond; it makes waves and disturbs the peace of everything around it. My father is a Taoist. He said balance in this world comes from not wanting anything and not thinking of yourself. My father told me to move through life like a bee gathering honey; it doesn't hurt the flowers, and it doesn't take away their color or smell. Even your own God says bad things about how you Americans act. He says, *not by might, nor by power, but by Spirit.*"

I was left speechless. I tried doing the right thing, but she turned everything around and threw the gospel back in my face. I knew then, just as I did back in the chapel at boot camp, that God wasn't with us in this fucking war, and we would all be damned because of it. America couldn't help the Vietnamese any more than I could help her. We were destroying not only others but ourselves as well.

Recalling my emotions from that night covered me like our bed sheets. They were crisp and clean but not nearly as warm and comforting. I reached out for Cynthia's hand and, once again, thanked God for sending her to me.

CHAPTER 31: GOOD NIGHT

I flipped over to my side of the bed and fluffed up the pillow. "Can't sleep, Will? Want to talk about it?"

I couldn't see her in the dark but felt her presence. "Too much stuff dredged up today about the past: first, it was Johann and the old woman talking about their war; then it was Johann's friend talking about his time in Vietnam; and then that conversation with Larry and Adriana about the war with Mexico. You just get sick of it after a while... all the wars, the urge to acquire more and more, the lack of compassion, the hate and anger. It seems like it's never going to end."

I turned to face her. "It's over." She said softly, reaching over to touch my cheek.

"It's never over." I turned my eyes back to the ceiling. "Most people never see outside themselves; they take all their hurt and anger and blindly lash out whenever they feel threatened or they selfishly take whatever they want, regardless of who gets hurt. Either way, they just want to satisfy themselves, and when they're done, they may say 'we're sorry,' but they'll do it all over again whenever they feel the need."

I paused to temper myself before resuming. "This old woman today, Lena, told Johann about her time in the camps. She went in when she was fourteen and lost her entire family by the time she was eighteen. She told us how angry she was at God and the world after the war was over. I don't know what happened to her afterward, but now, she's all alone in a wheelchair and carrying a lot of memories."

I tried again to see Cynthia's face in the dark but couldn't. All I could do was imagine her face as it was 30 years ago, and the memory warmed my heart and calmed me down. "I'm glad I found you." I thought a bit more about that and quickly added, "But it's probably better to say I was lucky you found me."

"We both were lucky."

"No, I was the lucky one. You trusted me enough to marry me, and I let you down. I always loved you, Cynthia, but I was selfish. I only thought of myself before the stroke. Back then, I knew what I was doing was wrong and, believe it or not, it tore me up every day worrying about how hurt you would be if you knew. But I did it anyway, and then you found out about it, which turned into a blessing after all."

I could hear and feel her breathing beside me while she digested my words. "I was always angry before the stroke, and I was always angry about being angry ... I was just frustrated with my life. I felt like there was no justice in this world." I reached for her hand, and she didn't pull it away. "My father pushed me into my own world while my mother watched what was happening without saying a word. I tried my best to get my parents' attention, and when that didn't work, I had to go out and find other ways to get love and attention."

"They're dead, Will. It doesn't matter now."

"I know, but it should matter." The old familiar urge to square accounts began to rise; it had been absent since the stroke. "I'm sick of all the angry, selfish people who screw the world over for their own selfish needs. They should be called to account for their lies and bad behavior. Each generation suffers because of them... people die or are damaged because they go after what they want, regardless of how much others suffer. And then, the next generation of those who suffered comes along demanding justice for themselves and their parents. And then, the whole cycle begins all over again. One man's idea of right is another man's idea of wrong, and off we go."

Cynthia reached out to touch my face. "Calm down, Will. Those kinds of people will always be with us, and there's nothing anyone can do about them."

Her touch made my anger and sadness dissipate. I moved closer and cradled my arm around her waist. "I'm calm, honey. No worries. I'm thankful you stuck by me... you gave me a chance to escape that cycle."

"Well, you should stop getting yourself all worked up over the past. You have to let go of it and take each day as it comes. Appreciate what you have."

"I know, but I can't whenever I think about all the people who died and all the money that was spent on that goddamn war. It could have been used to help others instead of destroying lives. And we're still doing it today America's spending more than ever on wars and sending our military all over the world so we can become a global empire while everything else inside this country is going to hell in a handbasket."

"Will, what do you say to Doris and Daisy each night?"

"What do you mean?"

"What do you tell them every night when we turn off the TV and head to the bedroom?"

"Get in bed?"

"Exactly. That's enough for one night. Now go to sleep."

She was right. I had to get my rest. I rolled over on my back and smiled. It felt good to be engaged. There was a lot of reading and research to be done tomorrow. I was anxious to see if Johann was speaking the truth to me or not.

CHAPTER 32: A LACK OF INTEGRITY

The dogs woke me earlier than usual. I finished our morning drill, brewed a second cup of coffee, and ducked into my study before Cynthia woke up.

I sat down at my desk, opened my notebook, and the first entry made me smile. It was Johann's mention of Enya. I turned to my computer and selected *A Day Without Rain* from her playlist. It was a comforting way to start reviewing a painful subject.

There were two starred items in my notes that I wanted to pursue further. The first item was Johann's mention of the Allies forging documents at the Nuremberg Tribunal. The second item concerned the torturing of German PoWs to obtain incriminating evidence. I had a hard time believing either item. The authorities had plenty of witnesses, captured documents, films, and photos to support the Allies' case against the Nazi leaders. Why did they feel the need to do this as well? If Johann was lying about this, that would be the end of any further visits. If he was correct, then I would want to hear more.

The next week or so was spent poring through the Tribunal's records. My first step was to check the rules regarding evidence. This was important because it would show they oversaw its submission and how they maintained its integrity during the trial. Both would be key to proving or disproving Johann's allegations.

The Tribunal's Charter contained only two very brief Articles concerning this subject. *Article 19. The Tribunal shall not be bound by technical rules of evidence. It shall adopt and apply to the greatest possible extent expeditious and non-technical procedure and shall admit any evidence, which it deems to have probative value...* "and *"Article 21. The Tribunal shall not require proof of facts of common knowledge but shall take judicial notice thereof.* [1]

Article 19 set the tone by stating that the proceedings were *not bound by any technical rules of evidence.* By contrast, our Federal Rules concerning evidence spanned over forty pages and provide clear instructions for governing the admissibility, authentication, relevance, identification, and handling of physical evidence.[2]

Article 19 meant that any Allied government could submit any piece of evidence without any control over its authenticity. When I read this, I knew there would be questions regarding their integrity. Article 21 followed suit by not requiring factual proof to validate a claim of common knowledge. In a federal trial, the claim of "common knowledge" could be challenged, and whoever made such a claim must provide proof of facts to substantiate it.

The Tribunal had multiple nations with different cultures, beliefs, and experiences with the enemy during the war. Any claim of "common knowledge" would be a tough sell. However, the prosecution used it numerous times to incriminate a defendant. When a defendant challenged any claim of common knowledge among the Allies, the four judges weren't bound to require any proof from the prosecution. It was rare that they did since the judges and the prosecutors both came from the same countries.

Now that I knew the ground rules, I began searching for any references to forged documents. The name Carlos Porter kept coming up in my searches. He was an attorney and a professional translator of German, French, Italian, Spanish, and Portuguese documents. He wrote several books and articles about the Allies forging German documents and submitting them as evidence at Nuremberg. His research was thorough and well-documented. Unfortunately, he was an obvious racist and a self-proclaimed antisemite, which undoubtedly detracted from an acceptance of his findings.

Udo Walendy meticulously researched the authenticity of Soviet photographs submitted to the Tribunal as evidence of German war crimes. His book, *Forged War Crimes*, outlined how those pictures were deliberately doctored or forged. Walendy was later convicted of violating Germany's "anti-hate" law (*Volksverhetzung*) for his views. His book was published on the Internet. I skimmed through it and didn't see any instances of hate, only a strong case for forgery and fraud against the Soviets.

Sefton Delmer was another name I stumbled across in researching forged documents at the Nuremberg Tribunal. He headed the Political Warfare Executive Office (PWE) of the British Intelligence Service during the war. The PWE's mission was to create "black propaganda" against the Nazis. Black propaganda is described as *false information and material that purports to be from a source on one side of a conflict, but is actually from the opposing side… typically used to vilify, embarrass, or misrepresent the enemy… [and] relies on the willingness of the receiver to accept the credibility of the source.*[3]

Journalist Marc Wortman described the role of the PWE and its operations as *a veritable fake news mill. Teams of artists, printers, and writers also published fake German newspapers and printed up thousands of illustrated leaflets full of believable, yet mostly false, 'news,' as well as pornographic illustrations, forged leave passes for soldiers, and other documents designed to crack apart German unity.*[4]

Delmer continued working for the British government after the war along with his associate, Otto John. I found a report in the CIA's archives that mentioned both men. Otto John had fled Germany after the July 20, 1944 assassination plot against Hitler. He was turned over to Sefton Delmer and lived with him for 10 months. The CIA report stated John worked for the British in various capacities during 1945 and 1946, on intelligence matters, on the POW reorientation program at Wilton Park, and on research for something that was redacted in the CIA's report, presumably for national security.

The CIA report stated that after the surrender in May 1945, John worked for the British War and Foreign Offices, interrogating German generals in the "Kensington cage" and helping to prepare legal documents for the Nuremberg trials. At Nuremberg, he worked as an adviser to the UK prosecution staff.[5] The CIA did not specify what legal documents were prepared by Delmer and John for the approaching Nuremberg trials or what advice they gave to the UK prosecution team. It was also interesting that the CIA noticed that Otto John had failed to mention his work for the UK prosecution in his CV.

The last thing to surface came from Gerd Schultze-Rhonhof, a retired Generalmajor in the German Bundeswehr (the postwar Wehrmacht). He found evidence in the British Archives of forged German documents that were submitted to the Tribunal. He wrote about them in his book, *The War Which Had Many Fathers.* [6]

That was the end of the line for me. The old man seemed to be right about the forged documents, but I still wondered why it was necessary. It was time to turn my attention to the torturing of German POWs.

CHAPTER 33: "TOO SANCTIMONIOUS A FRAUD"

It didn't take long to find information about the torturing of German prisoners. The most telling source was an article in *The Daily Mail* entitled *How Britain Tortured Nazi POWs*. The author wrote, *Thousands of Germans passed through the unit that became known as the London Cage, where they were beaten, deprived of sleep and forced to assume stress positions for days at a time.*[1]

The author said the facility belonged to *a network of nine 'cages' around Britain run by the Prisoner of War Interrogation Section (PWIS), which came under the jurisdiction of the Directorate of Military Intelligence… Of 3,573 prisoners who passed through Kensington Palace Gardens, more than 1,000 were persuaded to sign a confession or give a witness statement for use in war crimes prosecutions.*[2]

The article referenced enough published sources and first-person interviews to convince me that Johann's allegations were, once again, true. A quote from Harlan Fiske Stone, a United States Supreme Court justice who later became its chief justice, cemented Johann's case for me. On December 4, 1945, he wrote to a colleague about Robert Jackson, the American chief prosecutor at Nuremberg: *Jackson is away conducting his high-grade lynching party in Nuremberg. I don't mind what he does to the Nazis, but I hate to see the pretense that he is running a court and proceeding according to common law. This is a little too sanctimonious a fraud to meet my old-fashioned ideas.*[3]

The question of why the Allies felt it necessary to hold a Tribunal still nagged me. The presence of forged documents and brutally coerced testimony made it obvious that they weren't interested in getting to the truth. Why not save everyone the trouble and be done with it?

The only logical explanation I could think of was twofold. First, the Allies wanted to show the world how overwhelmingly evil National Socialism was. Second, they wanted to show the world how overwhelmingly righteous they were in defeating it.

I saw Larry later in the day and shared my findings. He chuckled and said the Nazis were lucky that they even had a trial because Churchill, Roosevelt, and Stalin favored summary executions. However, this plan was leaked and resulted in a public outcry. Larry was convinced that backdoor lobbyists pressured the politicians into thinking a Tribunal would better serve everybody's interests. And now I completely understand why.

The next several days were spent researching Johann's comments about America's medical experiments and eugenics programs. Here again, little information was available, but all of it agreed with what he had told me. I immediately thought of one of Johnny Cash's songs, *What is Truth.*

I looked up the song's history and found that Cash wrote it in 1970 and performed it at a White House function in 1972. One reporter wrote that its anti-war message made President Nixon and his guests appear uncomfortable. His observation made me think of something St. Augustine wrote, *And so they hate the truth for the sake of the object which they love, instead of the truth.*

So what was I to do with all of this? Perhaps Cynthia was right. Nobody cared about the past, especially about Nazi Germany; their regime was totally discredited. But what about the Allies? They had empowered the Tribunal to try Nazi leaders and punish them. But a trial presupposes fairness in seeking the truth to arrive at justice. Forgery and torture aren't part of that equation.

Something was missing, and it disturbed me a great deal. Johann pointed out that the West had committed the same crimes as the Nazis did in building their empires. In fact, he cited some instances where the Nazis had consciously followed Western tactics in building their empires. But yet, the West's crimes were never mentioned at Nuremberg. They were left blameless at the end of the proceedings. It appeared that the Allies loved their newly expanded international order more than they loved finding the truth, the root causes of the Nazi war crimes.

A portion of the Superman theme began playing in my head. My generation grew up watching the Superman TV show, where he fought *a never-ending battle for truth, justice, and the American way.* Maybe I was being naïve, but I believed that truth and justice were part and parcel of the American way.

My sense of naivete turned to anger once I realized that the Allies' failure to uncover the root causes behind the Nazi war crimes led to our war and our war crimes in Vietnam. Maybe their pride prevented them from seeing or confessing to their own sins. Or maybe it was something else.

I was now more determined than ever to hear Johann out. If his findings held true, it might show why our country committed such evil acts and why I participated in them. I called Johann and asked if it was okay to visit him tomorrow. He said it was about time.

~ 4TH VISIT ~

CHAPTER 34: AUGGIE

I drove up the next morning to see Johann, determined to hear his remaining points. There was no sign of Lena when I arrived, but Johann was sitting in his usual chair. He saw me enter and stood up to greet me. After we spent some time catching up with one another, I asked if he had seen Lena since my last visit.

"I've seen her around and waved hello, but we haven't talked much." He looked at me and smiled. "As I said before, she seems to like you more than me."

No kidding. I shrugged off his remark and got serious. "Johann, I went over my notes and wanted to clarify your second point about all men being alike. Were you saying that all men are created equal like it says in our Declaration of Independence?"

He furrowed his brows and shook his head. "Not exactly, Willi. I meant that all men are born alike, not equal. This leads to my third point: all men are born with God's spirit. It's what makes us all alike. It's His spirit that animates our bodies; it's what we call our soul. It gives us our consciousness and free will. Apart from that, each of us is unique, like a snowflake. We have different physical attributes and abilities, but we all have the free will to use them for good or evil.

"I grew up Catholic. I believe doing good is serving God, and serving God means serving humanity because, as I said, God is in all of us. Doing evil is using our free will to *not* serve God. This is sinning. It separates us from God. Sinning is selfish because it serves the self rather than God."

I was familiar with his point. "Yes, I understand, Johann. I converted to Catholicism a few years ago, but what does all this have to do with your story?"

"Everything. Because it started my war, which defined my life. And yours as well, Willi." He held up his hand to stave off any questions. "Now, let me continue telling you the rest of my story. He bowed his head briefly to scan his iPad. "I was quite young back in the early Thirties, but I remember the National Socialists' rise to power after the Depression began. It was devastating, but by the end of 1934, we were well on our way to rebuilding our nation. It was an interesting and exciting time for our people, Willi."

He smiled as he paused to collect his thoughts. "The goal of National Socialism was to make Germany a classless society. They wanted to provide equal opportunities in education and employment for all citizens, regardless of their birth or rank. There was still an upper class who resented this sort of leveling. However, once the new programs took hold, most citizens felt good about belonging to a national community that offered everyone a stake in its future."

He paused to take a sip of coffee and seemed to have forgotten what Lena said about the other Germans who happened to be Jewish. They didn't fare so well.

I looked up when I saw someone approaching Johann from behind.

"Dad?"

Johann recognized the voice, turned around, and slowly stood up. "Auggie, *willkommen!*"

I stood up as well and nodded at his son, who appeared slightly younger than me. He was trim, like his father, with a full head of graying hair.

"Willi, this is my son, August. I almost forgot he was coming today. And Auggie, this is Willi. He's another Knoske. Our long lost relative."

I reached out to shake his hand. "Hi, I'm Will. But I guess you should call me Willi since your father's been calling me that. And besides, it sounds pretty good the way he says it."

He laughed and slapped my shoulder. "I'm pleased to meet you, Willi. I get to come up here every week to see my father, whether he likes it or not."

"My son likes to joke, Willi. I can only take his company once a week anyway." He swiveled his head between us and then announced, "Before we sit down, let's get a cup of coffee, and then we can chat."

After filling our cups, we sat down, and the two started talking about Auggie's family while I listened in. It was pleasant to watch them converse and interact. I never had that pleasure with my father. He never took the time to share a cup of coffee with me, much less spend any time talking with me.

Johann jostled my arm and brought me back to reality. "Willi just retired recently. As I told you before, he's been doing family history and came here to interview me."

Auggie looked over at me. "You lucky duck; I plan on retiring myself in a few years."

"What line of work are you in, August?"

"Just call me Auggie, okay? August is a great name, but it's too formal. Anyway, I'm a machinist like my dad was. I do custom work for local companies in the area."

"Auggie was born in Germany, Willi. We lived in Hagen, a town in the state of Westphalia. We came here when he was about two years old."

Auggie smiled. "I don't remember much about Germany, Willi, and we've never been back. Have you been there?"

"Yes, but only on brief business trips. I remember being in Frankfurt, Marburg, Munich, and Liederbach. I also spent some time in Berschweiler bei Baumholder visiting a friend."

Johann nodded and said Hagen was northwest of those cities. "Willi and I have been talking about German history, Auggie."

"That's no big surprise." He turned around to face me. "He's been at this since he's retired."

Johann sat back and broke out into a wide smile. "Willi has been learning new things he hasn't heard before."

I nodded in agreement while the two smiled at each other.

"Dad's always talking about history. He talked about it over the dinner table when I was growing up, and he always took the time to answer all my questions." He smiled and patted his father's hand. "I heard you two talking about National Socialism. Have you talked about finances and the economy yet, Pop?"

"We only just started, Auggie." He sat up and smiled broadly at me. "Auggie is fascinated by what was done with the economy back then, especially with what's happening in America today. Are you ready to get into it, Willi?"

I looked at my watch. It was a little past nine. I had another two hours before it was time to head home. "Sure."

"Well, good because all this is part of the family history, Willi. Let's spend this visit focusing on how I grew up and how our two countries' business and government leaders used their free will to lead their countries. I think you will learn something."

CHAPTER 35: GERMAN SOCIALISM

Johann looked over at Auggie and smiled knowingly, then he turned to face me. "Many people, Willi, believe the Western capitalists wanted to remove our party because it was a threat to democracy and because of its anti-Semitism. But I believe the real reason was that our system offered an attractive alternative to their dog-eat-dog world of capitalism.

"Our economic model offered parity to our workers and aimed to benefit society. And, during the Thirties, we proved the success of our model by taking care of our workers and overcoming the Depression while the West did neither."

Johann must have seen a sour look emerge on my face because he quickly said, "Don't worry, Willi, we'll address the Jewish matter later. I promise." I looked away in disgust. We started this visit on such a good note, but this last comment made me wonder where it was going. Auggie looked at me, then at his father, with a concerned look on his face.

The old man pressed on with his lecture. "In fact, we'll talk about it when Lena is with us, but first, let's focus on the economy and what good things the party brought to our country. The first thing the party did after coming to power was to remove the so-called invisible hand that governed the capitalist marketplace. We took things into our own hands and established state-run programs that directed how the economy would serve the people instead of the wealthy investors. The goals and objectives of our government and the economy were not hidden but clear and understandable.

"The foreign and domestic capitalist leaders could no longer work with our banks to invest their money wherever it suited their interests. Our state-run economy directed that their capital investments had to be placed into programs that met the people's needs. Our party established national organizations that monitored the activities of private industries, farmers, and especially the banks. This was to facilitate their compliance with government programs."

I stopped writing to digest what he just said. If the government was going to take over and direct the economy, then everyone needed to get with the program – or else. The whole system and the notion of *Volksgemeinschaft* was anchored by the party slogan *Ein volk, ein Reich, ein Fuhrer.* You were either on-board with the program, or you had a real problem if you weren't. Was this his idea of free will?

I looked past Auggie, trying to find Lena but could find no sign of her. I'm sure she would have been able to rebut Johann arguments because, quite frankly, I wasn't up to it. I was having a hard enough time just keeping up with my notes.

Auggie, however, didn't falter in support of his father. "That's right, Pop. No one in this country ever questions what the wealthy do with their money. They can invest wherever they want, whether it benefits society or not. And if things go sour for them in one industry or country, they can pull out their capital and move on. The people left behind are stuck picking up the pieces and finding another way to survive."

Johann nodded. "That's right, Auggie; that's why the party took the reins. They saw what happened during the Twenties and wanted to make sure investors put their capital into serving the public's interest, such as constructing the Autobahn, building factories, or constructing homes for working people. This was the basis for Germany's economic revival while America suffered through the Depression."

During this whole time, Johann never looked down at his iPad. He had his justification for the party's existence down pat and proceeded to educate us on the development of his worldview.

"The party implemented many of the financial principles laid out by Gottfried Feder in his book, *The Manifesto for Breaking the Interest Bondage of Money*. His book stated that private bankers encouraged nations and people to take on loans so they could earn interest payments. The increase in debt devalues the money that working people earn and, as a result, the only way they can maintain their standard of living is to borrow more money. You can see a vicious cycle developing."

I wrote down and put a star next to Mr. Feder's name in my notes. I wanted to look him up later. This notion of accumulated debt was interesting, especially given our country's current economic situation.

Auggie must have been reading my mind. "I think this is exactly what's been happening in our country today, Pop." Auggie looked at his father and received an affirmative nod, "The working middle class, which is me, is getting squeezed out. Things are getting more expensive while our debt rises with it."

I leaned back in my chair. This was getting interesting, but it also sounded somewhat simplistic. "So, Johann, was the party able to put Feder's ideas into practice? Because if they did, it would have been a huge switch to make. Were they able to enlist the private sector into joining this program? And were they able to keep the peoples' interests a priority?"

"Well, Willi, there's no doubt this was a real balancing act, but we can only look at the results. One of the party's main goals was to get people back to work by restoring the Reich's economy. One of the ways the party did that was to set high tariffs on imports which would drive the economy to be more self-sufficient. These tariffs did reduce foreign trade and kept capital in the country, but it did cause rationing. However, unemployment did go down, and wages increased by almost eleven percent from 1933-1939, and Germany's GNP also increased by one hundred percent during the same time.

"Another goal was establishing basic social services to meet the worker's needs. The National Socialist People's Welfare (NSV) agency was established in 1933. It grew to include programs such as old age insurance, rent supplements, unemployment and disability benefits, old-age homes, interest-free loans for married couples, and healthcare insurance. This Agency provided relief for the elderly, the homeless, alcoholics, and ex-convicts. It also set up travelers' aid facilities at many rail stations."

Auggie kept nodding as his father rattled off one fact after another. "By 1939, the NSV had set up over eight-thousand daycare nurseries, funded housing for single mothers, and distributed food to larger families who needed it. By that same year, seventeen million Germans received some form of social assistance. Two years later, the Office of Youth Relief had thirty-thousand offices providing social workers, training, and counseling to prevent juvenile delinquency.

"We harnessed our free will to rebuild our country and maintain our culture during this time. And we celebrated our accomplishments in the 1935 documentary, *Triumph of the Will.* "

Suddenly, long-forgotten memories from my childhood came back to me. I read a lot of books when I was young about World War II. I was captivated by the pictures of Nazi Germany taken during this time. The colors, the crowds and flags made a big impression on me as well as the title of that movie. They all told me that anything was possible if only you exerted your will.

"I remember seeing photos from that documentary when I was a child, Johann. I couldn't believe all the people that were there and all the colorful flags and banners." Johann and Auggie watched me as I hurriedly bent over to scribble down my thoughts. I finished, looked up, and saw them smiling at me.

Auggie grinned and remarked, "It sounds like you're describing a MAGA rally, Willi."

I didn't know if he was joking or serious, but I didn't want to get pulled into current-day politics. Johann was also non-committal and continued. "So, you can see, Willi, before the war, the Nazis weren't entirely the evil party portrayed by some. The working people strongly felt that the Fuhrer and the Reich were taking care of them. The sense of *Volksgemeinschaft* became very real for us as everyone was back at work and sharing in the country's economic success."

I stopped writing as I remembered what Nazi Germany did to the Jews and all the political dissidents. "Wait a minute, Johann. A lot of effort was needed to build those autobahns and other large-scale projects. Didn't the country use forced labor from all the concentration camps? Those people weren't exercising their free will to do that."

He surprised me by smiling. "Yes, that's true. But tell me, Willi, how did you think the roads down South were built and maintained? I'll tell you. It was the chain gangs, and I'm sure they weren't out there working of their own free will. And I'll tell you something else, America today has the highest incarceration rate of any modern country. There are all kinds of dissidents, Willi. Ours were political; America's is economical.

"In any event, by 1939, our unemployment was practically zero. However, our national debt did rise to thirty-eight billion marks or fifteen billion US dollars. But America, by contrast, still had an unemployment rate of nineteen percent with a forty-billion-dollar debt.

"Germany's economic success far outstripped America's during the Thirties. It was only a matter of time before their capitalist leaders began moves to eliminate our system before it became a real threat."

CHAPTER 36: AMERICAN CAPITALISM

Johann paused to grab his coffee cup, took a sip, and then continued on his rant. "FDR and his capitalist backers were concerned that our system would eclipse their own. They collaborated to undermine us and finally pushed us into war to overcome the threat to their system."

I was stupefied. He was turning the tables again. He was making Nazi Germany sound like a progressive regime. However, his mentioning that FDR pushed Germany into war piqued my interest. I just mentioned this to Cynthia and wondered how he would rationalize this.

He turned his eyes back to his iPad, and his brows came together in thought as he scrolled through lines of text. "And just to show you that I'm not talking out of my hat, Willi, listen to what the Treasury Secretary, Henry Morgenthau Jr., said to the House Ways and Means Committee on May 9, 1939, about the state of the American economy, *We have tried spending money. We are spending more than we have ever spent before, and it does not work...I want to see this country prosperous. I want to see people get a job. I want to see people get enough to eat. We have never made good on our promises ... I say after eight years of this Administration, we have just as much unemployment as when we started ... And an enormous debt to boot!*[1]

"In 1932, unemployment in Germany was reported to be thirty percent while America's was just under twenty-five percent. In 1933, both FDR and Hitler started massive social and public work programs."

"But as you said," I interjected sarcastically, "after that, the similarity ended. Correct?"

"But not in the way you think," Johann quickly replied, ignoring my sarcasm. "Whereas both countries entered the thirties with a huge amount of government debt, most of Germany's debt was owed to foreign banks to pay for reparations and rebuilding during the Twenties. FDR's debt, however, was primarily held by the privately-owned Federal Reserve Banks.

"Hitler demanded in 1933 that Germany achieve a balanced budget and reduce Germany's dependence on foreign-owned debt. Our government began enacting the necessary controls to achieve that by reforming its monetary policy. In 1935, the government issued Labor Treasury Certificates, a debt-free and interest-free currency used to pay laborers on public work programs.

"Laborers used these notes to buy their goods and services, eliminating the government's need to borrow capital from private bankers. In addition, a good deal of Germany's debt also came from government-issued Offa and Mefo bonds, which were used to fund state-run public programs without any privately borrowed capital. FDR's national debt, on the other hand, was held by the banking community, and he continued to use capital funds borrowed from banks to fund his programs. When he increased the national debt, he made the bankers wealthier due to the increase in interest payments, just as Feder said."

Auggie interjected at this point. "Doesn't it sound like Germany had a great system, Willi? Everybody benefitted from making the economy successful."

I had to stop both of them. "What's the point of all this economic talk, Johann? What does it have to do with anything, especially our family history?"

He let out a long, vocal sigh. "All this tension between the two systems led to a devastating war, Willi. And while our system was eliminated in defeat, America's victory assured that their system would continue to prosper. Ultimately, it led to your war and all the wars that followed. God only knows where it's going next. But you and Auggie must understand that system because you live in and support it. Now, if you want to explore this further, I'll be happy to continue."

I looked over at Auggie and shrugged. He cocked his head with a quizzical look on his face. This was obviously the first time he had heard this from his father. "Sure, Pop. Let's hear what you have to say." I gave a half-hearted assent as well. Auggie seemed to be a nice guy but a little too naïve for my taste. Johann was pleased with his son's enthusiastic support and pressed on.

"So, you see, boys," his eyes switching back and forth between Auggie and me, "both Germany and Japan shifted over to state-run financing so their governments could direct their economies and own their debt while the United States continued to have its government dependent on borrowed capital from private banks, like the Federal Reserve Banks, to run theirs.

"There was, and still is, a synergy between American government officials and their capitalist investors. The capitalists fund the politicians' campaigns, and the politicians, once elected, enact policies and programs that benefit their financial backers. These capitalist investors and politicians had every reason to oppose Japan's and Germany's state-run economies during the Thirties.

"One of the first things that America and the capitalist West did during the Thirties was to undermine both Japan's and Germany's governments with negative press reports and propaganda. And when that tactic didn't work, the West drew a line in the sand. They told them to throttle their systems and submit to their economic dominance, or they would face war."

Auggie jumped in to quickly buttress Johann's argument. "That's right, Pop. During the Thirties, the capitalists and their governments wanted to hold onto the empires they had built over the past centuries. Their empires were built on conquest and by unfair treaties that took advantage of other, poorer countries. They weren't about to negotiate away any control to Japan or Germany."

Johann smiled. "You're right about that, Auggie. Both sides became locked into their ideological positions, and war became the only way to break the deadlock." He sat back and threw up his hands. "And war, after all, served the capitalists' interests. First, it would eliminate the competing systems, and second, the capitalist governments would need more funding to wage it, translating into more debt and increased interest payments to the banks."

My blood was starting to boil. "This sounds too simplistic for my taste. You make it sound like the state-run economies were progressive and benefitted their citizens while the capitalist systems were just ripping their citizens off while making a few wealthier."

Instead of getting angry, Johann cracked a smile. You just made my point, Willi. You and the Western capitalists just turned around what I said to make themselves look good while painting us as the bad guys. They never tried to work with us to accommodate both systems. They didn't have to; they were powerful enough to maintain the status quo, regardless of our system's merits."

"Johann, don't try to be clever with me. You know what I mean."

"I'm not being clever. This is what I found! All of this started my war. And it's started yours. And if you still think I'm being simplistic, then we'll have to dig deeper."

CHAPTER 37: "CORPORATE SOCIALISM"

Now he had my interest. "Okay, Johann. Let's dig deeper. Economic disputes may have led to our wars, but something else must be behind all that violence and brutality. And by the way, did I hear you right? Did you say the Federal Reserve Banks were privately owned?"

Johann smiled. "Ah, very good, Willi! That shows you're listening. Well, America did push Germany into war, not so much over economic differences but over who would dominate them. But we'll talk about that later. And, just so you know, the Federal Reserve Banks are, in fact, privately owned."

While Johann paused to look up something, Auggie looked over at me, and both our faces registered surprise at this revelation. "Here we are. Now listen, boys, the United States Court of Appeals ruled in 1982 that *Federal reserve banks are not federal instrumentalities for purposes of a Federal Tort Claims Act, but are independent privately owned and locally controlled corporations...* However, the Court also ruled that *the Reserve Banks are deemed to be federal instrumentalities for purposes of immunity from state taxation.* So, you see, Willi, in the capitalist system, the bankers can have their cake and eat it too."[1]

I shook my head, and Auggie chuckled. When I heard that, my anger began turning in another direction. I never learned that the Federal Reserve Banks were privately owned and that they were tax-exempt on top of that. They sure as hell seemed to have a lot of power and influence over what the government did or didn't do.

What the heck else did I have to learn before I gained a complete understanding of our system? It seemed like every time I visited Johann, things got turned on their head. I felt like I had believed the earth was flat until I met this guy.

"But now, boys, things get a bit murky." Johann looked over at his son. "I never mentioned this to you before, Auggie, because finance is distasteful to me, and I have no real interest in it. But recently, America's national debt exceeded twenty trillion dollars. I decided to look into that and found one man who used his free will to uncover what's really going on in this capitalist system."

He paused to take a sip of coffee, then put his cup down and picked up his iPad. "You know, boys, not too many people have an interest in international finance, how it evolved over time, and how it currently works today. It's hard to understand, and on top of that, it's a very dry subject."

Auggie and I both nodded, but this particular story had promise. We both sat in rapt attention.

"The ways of finding out who owns what and how cash flows through different channels to fund major transactions are deliberately kept complex in the capitalist system. Bankers and lawyers like to keep it that way because it covers their tracks and as an added dividend, increases their hourly fees. However, one man used his free will to study your country's system. He didn't do that to benefit himself but to expose the evil in it. That man's name was Antony Sutton."

The name sounded English or American, but I had never heard of him. "Who is he, Johann?"

Auggie beat him to the punch. His face lit up with a gleeful expression and made me wonder whether he would wind up looking like his father when he was 91 years old. "So you never heard of him, Willi? I'm not surprised. I'm glad Pop brought him up. He wrote four or five books about the relationship between finance and our government but none of them made any best-seller lists."

Johann showed me his picture on the iPad. "Antony Sutton was one of the few financial historians in the world at the time. He was an economics professor at UCLA and a Research Fellow at Stanford's Hoover Institution from 1968 to 1973. As Auggie said, he wrote several books about how this relationship evolved in the 20th Century.

"Richard Pipes, a Baird Professor Emeritus of History from Harvard University, wrote this about him in 1984: *Sutton comes to conclusions that are uncomfortable for many businessmen and economists. For this reason, his work tends to be either dismissed out of hand as 'extreme' or, more often, simply ignored.* [2]

"Sutton's book, *FDR and Wall Street,* notes that Roosevelt was the director of eleven corporations headquartered on Wall Street between 1921 and 1928 and was president of a major trade association before becoming the governor of New York in 1928. He wrote that FDR was president of United European Investors from 1921-1922.

"This was exactly when this company helped drive up hyperinflation in Germany and profited from it. They used German marks deposited in the United States to buy property in Germany at a discount from impoverished Germans.[3] Our people were forced into selling their property to feed their families. And all this contributed to the ultimate collapse of the German mark in 1923, which ruined and embittered the German middle class.

"You'll remember that I mentioned this briefly during our first visit, Willi. This book also notes that FDR confirmed the relationship between finance and government in a letter he wrote to Colonel House, one of his close confidantes, in 1933: *The real truth of the matter is, as you and I know, that a financial element in the larger centers has owned the Government ever since the days of Andrew Jackson—and I am not wholly excepting the Administration of W.W."* [4]

Auggie quickly burst in and explained that WW was Woodrow Wilson while Johann scanned his iPad.

"Yes, that's right, Auggie." Johann commended his son and continued to read the letter. "FDR told House that *the country is going through a repetition of Jackson's fight with the Bank of the United States—only on a far bigger and broader basis.* Well, boys, in that early fight with the banks, Jackson took the side of the workers and fought for the government to take control of the country's finances from the bankers. He won the first round, but the bankers ultimately prevailed.

"FDR, on the other hand, was part of that *financial element*. He grew up in that world and worked with that *financial element* to gain the presidency. According to Sutton, FDR's New Deal, and its related NRA legislation *made society go to work for Wall Street.* These programs were the beginning of what Sutton called *Corporate Socialism.* He said, and I quote, *The economic recovery part of the New Deal was a creation of Wall Street—specifically Bernard Baruch and Gerard Swope of General Electric—in the form of the Swope Plan ... In brief, Wall Street has a vested interest in politics because, through politics, it can make society go to work for Wall Street. It can also thus avoid the penalties and risks of the marketplace.*[5]

"The system he describes in this book is still going strong. In fact, there was an article recently in the *New Republic* that says as much if you want me to read it."[6]

I kept writing and waved away his offer with my left hand but made a note to look it up later.

He paused to sip his coffee. "I'm not trying to lecture you on economics, Willi. I only wanted to show you why National Socialism posed such a huge threat to Western capitalist leaders. For the last five-hundred years, private bankers worked closely with the American, British, and French governments to bankroll the expansion of their empires. And both groups in these capitalist systems wanted to keep the status quo in place by discrediting and ultimately eliminating any other system that threatened their standing."

I waited for him to mention the Nazi's favorite whipping boy, but he seemed to be avoiding the subject so far.

CHAPTER 38: UNGLOVED

"Okay, so now you have some background. Next, we're going to dig deeper and see the 'invisible hand' that guides the capitalists' marketplace; it momentarily appeared during the Thirties before it quickly disappeared again. This story should interest you since it involves a high-ranking Marine."

"Ollie North?" He was the only one I could think of that was involved in this kind of mess.

He chuckled and slapped my knee. "No, no. He's not that old. And this fellow had a higher rank than Colonel."

Now he had my interest.

"Have you heard of Smedley Butler, Willi?"

"That's like asking a kid if he ever heard of Santa Claus. Of course, I had. Every Marine learned about him in boot camp."

"Well, Antony Sutton devoted a chapter to him called *The Butler Affair.* Here's an extract from it: *According to General Smedley Butler's testimony to Congress, supported by independent witnesses, there was a plan to install a dictator in the White House. President Roosevelt was to be kicked upstairs and a new General Secretary ... General Butler was offered the post ...to take over the economy on behalf of Wall Street."* [1]

I almost fell out of my chair. Was the hero of all the Banana Wars involved in this kind of crap?

"This Butler Affair was interesting to me, boys, because it represented a real misstep for the bankers who usually keep these types of dealings well hidden. This incident might have gone undetected if not for this honorable man, General Butler. He was smart enough to string them along until he got the details behind their plans.

"He testified before Congress that he was first approached in mid-1933 by Gerald MacGuire, a bond salesman for Grayson M. P. Murphy & Co, which was then part of the JP Morgan Company. MacGuire told Butler they wanted to install a person with real power under Roosevelt to be the Secretary of General Affairs and then run the government the way Wall Street wanted.

"Let me read an extract from a Statement to the Congressional Committee on Un-American Activities that took place on November 24, 1934: *MacGuire then, according to Butler's testimony, stated, 'We have the President with us now. He has got to have more money. There is no more money to give him. Eighty percent of the money now is in Government bonds, and he cannot keep this racket up much longer. He has got to do something about it. He, Roosevelt, has either got to get more money out of us or has got to change the method of financing the Government, and we are going to see to it that he does not change the methods. He will not change it. He is with us now.'* [2]

"Further on, the plotters make an interesting admission revealed in Butler's testimony: *General Butler: They had both talked about the same kind of relief that ought to be given the President, and he said: 'You know the American people will swallow that. We have got the newspapers. We will start a campaign that the President's health is failing. Everybody can tell that by looking at him, and the dumb American people will fall for it in a second... And I could see it. They had that sympathy racket ... they were going to have somebody take the patronage off of his shoulders and take all the worries and details off of his shoulders...'* [3]

"Isn't it interesting, Willi, that they said they had the newspapers in their pockets? I won't go into all the details, but an important part of Butler's testimony came when he identified several other individuals involved in the plot. While the lesser-known individuals were summoned to testify, none of the more powerful figures that he mentioned like Grayson Murphy, Thomas Lamont, and J.P. Morgan ever were. The Committee actually deleted portions of Butler's testimony where he mentioned those other leading Wall Street bankers."

I was flabbergasted. Once again, I couldn't believe what I was hearing. We were talking about our country, not some third-world country. "I'm shocked, Johann. I can't believe I never heard about this, especially since it involved Smedley Butler, the most decorated officer in Marine Corps history who served as our Commandant."

"Well, Willi, the Butler Affair was swept away very quickly and quietly. But the capitalist powerbrokers did find somebody to take over the economy on behalf of Wall Street. It was the president. As MacGuire said, 'We have the president now.' "

CHAPTER 39: "WAR IS A RACKET"

Johann smiled as he bent over his iPad. "They had FDR, all right. He needed more money to fund his New Deal programs and had no choice but to follow Wall Street's lead to get it. They told him that if he wanted to get more money, then he would have to take gold out of circulation. Do you know why they told him that, Willi?"

His question caught me off guard. I had no idea. I just shrugged and let Johann answer his own question.

"Well, I'll tell you why. Before 1933, the American financial system was based on the gold standard, and gold currency was still in circulation. If FDR wanted to print more greenbacks to fund his programs, then the Treasury would have to increase the gold supply to keep up with the increase in greenbacks. But that wasn't an option, Willi, because the government was broke. There was no way to secure that much gold.

"So, the only way to increase the money supply to fund FDR's programs was to take gold out of circulation, which the president did by Executive Order in 1933. Putting more greenbacks into circulation devalued the dollar relative to the gold supply, but it didn't matter because citizens could no longer exchange their greenbacks for gold. They were stuck!

"The bankers didn't care about the average citizen being stuck because now they could increase the money supply, which would increase the national debt and the interest payments that the government paid them. The increased debt level also increased the bankers' leverage over how the government spent their borrowed money; they wanted to ensure it aligned with their interests. It was all about satisfying their self-interests, Willi.

"Do you remember when I quoted Morgenthau earlier? He said that after eight years of FDR's administration, there was just as much unemployment as when they started, and they were left with an enormous debt to boot! This was criminal, boys. FDR's national debt funded many of his social programs and made him look good in the press, but by 1939, we saw that it didn't do much to help the unemployed or the nation's economy."

Auggie eagerly agreed. "That's right, Pop. I'm only a machinist, Willi, but I know this stuff cold. The money supply grew by over ten percent from 1933 to 1937. Keynesian economics states that the best way to fight an economic downturn is to inflate the money supply, but that didn't work for the average American because the money never trickled down enough to make a difference."

I gave him a nod and made a note to look up Keynes' theory to see if he knew what he was talking about. Meanwhile, Johann took back the reins.

"Willi, allow me to show you where I am going with this by sharing something else about General Butler. He wrote a book called *War Is a Racket* in 1935, and here's a quote from it: *War is a racket. It always has been…A racket is best described, I believe, as something that is not what it seems to the majority of the people. Only a small "inside" group knows what it is about. It is conducted for the benefit of the very few at the expense of the very many… In the World War, a mere handful garnered the profits of the conflict. At least 21,000 new millionaires and billionaires were made in the United States during the World War… How many of these war millionaires shouldered a rifle?*

How many of them dug a trench?" [1] Johann was watching me closely. "Surprised, Willi?"

"I sure am. He sounds more like another pissed-off grunt than a Commandant."

"Well, he was every bit as disillusioned as you are. Here's another quote from an article he wrote in the November 1935 issue of *Common Sense, I spent 33 years and four months in active military service and during that period I spent most of my time as a high-class muscle man for Big Business, for Wall Street and the bankers. In short, I was a racketeer, a gangster for capitalism.*

I helped make Mexico and especially Tampico safe for American oil interests in 1914. I helped make Haiti and Cuba a decent place for the National City Bank boys to collect revenues in. I helped in the raping of half a dozen Central American republics for the benefit of Wall Street. I helped purify Nicaragua for the International Banking House of Brown Brothers in 1902–1912. I brought light to the Dominican Republic for the American sugar interests in 1916. I helped make Honduras right for the American fruit companies in 1903. In China in 1927, I helped see to it that Standard Oil went on its way unmolested." [2]

I fell back in my chair. I couldn't believe what I was hearing. During boot camp, we heard all about Smedley Butler's military exploits in the Banana Wars, but we never heard anything like this.

"I told you it would be interesting, Willi. But we're not finished. Sutton wrote another book called Wall Street and the Bolshevik Revolution. It itemizes how the U.S. capitalists invested in the industrial development of Soviet Russia since its earliest days. He cites State Department files, the personal papers of key Wall Street figures, and other key sources to prove it.

"There was one instance when banking executives from JP Morgan illegally funneled Bolshevik gold into America. Another time, Wall Street investors intervened with foreign governments to free Leon Trotsky. And many major U.S. corporations were making business deals with Soviet Russia fifteen years before the U.S. ever recognized the Soviet regime.

"And now listen to this, Willi. In 1968, during the height of the Vietnam War, Sutton published his first book, *Western Technology, and Soviet Economic Development.* It documented how the U.S. provided the Soviets with the funds, materials, and expertise to develop their manufacturing infrastructure, which later included computers. Most of this development was largely underwritten by American investors who provided American technology and support. And this Russian infrastructure manufactured arms, military equipment, and supplies that were sent to North Vietnam to kill and wound American soldiers. In some cases, American taxpayer money was used by your government to assist American investors with their Russian ventures."

I was bent over, writing notes, when Johann made this last statement. Were we fighting and dying for the right of corporations and their investors to make a buck by supplying our enemy?

A song started playing in my head. It was *The Backstabbers.* It was sung by the O'Jays back in the early '70s and summed up my feelings of betrayal back then and now. I recalled Cynthia's harsh indictments against Johann and wished she were here to see the other side of evil.

CHAPTER 40: A GUARANTEED ANNUITY

Johann slowly leaned forward, looking first at Auggie and then at me. "Willi, what are you thinking about?"

"That was a lot to digest, Johann, I knew there were selfish people in this country, but this sounds like a plot for a bad movie."

"Well, it doesn't end there, Willi. The same thing happened again right before your war. Thirty years after FDR, LBJ had the same problem; he needed more money to fund his Great Society programs, the Space Program, and the growing conflict in Vietnam. And the bankers used his desires to grow their influence even more. They told LBJ the same thing they told FDR: we'll print more money to fund your programs, but first, you have to take silver certificates out of circulation. You see, Willi, just like with gold, the country couldn't afford to buy more silver to back up any increase in silver certificates.

"So, LBJ stopped issuing silver certificates in 1964 and began to retire existing ones. In 1965, he signed the Coinage Act of 1965, which reduced the amount of silver in coins. This clearly violated the Coinage Act of 1792 as it debased our currency, but nothing came of it. By 1968, the government restricted the redemption of existing silver certificates to only Federal Reserve Notes; they could no longer redeem them for silver. After taking these steps, LBJ got his wish, and the bankers got theirs: the national debt was increased by seventeen percent from $317 billion in 1965 to $371 billion in 1970.

"All this additional government spending led to crippling inflation in the Seventies. Even though neither gold nor silver was in circulation, America remained on the gold standard. As a result, the value of the increased dollars in circulation began to decrease in relation to the gold held by the government. American citizens could no longer redeem their devalued greenbacks for gold, but foreign governments still could. The rush was on to hurriedly redeem their greenbacks for gold, which started to drain our reserves.

"And guess what happened? Nixon severed the last cord and took us off the gold standard in 1971. He said it was only a *temporary* move to hold off international speculators, but it's still in effect today, forty-six years later.

"Today, our paper currency is labeled a 'Federal Reserve Note.' It's basically an IOU. Congress is now free to set the national debt level as high as they want, and the Federal Reserve will print as much paper money as they need. The only thing that maintains their value is the holder's faith in the stability of our system. We are well over twenty trillion dollars in debt today, and our government pays more than two-hundred and fifty billion dollars in interest annually to the Federal Reserve to service that debt. This is quite an annuity for the bankers and, more importantly, it increases their leverage over setting government foreign and domestic policies to meet their needs."

Johann paused to lean back in his chair. "So now, hopefully, you can see why the Western capitalists made their governments push Japan and Germany into a war. They couldn't afford to lose control of the world market because that's what kept their system running and kept paying them dividends."

We all rested on that final note, and then I saw Lena entering the room. I was the only one facing the entrance, and she looked directly into my eyes. She never waved at us or said a word until she joined us.

"Hello, Willi… Johann."

"Hello, Lena. It's good to see you again." And I really meant it. I needed a break from these two.

Johann smiled. "*Guten Tag*, Lena. I'd like to introduce you to my son, August."

"Everyone calls me Auggie, Lena."

"Pleased to meet you, Auggie," Lena said. "What were you gentlemen talking about?"

Johann took the lead. "We were talking about finances, Lena, how FDR got in bed with Wall Street to push Japan and Germany into war to put an end to their state-run economies."

Lena quickly interjected. "You know there's a lot more to it than that, Johann."

The old man grinned. "Well, maybe there was. But let me say just one more thing to the boys. After America won the war, they had the only working economy left in the world, while every other country had to rebuild. American bankers and investors were only too happy to rush in and extend them credit to buy American goods and services. And these investors secured their loans by making sure that the borrowing countries spent those funds on programs that aligned with their interests. And there's one more thing…"

He paused here to make sure he had everyone's attention. "If any of those indebted countries ever work off those loans and grow powerful enough to challenge the status quo, then you can bet they'll be dealt with just as Japan and Germany were. And this is exactly what is happening with China today! It's insidious."

He turned to Lena. "I'm glad you came, Lena, because I wanted to tell you and the boys that the party was wrong to blame the Jews for Germany's problems. It was these capitalist powerbrokers and their self-serving system that caused our economic problems. They were the ones responsible for starting that war."

I saw Lena stiffen while Auggie quickly intervened to avoid a confrontation.

CHAPTER 41: PICK YOUR POISON

"Well, Pop, look on the bright side of things; everything that happened has made America the most prosperous, most advanced country in the world."

Johann looked at his son with an expression of concern. "And *that* is what you want out of life? What about you, Willi?"

Ever since the stroke, I dreaded whenever someone asked me an open-ended question like that. I had to take time to process what was being asked and then take more time to develop a response. Lena was staring at me with a concerned look on her face while I tried to reply to Johann's question.

"I don't know what to think, Johann. You make it sound like we're living in times like H.G. Wells' *The Time Machine*. It's like we're the Eloi living like sheep above the ground while those powerbrokers are like the Morlocks living below. They distract us with extended credit lines and then cart off our young to fight in their wars."

Johann nodded and put on a knowing smile. "Ah! *Alte Füchse gehen schwer in die Falle.* This means *all the old foxes know a trap when they see it*. You're not too far off, Willi. One day we'll wake up and find ourselves in one giant global economy owned, underwritten, and run by these powerbrokers. "And" he continued, raising his finger in the air, "our form of representative government may still be around, but the only candidates who can afford to run will be those whose campaigns are funded by these powerbrokers.

"The Constitution and the Bill of Rights may also still be around. However, they will amend both if their interests are ever threatened. The only fear these powerbrokers will have is if the people finally realize what's happening. Then there'll be a revolt against them, much like the bourgeoisie did in the French Revolution."

Auggie looked over at me with a half-grin as if to excuse his father's performance. I could tell he wanted this to end as much as I did. I gave him a slight nod in agreement and looked over at Lena, who had been keeping her peace. "Well, Pop, you know what they say: Every rich man is a capitalist and every poor man a socialist. The two are incompatible and always will be. It's just human nature."

Lena managed a slight smile and seemed to relax a bit. "You're right, Auggie. Those two are birds of the same feather but with different stripes; their leaders are more concerned with their ideologies and what keeps them in power rather than the people in their so-called systems. To me, it's like pick your poison."

She inched herself up and leaned forward. "I mean, all this talk about money-hungry capitalists and public-minded socialists is nonsense. All any level-headed person wants to do is live free of any system or ideology. People just want to be secure in their own homes and not worry about their grandchildren's future. Some people think President Kennedy's quote, *Ask not what your country can do for you, ask what you can do for your country,* was enlightening. But it's exactly that type of blind thinking that got you two into fighting their wars."

Johann muttered, "*Gott im Himmel!* Would you rather have us all sit on our hands and not do anything for our society? Look at what National Socialism accomplished during the Thirties. It united our people to rebuild the country and made us strong enough to throw off that crippling Versailles Treaty! This never would have happened if everyone did just as they wanted."

Auggie and I looked at one another, entranced by their exchange.

Lena was quick to counter-punch. "But look where this terrible system led, Johann… millions died because your leaders wanted it to keep it alive. It became detached from the people it was supposed to serve. This became obvious when it started persecuting its Jewish citizens. Our people were German citizens when this all started. They not only contributed to the German culture and economy for centuries, but they defended it as well.

"And after your system removed them, it went on to sacrifice every other citizen by fighting the war to its bitter end. That war destroyed everything that your people so proudly built. And all of this was because your *Führer* wanted to maintain his so-called public-minded system at any cost!"

He was caught flatfooted and took her rebuttal right on the chin. He sat there silently, taking the count while she paused to take a quick sip from her water bottle before Johann cut in. She eyed him carefully as she put the bottle back into its holder.

"Top or bottom, rich or poor, it doesn't matter, Johann. People should just live the life they've been given with those they love. Stop all this bickering and fighting between systems and who has what and why! Rational people trust in reason to live together in peace. A government is only needed to maintain individual rights and protect the peace. And that's all! I made my point."

CHAPTER 42: A LOSS OF STANDARDS

Johann sat there slack-jawed. It took a moment or two for him to recover, but he came back with a different tack toward her. "You never did tell us what you did after the war, Lena. Why don't you share it with us?"

She eased back into her chair and took another sip of water. "After the war," she sighed, "my spirit was crushed. I had just spent the last five years being treated like vermin. The guards kept us at a distance because they didn't consider us human. We couldn't speak directly to them; anything that had to be said to them was done indirectly through the Kapo, who was also a prisoner. If the guards ever called you, it was either to shoot or beat you."

Her eyes closed for a moment. "It was terrible. While we were there, I heard the most unimaginable words that a child should hear from her mother: 'I wish I never had you.' " She paused again to wipe her eyes with a tissue. Neither of us was inclined to interrupt her with questions. "You were talking about standards, Johann. Well, those camps lost all standards of humanity. I was angry at God for what was happening there. I wondered where He was and why all this was happening. I felt so insignificant.

"After the war, the only thing I could think of was where should I go? How do I find out what happened to my family, friends, relatives, and neighbors? Where was I to sleep? There were many practical things to think about. We were finally saved by the British, but I left them soon after I recovered and went to the American zone because I had an uncle in New York City. I had learned English in school, so I worked as an interpreter for the Americans. I would have left Germany immediately, but the Displaced Persons Act didn't pass until 1948. When my number finally came up later that year, I left for New York. I was twenty-two, and the only family I had left was my uncle."

She winced and adjusted her position in the wheelchair. "My uncle had a friend who socialized with a group called the Class of Forty-Three. This group met every Saturday evening in Ayn Rand's apartment to talk philosophy. She was writing *Atlas Shrugged* at the time. My uncle always looked forward to hearing what was discussed there from his friend."

I was familiar with Ayn Rand; I finished *The Fountainhead* and *Atlas Shrugged* while I was in the Marines. They were fascinating stories that attracted and repelled me. I enjoyed reading about the strong-willed characters and their desire to succeed, but I was repelled by their lack of empathy for others who were less fortunate. Rand portrayed a real dog-eat-dog world. "Did you ever get to meet Ayn Rand?" I asked. "I read two of her books."

Lena broke into a smile. "Well, when I heard she was a Russian émigré, I asked my uncle's friend if I could meet her. He told her about me, and surprisingly, Ayn agreed to let me come and listen in. Ayn would expound on her Objectivist philosophy and read pages from her manuscript to the group. I became an acolyte, and the members of the group helped me get into Columbia, where I became involved in the New York ACLU when it was fighting McCarthyism. I eventually earned my J.D. and stayed there until I retired. It was an interesting life, and now I'm here. That's it"

Johann keyed something into his iPad and looked up at Lena. "What is this Objectivist philosophy? I never heard of it before."

"It's not easy to follow. Basically, it says all rational people have a common interest in personal freedom; the freedom to pursue what Rand called rational selfishness. For her, the ultimate goal in life is survival, and the best way to survive is to live as a rational being. If a person stays true to logic and acts rationally, then they will find true happiness. When I first heard her talk, it was like drinking cool spring water after surviving a trip through the desert.

"Rand went so far as to say that any government trying to redistribute wealth or set up social welfare programs wasn't acting rationally. It was using force to take away the freedom and property of one citizen to give to another less fortunate. After I became involved with the ACLU, I began to see that pure reason only goes so far, and Objectivism made no provision for charitable or selfless acts. In fact, these two activities were vices as far as Objectivism was concerned, so I eventually broke away from the group."[1]

Johann raised his eyebrows. "That philosophy sounds hard to defend. Everybody has their own logic and reasons for doing things. Who's to say what's reasonable or not? Who will finally sort them all out, so something gets done?"

Auggie looked even more baffled and didn't wait for anyone to answer his father's rhetorical question. "So where do you think this leaves us, Pop? Capitalism, Socialism, Communism, Fascism, Democracies, and now this Objectivism?"

I stifled a snicker. He seemed genuinely lost. I looked around and realized that we all had different perspectives on life: Johann believed in the state being greater than the individual, while Lena was the ultimate libertarian, championing the rights of the individual over the state. Auggie seemed clueless as far as I could tell, and I didn't give a shit about anything.

Johann's brows were knitted in thought as he put down the iPad and considered his son's question. "Well, Auggie, after years of looking for the truth, Lena may have put me on the right path. It doesn't matter what system we find ourselves in. The best thing we can do is render unto Caesar the things that are due to him and render unto God the things that are due Him."

His expression turned from one of pensiveness to one of paternal love and concern. He gazed at his son, then at me and finally, his eyes rested on Lena. Lena sat silently, returning his gaze until he broke away to look at Auggie.

"Let me ask you something, son. Do you enjoy your current lifestyle? Do all the things you own provide you with comfort and security? If they do, then good; you should enjoy them. You worked hard for them." His voice lost all the anger and resentment he had expressed earlier.

He looked over at me than back to Auggie and began speaking in a cautious but caring tone. "Just remember this, boys: always think for yourselves. Don't let the system run your life. Examine it and find out how it grew. Watch where it's going and see what sort of people are running it. Give the Devil his due, but always remember that you're born of God, and your soul is part of Him. Remember, He gave you the free will to act on your own accord. It's up to you to decide whether to serve good or evil, God or mammon."

His voice trailed off with these last few words while Auggie and I sat there wondering what was coming next. Auggie stole a glance at me, and I raised my eyes in bewilderment.

Lena finally broke the silence. "You two boys are smart enough to figure things out. My guess is that you'll continue to do so in the future." She paused and then rested her eyes on Johann. His eyes were downcast and did not return her gaze. "You look tired, Johann, so I'll excuse myself. I'm tired as well."

Johann raised his head and watched her wheel away. He did look exhausted. "I'm tired too, boys. But I have one more thing to show you before going back to my room."

CHAPTER 43: PEOPLE NEED TO KNOW

"Willi, do you remember during our second visit when I said evil begets evil? I told you the capitalist powerbrokers lied about the Fourteen Points to get us to sign the Armistice and then strongarmed us into signing that terrible peace treaty. After that, they caused hyperinflation in our country to make their profits. Their actions were evil and led to widespread resentment in Germany.

"And this evil led to another evil: the party blaming all of Germany's problems on the Jews. And this evil led to still another evil: the Western capitalists turning their backs on the Jews and letting them suffer for their sins. They never admitted it was their lies and greed that caused Germany's problems. They let the Jews take all the blame rather than confess and give up their ill-gotten gains.

"What they did instead was to stir up hatred against the party. And this incitement only caused more resentment against the Jews and caused further suffering. As an example, London's *Daily Express* published this headline on March 24, 1933: *Judea Declares War on Germany.* There was a trailing banner that read *Jews of all the World Unite. Boycott of German Goods. Mass Demonstrations.*[1] This announcement came less than three months after the Nazis came into power. And it only served to fan the flames of distrust and hatred on both sides until it led to war."

This boycott was news to me. God only knows whether it was engineered by the so-called "powerbrokers" trying to discredit National Socialism or by Jewish leaders trying to suppress anti-Semitism. "Wait a minute, Johann. If you want to say that one evil begets another evil, wasn't Germany responsible for starting World War I in the first place? They pushed Austria into declaring war on Serbia after Archduke Ferdinand was assassinated. After that, Russia, who was Serbia's ally, began to mobilize and Germany declared war on them as well as France, which was in alliance with Russia. And Germany struck first by attacking France through neutral Belgium and then Britain had to join the conflict because it was allied with Belgium."

I was shocked that I remembered all that. "So, yes, Johann, one evil did beget another. But how far back do we have to go? And what's the point? Nobody will ever forget what the Nazis did during the war, just like no one cares about any good they did before the war. It's all over and done with."

Johann's face turned red as he suddenly roared back to life. "Well, it does matter, Willi. And I will tell you why. People need to hear the truth about what happened to National Socialism. The capitalist powerbrokers can't get away with what they did to Germany at the end of the First World War. And we can't let them get away with allowing the Jews to be their sacrificial lambs for the crimes they committed.

"All the vitriol that was expressed in that headline went back and forth until it led to the Second World War. And the capitalist powerbrokers were never called to account for their behavior by the American press because, as MacGuire told General Butler, they had the newspapers in their pocket."

He suddenly clammed up and fell back into his chair. He was either exhausted or may have remembered what Lena had said earlier about stopping all the bickering and fighting.

"Our greatest fault," he said tiredly, "was that we had too much pride in our system. Our pride blinded us to everyone outside of it." He paused to rub away the moisture gathering in his eyes. "The book of Psalms says, *God loves justice and will not abandon His faithful ones.* We forgot to trust in God to provide us with justice. We became so wrapped up in our desire for redress and our pride in rebuilding that we lost sight of Him and everyone else."

I watched as he slid further back into his chair. It was like watching a mirror version of myself as I slumped into the couch from the stroke. I glanced over at Auggie, who was watching the past bear down on his father.

Johann's chest began heaving as he tried to hold back the tears.

Auggie leaned forward. "What's wrong, Pop?"

"I was thinking about your mother, Auggie." His eyes opened and were rimmed with tears. "She was right when she said it would be best to leave Germany and put the past behind us." He took a deep breath and continued. "She never once forgot about God or about caring for others. There were things she liked about National Socialism. She was encouraged by all the progress we made in the '30s, how quickly we rebuilt, and all the social programs that we started.

"But there were a lot of things she didn't like: the arrogance and swagger, how the racist theories divided people, and how the Jews were treated. She was devastated when war came and destroyed other countries and then our own."

He turned to face me. "You should have met her, Willi. Her name was Ida, and she was a kind and loving person. She wanted me to forget about the past, but the nagging sense of injustice never left me. She became upset when I started researching the war after retirement, but she supported me anyway."

Auggie reached out to hug his father. "She was a great woman, Pop. And you are a great father."

He acknowledged his son with a look of regret. "I wish I could have been more like her, for your sake, Auggie." He shook his head. "I never saw her angry. She had this unconditional sense of love, patience, and forgiveness. She always kept her faith and believed things would turn out for the best, regardless of what happened to us.

"But I could never afford that; I was too focused on getting justice for my country. But she was able to make me forget about that whenever I got too excited. She would calm me down, comfort me and make me feel loved. She gave me peace. I don't know what I would have done without her."

This wasn't the Johann that I knew. God only knows how he and his wife ever got together, so I asked. "How did you meet her, Johann?"

Auggie seemed startled by my question. He leaned back and waited to hear what his father would say.

"I can't talk about that now, Willi. I'm too tired, and that will only bring up more questions."

Auggie stood up, walked over to his father, and patted him on the shoulder. "That should wrap it up, Pop, don't you think? This was a lot more than either Willi or I had bargained for. What do you say, Willi?"

I offered a slight smile. "It's been a full day for me too, Auggie. It's time for me to head home. Anyway, you two probably want some alone time together."

Johann slowly stood up to shake my hand. "Willi, it was good to see you again." He gave me a tired smile. "I hope you learned something today. And remember, there are still more points that we have to discuss."

"Okay, Johann. And thanks for the history lesson today. I learned a few new things. And it was also good to hear from Lena. She said a few things that made me stop and think."

He nodded slowly. "I know. She made me think about things as well."

~ DRIVING HOME ~

CHAPTER 44: THE HORROR

On my way home, I wondered why I never heard about Smedley Butler's role in that plot. It sure seemed important enough. His statements seemed to verify everything that Johann was saying about our system. And it was equally shocking to hear that FDR was one of those "powerbrokers" who profited from Germany's troubles in the Twenties and colluded with Wall Street during the Thirties to drive up our debt. Why was neither of those brought up in our history books?

But the final shock came when Johann spoke about US investors giving Russia the funds and expertise to develop their manufacturing infrastructure. They used that to supply North Vietnam with the trucks, guns, missiles, and ammunition to be used against us.

Was Butler correct? Did Wall Street have the newspapers in their back pocket? Is that why this stuff was never reported? But what if they didn't? Was the story buried because the editors felt it wasn't interesting? But what if they did report it? Would it have changed the course of history, my father's life, and mine?

I looked over the traffic and saw the highway dip out of sight a few miles ahead. It made me feel like the world I knew was disappearing into a void. Was Johann telling me all this stuff on purpose? If so, what was it? Maybe he saw me struggling with my past and was trying, like a good father, to help me get over it and move forward, especially when he started quoting Scripture.

Lena seemed to be doing the same thing but in a different way. She saw right through me when I spoke about my need to survive boot camp. She saw my fear and weakness. I was humbled by her story about her mother, how she had sacrificed herself to feed her children.

I looked out over the highway and thought again about my need to survive boot camp. I thought about running around the track and telling myself that I would run over the guy in front of me if he fell in order to survive. And then I thought about my father and how he had squirreled himself away in the woods instead of returning to help his squad.

I grabbed a stick of gum from the center console and popped it into my mouth. The burst of spearmint wiped away the taste of stale coffee. It brought back memories of my uncle's farm. When I was a child, my brother and I would spend part of each summer there. My uncle taught me to pick spearmint leaves and chew on them to quench my thirst.

I went there every summer until I joined the Marines and didn't return until fifteen years later when my first marriage began to fall apart. I began to rethink that last trip because it was a pivotal moment in my life.

After the death of our daughter, I focused on finishing my honors paper while Alicia went back to work. I was in my senior year and applied for a *Monbusho* Scholarship from Japan to continue my studies there, but I didn't tell Alicia. When I was accepted, she said she didn't want to go to Japan, and she didn't congratulate me. That should have been my first clue about things to come.

My father grew closer to Alicia after the death of our child, and he wanted to make sure I could take good care of her after graduation. He used his connections at IBM to get me an interview. Remembering that interview made me chuckle. The interviewer wondered why someone with a degree in English and history would want a job at a computer company.

I explained my objective was to join a reputable company and build a successful career. I spun off all my achievements in the Marines and college and told him I was confident about doing equally well at IBM. That was all bullshit. I didn't want to work for IBM, but I couldn't afford to miss this opportunity. There were scant pickings for employment during the 70's recession. Fortunately, they hired me.

I applied the same single-minded focus to the new job that I used in boot camp and college. It was a matter of not only my surviving, but I now had a family. Nothing would stop me from keeping that job and succeeding. After four years of hard work, I won several awards and a promotion to management.

I squinted into the traffic ahead and tried to recall my relationship with Alicia during my time at IBM. I couldn't remember anything except my being proud of surviving the transition from college to win that promotion into management. Unfortunately, after that promotion, an unexplained fear arose in me. I didn't understand where it came from or how to deal with it. I became agitated and frustrated.

Looking back at it now, it was the same fear of dropping the ball when I was playing catch with my father. There was a sense of foreboding, a sense of something imminent coming that would cause me to fail in my new position. My frustration over this unknown fear led to angry outbursts at home, which made Alicia anxious and scared. I was able to keep my anger in check at work, but an increasing resentment arose against my peers. Their lives were peaceful, while mine was haunted by the war and something else I didn't understand.

It was around this time that *Apocalypse Now* was released. I went by myself to see it. The vision of Martin Sheen's camouflaged head emerging from the swamp stayed with me long after the movie ended. Later that night, I looked in the mirror and saw it superimposed on my face. The spectral voice of Colonel Kurtz whispered in the background, *The horror … the horror …*

I stared at the mirror until the vision disappeared. My expression slowly changed to one of anger as the beast surfaced. I made a vow to myself that nothing would break me, not my father, not the DIs, and not any goddamn unknown fear.

I decided it was time to get hard again. I began running and exercising each day. I retrieved my old boonie cover, camouflaged utilities, and jungle boots from my sea bag. I went to a nearby Army & Navy store and purchased a web belt with two canteens, two magazine pouches, an LC-1 "Alice" pack, and a Heckler & Koch 91 assault rifle. If something bad was about to happen, then I would be prepared for it.

Each weekend, I'd grab my gear and head out for the woods. I walked slowly among the trees with quiet deliberation as if stalking a deer. With each step, I could hear Colonel Kurtz whispering, *Crawling, slithering, along the edge of a straight razor … and surviving.* I knew that one small slip could be my last.

The sense of something ominous grew stronger every day. It was the early '80s, and America was changing as sex, drugs, and violence took center stage in the popular media. I felt like Travis Bickle, the deranged veteran in *Taxi Driver* who also worked out and carried guns to be ready for anything. I didn't like what I was becoming and decided to leave America.

I resigned from IBM and took a job in Saudi Arabia. Alicia and I settled into a company compound near Dhahran. Life was orderly and peaceful there. Things were getting back to normal, and both of us felt we could live there for a long time. But, after the first year, life became stale and mechanical. The same sense of foreboding returned and overshadowed an otherwise peaceful existence.

Only this time, there was no outlet to relieve my anxieties. My rifle and gear were back in the States; there were no forests here, only vast expanses of sand. I began to realize that leaving America hadn't solved anything. The threats weren't coming from outside; they were inside. It was the beast. My fear was not only feeding the beast but also generating anger against it. I was caught in a vicious cycle.

One night, my ex-boss at IBM called and asked if I wanted to rejoin the company as a system engineer. I was thirty-one and reluctant to switch careers, but Saudi Arabia wasn't doing me any good. Alicia was reluctant to leave, but she agreed as the Iran-Iraq war began to heat up.

For the next four years, I bore down again to learn new skills for the new job. I was competing with younger college graduates, so I bore down with the same single-minded focus. I was determined to succeed. And I did.

The following four years were very demanding. I had to travel every week to work on long and complex projects for our clients in different cities. But, in the end, it all paid off. It wasn't long before I led those large projects and generated new ones to help our business grow. I won numerous cash bonuses and was awarded invitations to the System Engineer's Symposium for two years in a row.

I glanced in the rearview mirror and felt the past coming up on me as fast as the cars behind me.

CHAPTER 45: DEAD SILENCE

My gum had lost its flavor. It became as stale as my first marriage after returning from Saudi Arabia. I opened the window and spit it out.

Alicia wasn't happy about the move or my new job with IBM back in the US. She never spoke about it, but her mood changed. She loved the peace and quiet of the company compound in Dhahran and became increasingly disenchanted with all the materialism being displayed in America during the '80s.

After my career started to take off, she shied away from everything related to it. She avoided office parties, socializing with my business associates, and wasn't interested in my work. She turned away from the changing world and wanted more of my time than I could give. I was too proud to ask what was wrong, or perhaps, I was too afraid of what she might say if I did. I wasn't sure which one it was, but things only got worse.

She retreated into an evangelical group that met frequently for Bible studies. She had a paperback book, *Good News for Modern Man*, that she took with her. It was a contemporary version of the New Testament. I glanced at it briefly, but it was like pablum compared to the King James version. She begged me to join her. I went once but left thinking they were a bunch of hillbillies. I never went again.

After that, Alicia started going her own way. I was glad she did because it left me alone to pursue my career.

Cars began passing me. I suddenly realized my thoughts had been distracting me. I quickly caught up with the traffic flow and returned to reflecting on my first marriage. It was rapidly declining, and to make matters worse, middle age began setting in. I remembered looking in the mirror and seeing, for the first time, a pudgy, balding civilian staring back at me. All my fears about losing my edge and failing returned. However, this time, my job was too demanding. There was no time for any sort of outlet I was too busy keeping up with too many clients.

Two incidents occurred that finally convinced me that something needed to change. The first happened when several guys from the office asked me to join them for drinks after work. After a few drinks, they started to piss me off with their light-hearted revelry. It all seemed too frivolous for me, so I left early.

I got into my red TR-7 sports car and raced home on the Interstate like a drunken Indy driver. Another car blew by me, and we began to pass one another until he cut me off a little too close for comfort. I jerked my car into the lane next to him, pulled a pistol out from under the car seat, and pointed it upward as a warning to back off.

The pistol was only a pellet gun, but it was made to resemble a .44 Magnum. I bought it years ago with money earned from my paper route. The other driver looked over at me, pulled out a pistol, and pointed it directly at me. I felt the cold embrace of death and eased off the gas as he sped away. I might have been drunk, angry, and a little crazy, but I wasn't stupid. He was not only angry but stupid. And stupid people with guns scare me.

The next incident occurred when Alicia invited our neighbors over for dinner. The husband and I drank a few more beers than we should have and went to the garage to grab a few more. The husband saw a Marine recruiting poster on the garage wall and asked if I was in the war. I said yes, and he said he was lucky enough not to get drafted. And then he asked if I was a good shot.

I quietly walked over to my footlocker and flung it open. He saw all my stored military gear and the H&K rifle with its stock collapsed. His eyes lit up when I took it out, extended the stock, and locked it into place with a resounding click.

I carried it out of the garage into the dark of the evening. There was a streetlight about 100 yards away. I asked if he thought I could hit it. He looked at me with a half-baked smile and said, "You've got to be kidding me." While he gawked, I told him to watch.

I loaded a bullet into the magazine, slammed the magazine into the rifle, and chambered a round. I lifted the rifle to my shoulder, aimed through the iron sights, and fired. The noise was deafening, and an orange flash burst from the barrel. The light exploded into a million pieces. The glass fragments showered down on the road. They illuminated the darkness with their reflections of moonlight.

I didn't wait for anyone's reaction. I lowered the rifle, pulled out the magazine, put it on safety, and picked up the spent cartridge. We headed back into the garage, and I stowed the rifle back in the chest.

When we walked back into the house, there was dead silence. Nobody said anything, but they must have heard the shot. As I think about it now, anyone would have been crazy to say anything to me after that.

CHAPTER 46: DOWN FROM THE MOUNTAIN

A truck roared by and shook my car. I was stunned but thankful for the interruption. I looked down at the dashboard clock. I was about halfway home with less than an hour to go. I smiled at the irony. Halfway home. After the streetlight incident, I knew my life was half over. I just couldn't imagine living the other half the same way.

A few days after that second incident, I told Alicia that I needed to take a break. I was going to my uncle's farm to camp out. She didn't question me. In fact, she rarely objected to anything I did anymore.

It didn't bother me to be alone in the woods. In fact, I embraced it. If I couldn't find a way to purge the beast up there, then that would be the end. Someone would have to drag my carcass out of the woods, just as I did with the deer.

I decided to fast during the trip, so there was little to pack. I took my H&K, ammo, knife, hatchet, flashlight, tent, sleeping bag, four canteens filled with water, web belt, and a box of cigars to keep the hunger away. I planned on staying no more than four days.

When my aunt and uncle saw me step out of the car in jungle utilities, jungle boots, and boonie hat, their discomfort was noticeable. I smiled, said hello, thanked them, and told them I would be back in four days or so.

It was a peaceful walk up the steep mountain. Most of the way up was through a meadow of knee-high grass that gave way to a short patch of scrub before the forest began. I walked a short distance into the woods until I found a suitable campsite. I cleared an area to pitch my tent and set up a fire pit. The quiet was calming. All the distractions of civilization were left behind, and the beast was still.

That night, I sat on a log beside the fire and smoked a cigar. I decided not to think about anything for the next few days. If a solution came, fine. If it didn't, then I knew what to do.

I woke up early the next morning and looked outside the tent. The sky was dark, with a hint of dawn in the distance. I turned on the flashlight, got into my clothes, and went to sit on the log by the fire pit.

The birds were the first to awake. They were followed soon after by deer who emerged from the woods to graze in the meadow. They weren't aware of me since I was upwind.

When sunlight began to break over the horizon, I lit a cigar and smoked it down to the bitter end. It tasted and smelled awful, but I intentionally brought cheap cigars to kill my appetite. And they were effective. After the cigar was done, I strapped on my web belt, slung my rifle over my shoulder, and started walking across the top of the mountain.

After a while, the sling began to chafe against my shoulder, so I unslung the rifle and sighted it in a large tree about 80 yards away. I sucked in a breath, held it, and squeezed off a round. There was a thundering boom, which reminded me of my first deer hunt. Then silence.

I stood there for some time before walking over to the tree. As I came up to it, I could see where the bullet had ripped open the bark. I was pleased that the bullet hit its mark, but as I came closer, the size and depth of the tree's shredded pulp made me regretful. I lost all desire to fire that rifle again.

Each morning, I set off walking across the top of the mountain until the sun got directly overhead. By then, the meadow had shed its coat of morning dew, and I could walk down the hill without getting soaking wet.

A wide stream ran around the base of the mountain. Once I got there, I would strip down and carefully wade through the rushing current to a large, dry rock in the middle of the stream. The water was refreshingly cold, but the sunbaked rock was wonderfully warm as I sat down. I gazed up at the clear, blue sky and took in the fresh country air.

After a while, I would get up to wash myself with a bar of Ivory soap. I took it because it was 99.44% pure. After rinsing off, I would return to the shore, find another rock, and sit back to dry off. After that, I would dress and sit down to smoke another cigar.

Once the shadows began to lengthen, I would gather my gear and return to the campsite. After sunset, I would start a fire, smoke another cigar, and wait for nightfall. When the stars came out, I went into the tent to sleep.

The first day was spent battling hunger. The second was spent resigning myself to being hungry and by the third day, the hunger had passed. I felt like I could fast for days.

During the night of my third day, a sense of bliss arrived. I sat by the fire surrounded by darkness, and a quote from Goethe came to mind: *And so long as you haven't experienced this: to die and so to grow, you are only a troubled guest on this dark earth.*

That was a good summation of my life. I had been a troubled guest on this earth since childhood. A wave of nausea came over me as I sensed the end was near. I watched as the sparks flew up into the darkness until their glow disappeared. The darkness left behind revealed more stars than I had ever seen before.

The infinite number of stars reminded me of God, and suddenly, my nausea vanished. I remember that moment as if it were here today. I sat in the darkness and recalled a sign that Carl Jung had hung over his study door: *Bidden or unbidden, God is always present.*

It was God's divine spark that had fused my father's cell to my mother's and began my journey here on earth. He was the First Cause, and He would be the Last. He gave me life, and He would be the one to end it, not me. I took comfort in that thought. Suddenly, my life felt precious.

I woke up on the fourth day with my mind made up. I would leave the past behind and start my life anew. I marched down that mountain with the same steely-eyed focus that had taken me through so many challenges before, convinced that this course of action would be the best for all concerned.

I arrived home later that day and promptly told Alicia our relationship was over. I promised to support her until she could start a new life. She broke down crying and sank to the floor. I had foreseen this tragedy twelve years ago when I first crawled into bed with her. I thought I could redeem both of us, but as it turned out, I was only half-right.

My exit sign appeared, and I exhaled a sigh of relief. This visit and the drive back had been mentally and spiritually exhausting. As the car slowed down, I opened the window. A rush of fresh air came in and made me think again about my steely-eyed focus as I came down that mountain. My decision to stay alive may have been divinely inspired, but I was suddenly convinced that the decision to leave my past came from the beast. It had used my pride to deceive me into believing I could overcome anything, even my past. And that thought angered me.

I quickly closed the window. The stillness inside the car made me think of the *Triumph of the Will*. That movie and all it represented was another deception, only that time it was borne out of a nation's pride. The beast had made Germany believe that it could overcome anything.

I stared ahead at the oncoming exit ramp while a Bible verse slammed head-on into me: *"Pride goeth before destruction and a haughty spirit before a fall."* Truer words were never spoken.

CYCLE III: *DIE NIEDERLAGE*

Gott lässt uns wohl sinken, aber nicht ertrinken.
(God lets us sink but not drown.)
An old German Proverb

~ AT HOME ~

CHAPTER 47: FACT CHECKING

I spent the rest of the ride home wondering about Johann. Was he a resurrection of the beast? Was he too being deceptive and trying to set me up for something to come? But if so, why? There was no doubt that he was repackaging history, but was he also trying to repackage me as well?

I pulled into the garage, turned off the car, and my mind went back to Alicia. I wanted to end things quickly with her. I made the announcement short, thinking it would be merciful for both our sakes. But now Lena's words came back to chastise me for my lack of compassion.

She was right. I had bulled my way through everything, including my first marriage, until the stroke hit. And now, I suddenly realized how selfish I had been. A silent refrain began playing over and over in my head as I sat in the silence of the garage. *An unexamined life is not worth living.* I had thought of this phrase once before, during my second visit with Johann. It did not come from the beast. It came from my conscience.

Cynthia opened the door into the garage with a worried look on her face. I quickly jumped out of the car to give her a warm greeting. I was happy to see her expression change to a welcoming smile.

We spent the rest of the day outside, sprucing up the yard and taking occasional breaks on the patio with Doris and Daisy. I kept waiting for her to ask about the visit, but she never did. I finally broke the ice at dinner. "Well, I got to meet Johann's son today. He's quite a character as well." I grinned, hoping to disarm her anticipated response. It didn't work.

"I still don't understand why you need to go there, Will. And now you're getting in deeper by meeting his son. When will all this end?"

I looked down at my plate. My appetite was diminishing, along with the warmth of my dinner. "I don't know, Cindy. Today he was spouting off about pre-war Germany, which he said was an economic miracle. He compared it to America, which was being run into the ground by a bunch of scheming crooks who profited from the Depression. Can you believe that?"

She looked exasperated. "He's an old man, Will. He's probably senile and got his facts all mixed up with all that Nazi crap he grew up with. Why don't you just forget about all this and move on?"

"I don't think that's the case. He's pretty darn sharp. He's still reading and uses computers. A lot of 90-year-olds have kept it together, like Clint Eastwood, Pablo Picasso, and even Betty White. He's been researching this stuff for twenty-five years, so he probably knows what he's talking about."

She put her glass down, and her face grew harsh. "But everything that man stands for is evil, Will, and you shouldn't be listening to him. God knows I'm tired of listening to you talk about him."

I surprised myself by getting defensive. "Well, everything he's said so far has checked out. But" I admitted, "he really went way over the top today. I'm going to have to research my notes to check out everything he said. But you shouldn't force him into a box, Cynthia. Not everything is so black and white."

Cynthia didn't relent. "I'm not forcing anything, Will. This is not rocket science; what happened back then is as plain as the nose on your face."

"I don't know that anymore. Everything we've learned in life is only what we've been told, and I'm learning now that there's more to it than that." I looked away, pissed off that Johann was coming between us. My life got screwed up because of the beast. I wasn't about to let that happen again with Johann. I was going to see if there was any truth to his remarks. I looked over at Cynthia, who was still staring at me.

"I suppose you plan to go back?"

"I don't know. I have to check out what he said today, and then we'll see."

The next few weeks were spent fact-checking my notes. I found Sutton's books online and spent the next few days checking out Johann's references to him. They all tied out. Then, my special-order book came in. It confirmed FDR's positions in the investment companies during the Twenties, including the one involved in Germany's hyperinflation. I closed the book on that subject but then had another thought. If FDR wasn't what he appeared to be, what about Hitler? Was he really a dedicated socialist?

The best source to check this out was a book by Ernst Hanfstaengl, *Hitler: The Memoir of the Nazi Insider Who Turned Against the Fuhrer.* Hanfstaengl's father was German, and his mother was American. Hanfstaengl had graduated from Harvard, met Hitler in the early twenties, and became enamored of the National Socialist program. He served as the Party's first foreign press secretary until 1937 when he had to flee Germany in fear for his life.

Hanfstaengl wrote that Hitler transformed from a dedicated national socialist during the '20s to a self-obsessed megalomaniac after becoming a dictator. Hitler apparently became enamored with the power and wealth of his position and made millions as the *Führer*.

The government purchased millions of copies of *Mein Kampf* for distribution to soldiers and citizens. In addition to earning royalties from those book sales, Hitler also licensed his image for postage stamps and posters that were plastered all over the country. And on top of it all, he ordered the Ministry of Finance to classify him as tax-exempt in 1934.

Mr. Hanfstaengl said Hitler was a complex man who worked tirelessly to elevate the country's stature by promoting his own image. Although he lived like an ascetic, he owned an extensive collection of rare art objects as well as a collection of high-priced Mercedes-Benz cars. He was also known for giving expensive gifts to friends and associates.

I also found an interesting article that uncovered the disparity between what National Socialism promised and what it delivered. The author wrote, t*he Nazi economy can hardly be looked upon as a "socialist" regime so far as ownership of private property is concerned. Whatever may have been the specific reasons, whatever may have been the changes in identity of individuals owning property, the average inequality in the distribution of wealth was greater in 1935 than in 1931.*[1]

I planned to lord this over Johann but then thought the better of it. There was no point in rubbing the old man's face in it. He was a dyed-in-the-wool National Socialist who saw first-hand how it spurred his people to rebuild their nation. What he didn't see, however, was the corruption that came with the party's rapid rise and the suffering it heaped on its Jewish citizens. There were simply no checks and balances on the Nazi leaders after they came into power.

I researched the other characters in my notes, including Feder and Butler. Everything Johann said about them checked out. Then, I found the full, unexpurgated version of Butler's testimony before the McCormack-Dickstein Committee. It was never published in the Congressional Record but was given in error to an investigative journalist. It was printed in an obscure periodical, *New Masses,* on February 5, 1935. Johann was right about Butler naming some prominent people in the financial community who were involved. But, as he said, nothing ever came of it. None of the leading newspapers or periodicals ever published that version.

There was only one more thing left to check out. Johann asserted that America pushed Germany into World War II. It didn't seem plausible to me from what I knew, but I wanted to see if there was any truth to his statement.

CHAPTER 48: ABSTRACT DIFFICULTIES

I didn't know where to start. Unlike the US oil embargo that pushed Japan into attacking us, I couldn't think of anything FDR did that may have pushed Germany into war. Perhaps the best place to start looking was in the Nuremberg transcripts. They may offer insight into the events that led to war.

Robert Jackson, the chief American prosecutor at Nuremberg, put forward the first charge against Germany's leaders for their *preparation and waging of wars of aggression.* He stated, *We need not trouble ourselves about the many abstract difficulties that can be conjured up about what constitutes aggression in doubtful cases. I shall show you… these were unlawful wars of aggression in breach of treaties and in violation of assurances.*[1] I decided to research each of these breaches in chronological order to see if Johann's assertion held any water.

The first breach came on October 23, 1933, when Germany announced its intention to begin rearming, a violation of the Versailles Peace Treaty. It also stated its intent to withdraw from the League of Nations. Both actions resulted from the Allies' failure to comply with Article 8 of the League of Nations Covenant, which required all signatories to progressively disarm over time *to the lowest point consistent with national safety and the enforcement by common action of international obligations.* This was the first hint that the Allies were pushing Germany toward war by their refusal to disarm.

UPI reported the same day, *Germany adamantly demands that she be permitted to increase her armaments or that the allies, meaning France and Poland particularly, reduce theirs. France, with the backing of the United States and Britain, refuses to disarm before a test period of international armaments control. Germany was refused coldly her requested permission for rearmament.* [2]

Although the signatories to the Versailles Peace Treaty had held numerous disarmament conferences over the past thirteen years, the Western Allies had accomplished nothing. In fact, they had modernized and expanded their military capabilities while Germany was left disarmed and defenseless during the same time period.

Jackson didn't mention any of this at the Tribunal, nor did he mention that the Allies did nothing when Germany started to rearm after that. I thought about Mr. Sutton's book and wondered who provided Germany with the necessary finances, resources, and technology to rearm. Germany was still recovering in 1935, but I deferred answering that question for now.

Germany's second breach came on March 16, 1935, when Hitler denounced all the military clauses of the Versailles Treaty and proclaimed that Germany would immediately start military conscription. He based his decision, once again, on the failure of other signatories to disarm.

UPI reported that Germany's announcement *rocked Europe, already tense with the increasing momentum of an arms race among the chief powers. France and Great Britain already had moved this week toward increased armed strength.* [3] And once more, the Western Allies did nothing to punish Germany for this second breach.

Germany's third breach followed two months later, in May, when German forces marched into the Rhineland to displace the occupying French troops. Jackson didn't mention that France and Russia precipitated this action when they signed the Franco-Soviet

Treaty of Mutual Assistance. This was a bilateral treaty aimed at enveloping Nazi Germany in the event of unprovoked aggression. Germany displaced the occupying French troops because it didn't want a potential enemy posted within its territory.

David Lloyd George, who was Britain's Prime Minister during World War I and also helped draft the Versailles Treaty, agreed with Germany, and said as much in a speech to the House of Commons on July 27, 1936: *The moment the Russo-French Pact was signed, no one responsible for the security of Germany could leave its most important industrial province* [the Rhineland] *without defense of any sort or kind when…France had built the most gigantic fortifications ever seen in any land, where, almost 100 feet underground, you could keep an army of over 100,000 and where you have guns that can fire straight into Germany. Yet the Germans are supposed to remain without even a garrison, without a trench. I am going to say here that if Herr Hitler had… allowed that to go without protecting his country he would have been a traitor to the Fatherland.* [4]

Johann seemed to be on the right track. And it was odd that, once again, the Allies took no punitive action against Germany for this third breach. The fourth breach came on March 12, 1938, when the *Anschluss* was completed between Germany and Austria. Shortly afterward, Austria held a mandate on the union and received an overwhelming endorsement.

Although the Versailles Peace Treaty specifically prohibited this action, no punitive action was taken by the Allies, which sent a strong signal to Germany that the Allies didn't feel the Treaty was worth salvaging after this last breach.

The fifth breach followed quickly on the heels of several events that involved Czechoslovakia. This was a new nation created by the Versailles Peace Treaty after the Austro-Hungarian Empire was dismantled. The first of these events was the Munich Agreement signed on September 30th of, 1938. It further eroded the Versailles Peace Treaty, which reverted a portion of Czechoslovakia, the Sudetenland, back to Germany.

The second event followed two months later when the Allies signed off on a treaty that ceded two more portions of Czechoslovakia; one went to Hungary and the other to Poland.

The third and fourth events followed soon after. On March 14, 1939, another piece of Czechoslovakia was dismembered when the province of Slovakia broke away and declared its independence. The next day, the Carpatho-Ukraine region followed suit. However, it was quickly annexed and occupied by Hungary soon after.

The fifth breach came within days of those two events. Germany forced the Czech president to sign over what was left of Czechoslovakia to them out of fear of political unrest. Germany invaded and took control of the now-defunct state the next day. There were no Allied repercussions against Germany for this action.

By mid-1939, many of the terms in the Versailles Peace Treaty were completely undone. Mr. Jackson never mentioned this in his charges, nor did he provide any context behind the five breaches. However, his role at the Tribunal was that of a prosecuting attorney. His job was to secure a conviction; it was not to deal with any of the *abstract difficulties* that would help uncover the truth of what actually happened.

The problem, however, was that his one-sided explanation worked its way into the mainstream of current history. What happened to the other historians, journalists, and academics since then? They apparently treated Jackson's prosecutorial summation as fact and incorporated his spirit and tone into their published accounts. Why hadn't they bothered to research it as I did?

I thought again about Antony Sutton. Why weren't his writings more well-known? And why on earth did I have to learn all this from someone like Johann? I began feeling uneasy about my findings.

Something didn't seem quite right. It seemed like something was missing.

There was the version of history that I grew up, and now there was this other version that Johann was serving up. Each had their own set of facts and rationale, but neither seemed to be completely accurate. But if both sides were somewhat flawed, then where did the truth fit in? I didn't want the old guy to be right, but it seemed as if the Allies had sidestepped a good part of the truth during the Nuremberg Tribunal. Perhaps Germany wasn't pushed into war by the Allies, but it did seem like they were drawing Germany into starting one, consciously or not.

There was one more breach left to explore. It was the one that broke the camel's back: the invasion of Poland in September 1939.

CHAPTER 49: PRACTICAL DIFFICULTIES

I looked down and saw my third cup of coffee was drained. So was I. Researching Germany's invasion of Poland would have to wait until tomorrow. I shuffled all my papers into a neat pile and then set off to find Cynthia.

She wasn't in the kitchen, so I headed to her study. I found her sitting at her desk, peering into her laptop. She didn't hear me arrive, so I just stood there, watching her, and remembering the first time we met. She was different from Alicia in so many ways. She had a strong belief system and was very vocal about expressing it, whereas Alicia was ambivalent about most things and never voiced an opinion about anything unless asked.

"Will, I didn't hear you come in. Are you done for the day?" She flipped her glasses back on her head and smiled. I nodded and smirked. She started wearing glasses a year ago, and frankly, I liked the look on her.

"Yeah. I'm done for the day, but I still have more research to do. So far, everything Johann said has turned out to be true. It's unbelievable what kind of bullshit I had to wade through to find what I did. None of it was in any history books I ever had in school, although he did miss a few things about his own country."

She frowned at my profanity. "Sorry, honey, but it's hard to believe what Germany was put through by the Allies after the First World War. It's no wonder things led to the Second."

"Will, don't you think the Allies knew what they were doing? They didn't trust the Germans. Germany started the First World War. And after that, they wanted to make sure Germany didn't start another, but that's what happened! I took some history courses, too, Will. So what are you trying to do? Rewrite history? Do you think there's any great earth-shattering discovery to be made? And if there was, do you think anyone's going to care?"

All I could think about while she was raising her voice was Johann's first point: evil begets evil. There was no point in arguing this any further. Her mind was made up. "I don't care about making any big discoveries, honey. I just need to work through this for myself. Let's call it a day and go outside with a glass of wine."

"Okay, I'll stop. C'mon, girls." She shepherded Doris and Daisy outside while I poured the wine.

We spent the rest of the evening outside talking until the sun slipped below the horizon, leaving a dark orange hue in its wake. It was pleasant sitting with her and not thinking about anything too seriously. It made me feel whole again.

The next morning, Doris and Daisy were jumping and whining at my side of the bed. It was 4:00 a.m. When we finally finished our daily drill and walked in the door, Cynthia was already up. She and I sat down with our coffee to watch and chat about the news. After that, I made another cup and headed back to my study to pick up where I left off, Germany's invasion of Poland.

Jackson summarized Germany's last breach of the Versailles Peace Treaty in a short, direct statement: *commencing in September 1939, in a series of undeclared wars against nations with, which Germany had arbitration and nonaggression treaties, and in violation of repeated assurances ... Germany attacked Poland.*

While Jackson did not have to deal with any of the *abstract difficulties* caused by the Versailles Peace Treaty, Germany had to deal with many of the practical difficulties associated with it. One of the biggest was the Republic of Poland, a new nation established by that Treaty from German soil.

This new country had a thin stretch of land called the Polish Corridor that separated the German state of East Prussia from the rest of the German nation. It was about twenty miles wide at its northernmost tip and seventy miles wide on its southern end.

In addition, several postwar treaties established the former German city of Danzig into a new "free" city-state, making it a ward of the League of Nations. However, Poland was given administrative control of many of its day-to-day operations. In 1938, ninety-eight percent of this city-state's citizens were reported as German-born.

This piece of geopolitical engineering astounded me. A comparable analogy in the United States would be to slice off a thin piece of eastern New York state, running from north to south, and give it to Canada; that thin slice would be called the Canadian Corridor. The Canadian Corridor would lie between the New England states and all the other states in the USA, leaving New England separated from the rest of the country. To top it off, New York City would be designated a "free city-state." It would be governed by the United Nations and administered by Canada. I could only imagine what a nightmare scenario that would be!

The establishment of the Polish Republic was completed in 1920. Nazi Germany formalized relations with it on January 26, 1934, when the two countries signed a ten-year non-aggression pact. Germany approached Poland in October 1938 to renegotiate that Pact. There were two very practical reasons. First, it wanted to extend its newly built autobahn across the Polish Corridor to connect to East Prussia. Second, it sought Poland's support to regain control of Danzig and its German-born residents. Germany offered, in return, to renounce any future claims on its former territories now held by Poland.

These negotiations continued into 1939 when Hitler met with Poland's foreign minister on January 5th. Germany's foreign minister, Von Ribbentrop, followed up on these talks with negotiations in Warsaw. The negotiations continued until March 31st, 1939 when Poland suddenly stiffened its position. Britain and France had just guaranteed Poland's sovereignty if they were ever attacked, providing them with a safety net.

I wondered why this was necessary since Poland already had its sovereignty guaranteed by a variety of postwar treaties, especially under the League of Nations' Covenant, Articles 16 and 17. Why did they need another?

Something didn't sound right to me. As Johann said, it was time to dig a little deeper.

CHAPTER 50: FALSE FLAG

It took three days of digging until I stumbled on something promising. It was a book called the *German White Book* that had the subtitle: *Documents Concerning the last phase of the German-Polish Crisis*. It contained a collection of documents written by Polish diplomats during the 1938-1939 negotiations.

The Germans seized these documents after the 1939 invasion and published them in April 1940. I was ready to dismiss their credibility until I found that Edward Raczyński, the Polish ambassador to London from 1934 to 1945, confirmed their authenticity in his diary.[1]

These documents showed that Polish diplomats knew that America had pressured Britain and France to issue that guarantee. In fact, the US promised to give military support if war did occur. Was this FDR's way of pushing Britain and France to start a war with Germany?

After that guarantee was issued, the Poles stiffened their negotiating position with Germany. They also accelerated their persecution of the more than one million Germans left behind in their country after the First World War. According to Richard Blanke, a history professor from the University of Maine, this persecution had been going on for some time. Blanke authored a book called *Orphans of Versailles: The Germans in Western Poland 1918-1939*. Here is an interesting extract: *It is hard to avoid the conclusion that the Polish state was bent on the elimination of most of the*

German minority in Western Poland … Moreover, this goal was well underway to being achieved by 1939 … [2]

Germany did not react well to the hardening of the Polish position or to the accelerated persecution of its German-born citizens. After realizing there was no chance of obtaining a peaceful resolution to either situation, Germany invaded Poland on the first of September.

Hitler told the Reichstag on that same day that he was *determined to solve (1) the Danzig question; (2) the question of the Corridor; and (3) to see to it that a change is made in the relationship between Germany and Poland that shall ensure a peaceful co-existence. In this, I am resolved to continue to fight until either the present Polish government is willing to continue to bring about this change or until another Polish Government is ready to do so.* [3]

Britain and France immediately declared war on Germany but took no other meaningful action to back up their guarantee. Their lack of action went down in Polish history as the "Great Betrayal." Russia also invaded Poland from the east on September 17[th,] but neither Britain nor France declared war on them despite their unconditional guarantee.

Was Germany pushed into starting the Second World War? I couldn't say, but I read where the Nazi leaders were genuinely surprised by Britain's and France's reaction, a declaration of war; they were hoping for another pass after a series of other breaches or, at worst case, a negotiated resolution to the conflict.

My email pinged with the arrival of a new message. It was the daily feed from the *Smithsonian*. The subject line read *FDR's secret Hitler map.* I opened it and read that FDR made a speech on October 27, 1941, that was designed to inflame public opinion against Germany. His speech was widely reported in the domestic and foreign press.

FDR said that *a secret map* [was] *made in Germany by Hitler's government. It is a map of South America and a part of Central America, as Hitler proposes to reorganise it... This map makes clear the Nazi design not only against South America but against the United States itself.*

He continued by telling the audience, *Your government has in its possession another document made in Germany by Hitler's government. It is a plan to abolish all existing religions – Protestant, Catholic, Mohammedan, Hindu, Buddhist and Jewish alike.*[4]

The *Smithsonian* article stated that both documents were forgeries created by British intelligence. I immediately thought of the black propaganda that was churned out by Sefton Delmer and his associate Otto John. The Brits routed these documents to "Wild Bill" Donovan, who had direct access to FDR. The president recently appointed Donovan to head a new organization called the Office of the Coordinator of Information (the predecessor of the OSS, which grew into the CIA).

The article ended by saying it was highly likely that FDR knew the information was false. If that were true, then he was pushing the American citizenry into a war against Germany just as he did with Britain, France, and Poland when he pressed them to issue that guarantee in 1939.

Perhaps Johann was right after all. Perhaps FDR wanted to eliminate National Socialism, even at the expense of sacrificing Poland. Was that such a terrible thing? At least it kept our system intact. But was it worth all the loss of life?

I leaned back in my chair and gazed out the study window. Maybe Cynthia was right. What did I hope to get out of this? What was the point of all these discussions and research?

I turned to face my desk and thought again of stopping this. But as I flipped through my notebook, I realized this was no longer an option. I was in too deep. The worm had already turned. I had to let things run their course.

CHAPTER 51: *OUROBOROS*

The next morning, I woke up and to face one clear certainty: Doris and Daisy had to go outside. It was 3:45 a.m., and they were at my bedside, expressing themselves in no uncertain terms. We quietly padded our way out of the bedroom as Cynthia was a light sleeper. After they finished their business, we went inside. I warmed up their breakfast while they yapped at my heels. It was the least I could do for my old friends.

I watched them wolf down their food and realized that my motivation to do any more research was gone. I watched the news until 7:30 and then called Johann to see if I could visit. He agreed, adding that it had been too long since our last visit. After Cynthia and I finished our morning coffee together, I went to my study to grab my things for the trip.

On my way out, I noticed Howard Zinn's book, *A People's History of America,* sitting on my bookshelf. I had purchased it in the early '80s and remembered how refreshingly different it was. It laid out a critical view of America's history from a working person's perspective; it was not your traditional, top-down view that upheld our leaders and reinforced the myths that held our system together.

Zinn took a lot of criticism from mainstream historians at the time. This was to be expected since they wrote about and interacted with the top 10% who built up and benefitted most from the system. It was a classic case of one hand washing the other.

I was curious about Zinn and did a quick search on the Internet. He died in 2010 but wrote something interesting in 2005 that caught my eye: *We were not born critical of existing society. There was a moment in our lives (or a month, or a year) when certain facts appeared before us, startled us, and then caused us to question beliefs that were strongly fixed in our consciousness – embedded there by years of family prejudices, orthodox schooling, imbibing of newspapers, radio, and television. This would seem to lead to a simple conclusion: that we all have an enormous responsibility to bring to the attention of others information they do not have, which has the potential of causing them to rethink long-held ideas.*[1]

The Brits have a word that best describes my reaction to reading this: gobsmacked. Rethinking *long-held ideas* was exactly what I had been doing since meeting Johann. I suddenly remembered where I had heard that phrase about *the unexamined life*. It was in my college philosophy class. We were discussing Socrates' trial, and his defense was that an unexamined life was not worth living.

But how far back do you have to go to examine the truth behind anything? As I argued with Johann, one event always begets another, and you would have to go back in time *ad infinitum* to find the first cause of anything. But only God can do that. And I suppose that's why only He can truly judge.

I put down the book, headed out the door, and was on Interstate 81 in no-time. There was a long drive ahead of me but, at least, it gave me time to continue critiquing my past.

Things moved along quickly after leaving Alicia. We retained lawyers, had our property divided, and sold the house. I moved into a seedy apartment, stopped communicating with my parents, and quit my job at IBM. I joined a small management consulting firm to rebuild their technology practice.

It was fortunate timing because the Internet was taking off, and it took my new practice along for the ride. I was buried in work but happy to be focused on the present and detached from the past. Once again, I had to learn new skills and tools. My mind became as sharp as a rapier. I slashed my way through client problems with new technical solutions and parried the best efforts of my competition with charm and wit.

About a year later, I met Cynthia at a business conference. I was a speaker, and she came over after the session to ask me a question. She was very direct in describing her business problem. She asked pointed questions about my experience and how I would propose to solve them. She wasn't schmoozy like most attendees, and her earnestness made me smile. I offered to come to her location to better understand the situation and then work up a detailed proposal. The rest is history.

It didn't take long to see that Cynthia was a far better person than I could ever be. She was grounded. She saw things as they were, without any of the dark filters that shaded my life. She saw the good in others and never lost that goodness, even after she uncovered the beast.

After our business relationship ended, I asked if we could see each other socially, and she agreed. I worked hard to project the image of the All-American boy who went into the military and worked his way through college. I tried to avoid any details about my past.

She was unfailingly honest and direct with me, correcting me whenever I was rude or spoke out of turn. She had a positive effect on me, and there was nothing I wouldn't do for her or to spend time with her. She must have seen something good in me, although she did have some initial concerns. I would have to stop smoking and swearing if we were to have a relationship. As we continued to see each other, she continued to show concern for me and our relationship. She made me want to become a better person, and I was happy to comply.

I remembered thinking a few days ago that she was attracted to me because she saw a lost soul and saw it as her mission to save me. If that was the case, then she sure worked hard at it and her efforts gave me hope for the future.

We were married two years later, and my determination to leave the past and start anew seemed to be paying off. Life was good. I was finally feeling fulfilled with my new life. It stayed that way until it seemed too good for the likes of me and that's when the sense of imminent doom returned. I began to think that I didn't deserve anything from my new life: the successful consulting practice, a lovely wife, and no signs of the beast. The fear of failure began to reappear, leaving me constantly frustrated, which led to outbursts of anger when things didn't go my way.

Cynthia, unlike Alicia, didn't back down when my anger erupted. She stood her ground and asked me what was wrong. I was not used to being challenged, and her questions stopped me cold. She was the first person who cared enough to ask, and when she did, I didn't know how to respond. Instead, I would take a deep breath and tell her nothing was wrong.

But she never bought it. She pressed me to be honest, but I couldn't. I didn't completely understand where the anger was coming from. I had thought the beast was gone, but now I wasn't so sure. I feared she would leave me if I tried to explain it. Consequentially, each situation ended unresolved. Both of us would walk away frustrated.

Once again, I was able to keep my anger in check at work. My consulting practice grew to twelve consultants which gave me time to write for professional journals, speak at business conferences, and develop and deliver executive training courses. I constantly traveled cross-country. I began selling work that took me to the Caribbean islands, South America, and Europe.

I was at the top of my profession, The marketplace heaped tons of recognition on me, the firm rewarded me with more money, and I was married to a wonderful woman. However, underneath it all, I was turning into an emotional mess. My fear of keeping up in an increasingly competitive marketplace grew worse with each passing week.

I saw less and less of Cynthia, and life was rapidly becoming unbearable. The nights alone on the road were the worst. There were no outlets for my mounting anxieties. And it was during this time that I realized that the beast had returned. It was stoking my fears and anxiety while it pressed me to find a way to relieve them. It whispered that there was no reason to tell Cynthia and burden her with all my problems. It said she would think the less of me if I did. And besides, she was busy enough with her own career, taking care of our home and her aging parents.

So, I pushed myself harder and harder each day. And the more I succeeded, the more I knew how much would be lost if I failed. The spectral voice of Colonel Kurtz returned and reminded me that one small slip could end it all. It was a vicious cycle, and the feelings of imminent failure began to overshadow each day. I felt like a snake eating its own tail.

The highway in front of me suddenly got dark. I glanced into the rearview mirror and saw a huge, long dark cloud passing overhead. I gripped the steering wheel and shuddered, remembering where those bleak times led.

The exit for Johann's town appeared, and I gripped the wheel even tighter. The *long-held ideas* I had about surviving and excelling had almost led to my end, just as Johann's regime did for him. I looked up and saw more dark clouds moving rapidly in the direction of Johann's facility. I hoped it wasn't a portent of what was to come.

~ 5TH VISIT ~

CHAPTER 52: BEARING THE SINS OF OTHERS

I found a parking space close to the building. I pulled in and gave a sigh of relief. I was glad to be here. Dwelling on the past was proving to be an onerous task.

I strolled into the Garden Room a few minutes later and saw Lena reading her book on one side of the room and Johann snoozing on the other. I waved to Lena as I walked over to Johann. I gently touched him on the shoulder and asked if he was all right.

"I'm fine," he replied, turning his head to face me, and blinking his eyes open. "I may be old, but I'm not dead yet. What do you say we get a fresh cup of coffee? I could use a refill to wake up."

I smiled. He must have read my mind. We went over to the machine and made ourselves a cup. When we came back to sit down, Lena rolled over to join us. "Hello, Will, Johann. How is everyone today?"

Johann was sipping on his cup and nodded in return while I quickly replied. "I'm doing okay. Thanks for asking, Lena."

The worst-case scenario had just unfolded. It would have been best if Lena wasn't here as I intended to confront Johann about Nazi Germany's treatment of the Jews. She had already been through it and sure didn't need to hear it again. But she might help to keep him honest.

I had some hope of him offering new insights into the Holocaust for two reasons. First, I grew up in Pennsylvania Dutch country. It should really be named Pennsylvania Deutsch since many of the people had German roots. These folks were mostly kind and good-natured. I could not imagine people like that would be involved in the Holocaust. And secondly, I was one of them and couldn't imagine that I would ever be involved.

I briefly closed my eyes and jumped into the deep end of the pool. This was going to be a long day. "Well, Lena, I wanted to hear from Johann how the Germans treated the Jews, both before and during the war. I don't know if you want to stick around for that or not."

Lena's face went cold. She and Johann exchanged glances; neither were sure who was going to speak first. Then she replied, "Why would you want to discuss that, Will? Everyone knows what happened."

"I know what happened, Lena, but Johann told me things about Germany that I had never heard before. I want to know if the Germans were really as evil as everyone says they were. But I can understand if you want to leave."

Johann didn't wait for her to respond. He spoke up in a hurry. "Listen to me, Willi. It's not a question of Germans being evil; there are evil people everywhere ... they are scattered all over the world: the British, the Americans, French, Russians, and even the Jews. And this leads me to my fourth point, Willi: evil will always destroy itself. After all, how can anyone possibly justify its existence? In the end, evil will always turn on itself.

"Now, as you know, a good person can perform an evil act that causes others to suffer. They may do so believing that others must suffer to benefit the greater good. But an evil person commits an evil act solely for selfish reasons, without regard for anybody else.

But one of the worst things anyone can do is to blame an entire people for the actions of one or a few evil persons."

Lena stared at him with guarded interest and turned her eyes to face me. "I will stay here for now, Willi."

Johann straightened up and set his jaw. "*Gut!* Well, we can start then. I was only seven years old when National Socialism came into power. It was all I knew growing up. I don't think any of us felt like we were evil people, so the best I can do is tell you how we felt during those times. Is that fair enough?"

I nodded in agreement, and Lena did the same.

"Rightly or wrongly, Hitler was our leader, and we believed him when he said that the Bolshevik and Capitalist systems threatened our country and culture. They caused a lot of conflicts in our country during the '20s and early '30s. He was right to say that both of these systems were led and influenced by a few powerful individuals. Some of them may have been Jewish or not. But, I will say it again, the sins of a few shouldn't condemn a whole people. I have always believed in that!"

Lena was quick to chime in. "But that's always been the case. Hasn't it, Johann? We have always borne the sins of others. In this country, I learned how Protestants like the Carnegies, Rockefellers, Vanderbilts, Fords, and Mellons kept the Jews, Catholics, and Blacks out of their circles. They wanted to keep their society pure and excluded others. I fought this kind of thinking for years in the ACLU."

Johann smiled and nodded. "You have a point there, Lena. Most people in the West and Russia believed the Jews were financing and controlling governments to benefit themselves. And there's no doubt there are powerful people today who have undue influence over our governments, regardless of which religion they belong to. But as I said before, Germany was not the only country in history to persecute the Jews." He turned his head from side to side, looking at us and waiting for a reaction. I wasn't sure what Lena was thinking, but I didn't want to interrupt him at this point. I wanted him to keep going and see where he was headed. I didn't have long to wait.

"Hitler was right to hate all the profiteering and corruption that was going on in Germany, but he was wrong to blame every single Jewish person for it. All of our problems came from a few evil people who didn't practice any religion." He took a deep breath, swelled his chest, and then slowly exhaled through his nose like a bull about to charge. "I fought for our country because I, too, hated how Capitalism was trying to exploit Germany and how Bolshevism was trying to upend our society.

"I had no feelings about the Jews one way or the other back then. They were different, but they lived in peace with us. But I found during my research that there were a few prominent people from Jewish families that became lightning rods for fanatical Nazis, like Goebbels. Let me tell you about them and why they attracted the party's attention."

I looked over at Lena with raised eyebrows, expecting some kind of retort. She saw me and grabbed the arms of her chair. "Be careful of what you say, Johann. Remember, it takes two to tango."

CHAPTER 53: A LOT OF *MISHEGAS*

He nodded thoughtfully, as he scrolled through his iPad. "You may be right about that, Lena. But let me start by reading an extract from the Finance Section of the 1906 edition of the Jewish Encyclopedia: *With the peace of 1815 came the beginnings of international finance... The Jews, through their international position, were the first to combine into syndicates for such purposes, and the earlier stages of national loans and the larger industrial operations... the practise* [was] *initiated by the Rothschilds... followed by other Jewish financiers, like the Bischoffsheims, Pereires, Seligmans, Lazards, and others... By this means Jewish financiers obtained an increasing share of international finance during the middle and last quarter of the nineteenth century. The head of the whole group was the Rothschild family.*[1]

"Interestingly enough, this section refers to the Jews as a whole before it gets into singling out the wealthy ones that were responsible for financing Western imperialism. This same encyclopedia also had a Banking Section. It stated that the Rothschilds' London House issued loans to various countries totaling £21,800,000 between 1818 and 1832; that's a lot of money for those times.[2] Elsewhere in this section, it noted that the family made forty-eight loans to twenty different countries between 1817 and 1848, totaling $654,847,200. Their fortunes continued to rise after this encyclopedia was published, and I would say, their political influence as well.[3]

"Then, we go to the Twentieth Century and the Versailles Treaty." Johann stopped to lean forward between Lena and me as he checked his iPad. "Here's an article from *Haaretz*, the longest-running newspaper in Israel; it's dated September 25, 2015, and its title is: *Who Was the Most pro-Jewish U.S. President? Woodrow Wilson.*

"The article was an interview with Scott Berg. He recently completed his biography on Wilson and won the Pulitzer Prize for his biography on Charles Lindbergh. Here's an interesting extract from that interview: *Wilson supported the Balfour Declaration, the establishment in Palestine of a national home for the Jewish people. He did so despite the advice of his most trusted confidante, Col. Edward House…he was also the most pro-Jewish president the U.S. has ever had. He appointed the first Jew to the Supreme Court, Louis Brandeis, a fervent Zionist, who counseled Wilson about the Balfour Declaration… He brought the financier Bernard Baruch into government, and he appointed Henry Morgenthau as the ambassador to the Ottoman Empire during the First World War.*" [4]

What was Johann thinking by rattling this all off? It was like he was justifying everything that Dr. Goebbels' wrote about in Nazi propaganda. I decided to step in. "Wait a minute, Johann, what's this all about? You're making it sound like there's a basis for all this Nazi anti-Semitic propaganda. What's wrong with making loans to foreign governments, or what if Wilson was pro-Jewish? He was also a deeply religious person. In fact, if I'm not mistaken, he was an Elder in the Presbyterian Church."

Johann's face took on the expression of a frustrated teacher. "Haven't you been listening, Willi? I've said all along that the Jews had nothing to do with all of this! It was only a few wealthy powerbrokers who did, and they didn't practice any religion at all. They only followed their own self-interests and bought their way into government circles to get what they wanted. Some came from

Jewish families, and some didn't. But they all had one thing in common: they didn't care about any religion or country! Their only concern was to turn a profit for themselves!"

Lena's head shot back as if she were asking God for mercy. "Enough of this *mishegas*, Johann. What are you trying to say? Why mention the Jewish people at all if they have nothing to do with this? You're only cherry-picking names just like Dr. Goebbels did. Like Will just said, there were other wealthy individuals who did the same thing, and not all of them came from the financial world. I already mentioned a few of them, and most were Protestants like the Carnegies, Rockefellers, Vanderbilts, and Ford, all of whom discriminated against the Jews. Why don't you mention them as well?"

Johann looked exasperated. "Well, Lena, whether this is a lot of *mishegas* or not, people on both sides of this brewing conflict in the thirties took this Jewish issue very seriously."

She dismissed his remark with a wave of her hand. "You're right about one thing, Johann. Germany wasn't the only country responsible for what happened to us. America also bears guilt. And the *Motorschiff* St. Louis is a prime example. This boat was filled with our people seeking refuge from Germany after *Kristallnacht*. It left Germany for Cuba in 1939 but was denied entry.

"The captain appealed to FDR for asylum, but he refused to issue an executive order that would override the 1924 Immigration Act. He didn't do it for them or for any other Jews trying to flee Germany. He was getting ready to run for a third term. There was too much political pressure on him to keep immigrants out, especially the Jews from Eastern Europe!"

I forgot about this incident until Lena brought it up. However, her point about the political pressure on FDR was interesting, especially since it contradicted what Johann had said about the

Jewish influence on his government. I looked over to see if I could catch his eye, but he was listening intently.

"Many of those on board were finally returned to Europe and were lost during the Holocaust. Can you imagine if your wife was on that ship? Your son? And later, between 1942 and 1943, Jewish lobbyists met with FDR. They asked him to bomb the railways leading to the death camps, but nothing happened with that request either. Nobody was willing to go out on a limb for us."

Johann's surprised expression matched mine. "I forgot about that incident, Lena, but that's an excellent point. However, you're getting ahead of me. We need to follow the timeline on this subject to make sure we understand the context of these events. You mentioned at our last meeting that Western Europe forced the Jews out of their countries and into Eastern Europe, where Poland, Lithuania, Belarus, Ukraine, and Moldova are located today. Unfortunately, Russia took control of this territory during the late 1700s and early 1800s and this proved to be disastrous for both our futures."

CHAPTER 54: SOCIAL COMPRESSION

"That's my back yard, Johann," Lena interjected. "Those lands were known as The Pale of Settlement because they were outside the traditional borders of the Russian Empire. There were over five million Jews living there, and most of them were concentrated in urban areas like Łódź, my hometown.

"If you're going to talk about the Russian *pogroms*, Johann, I'll take over. These were violent acts conducted against us after Tsar Alexander II freed the serfs in 1861. Many of these serfs left their tenant farms in Russia to seek opportunities in the towns and cities of the newly acquired territories. And guess what happened? They got there and had to find work. They needed to trade or sell their goods or borrow money to buy property, equipment, and basic goods in order to survive. And guess where these Russian Orthodox serfs got these things? From the Jews who were already living there!"

Lena was holding court now, and we both dutifully sat as she continued. "All of a sudden, there were two different people with different religions and economic levels mixing together. And when someone has what someone else wants, guess what happens next? The *pogroms*.

"They began shortly after Tsar Alexander II was assassinated in 1881. The bomb that killed him was traced to a revolutionary group called the People's Will. One of the convicted assassins happened to be a Jew. The Russians blamed all the Jews for the Emperor's death and used that as an excuse to terrorize them. And, as usual, they looted and burned Jewish businesses and synagogues. They assaulted and murdered Jews who had lived there peacefully for many years. These *pogroms* continued until 1906 and drove two million Jews out of the Russian Empire back into Germany, Western Europe, Britain, and the U.S. The new rail systems and ocean liners helped this process."

Lena paused to take a sip from her water bottle, and Johann rushed right in. "So, Willi, you can see what happened next: first, the Jews were pushed into Eastern Europe by the West, and then they fled Eastern Europe to go back to the West because of these Russian *pogroms*."

Lena looked askance at Johann after he blithely summarized her discourse. "My parents spoke about our community tripling in size during the late 1800s as these people moved into Poland to escape the *pogroms*. The Nazis came later and finished the job for the Russians. And now, there is little trace of any Jews in Lódz. But many other Jews stayed in Russia. Jewish self-defense leagues and Jewish political organizations, like the General Jewish Labor Bund, began forming to protect and defend Jewish interests."

Johann leaned forward and quickly interjected, "The Bund is notable, Willi because it became involved with the Russian Social Democratic Labor Party, which eventually became the Bolsheviks who overthrew the Russian imperial government in 1917."

I paused to lay down my pen and quickly spoke up before they got at each other's throats. "This is all very interesting since I heard of these *pogroms* but never knew how they started. But it seems to me that this was more of a class struggle than religious persecution."

Lena jumped in. "No, Will. The word *pogrom* means an organized massacre of a specific ethnic group. And that's what they were, massacres against us. And, yes, we are an ethnic group, and yes, we are a religious group as well; we are a people. Never forget that!"

"Lena is right about that," Johann said with a tone of authority, reclaiming his position, "and things went downhill from there. There was a lot of violence and social upheaval as the Bolsheviks brought down the Russian Empire. The Russian Revolution and the overthrow of royalty upset the whole social order in Europe. The French Revolution happened a little over a century ago, and people still had fresh memories of that turmoil. People were afraid that a similar violent revolution would happen in their country as the Bolsheviks began exporting their ideology.

"And just to show you that people believed there was a connection between Jews and the Bolsheviks, let me tell you about Robert Wilton. He was an English newspaper reporter who worked for the *Times of London* in St. Petersburg, the capital of Imperial Russia. He covered the end of the empire and the start of the revolution.

"He wrote a book called *The Last Days of the Romanovs.* The first edition had an appendix that listed the names and nationalities of each member in each Soviet leadership group. I summed it up here on my iPad. Listen to this and you'll see why people made a connection between the Jews and the Bolsheviks. Nine of the twelve members in the Central Party were Jewish. Seventeen of the twenty-two members in the Council of People's Commissars were Jewish. Twenty-four of the thirty-six members of the Emergency Commission of Moscow, the Cheka, or secret police, were Jewish and forty-two of the sixty members of the Central Executive Committee were Jewish.

"Wilton wrote, *There is no reason to be surprised at the preponderant role of Jews in the assassination of the Imperial family. It is rather the opposite that would have been surprising.*[1] But here again, Wilton was just as guilty of anti-Semitism as Hitler was in blaming

252

all of the Jewish people. Fear was running rife during this time, and Jews became an easy target for people. Are you following all of this, Willi?"

I gave him a blank stare. I followed him all too well. I knew full well how fear could turn into frustration and then into anger.

Lena looked at my expression with concern, as if she knew my thoughts. She turned to face Johann and then shook her head in disgust. She didn't say a word to him but turned around and left. We watched her go. We were too surprised to say anything. I couldn't blame her for leaving. Johann didn't need to bring all of this up. But it did help to understand people's mindset at the time.

Johann sat still, watching her leave, then quietly said, "There is no reason or logic to this anti-Semitism, Willi. A lot of our generation grew up with it, and as I said, it wasn't isolated to Germany. A 2013 article in *The Los Angeles Times* reported that even FDR was guilty of it. The reporter interviewed several people who knew him well, and they spoke of several incidents where it happened.[2] But," he said with a wave of his hand, "enough of that for now. Do you still want me to go on with this, Willi?"

I was on the fence. If nothing else, I wanted to hear his thoughts on why the Holocaust happened. Discrimination has always been with us, but nothing ever came close to reaching the scale of the Holocaust. If he had some new insights, I wanted to hear about them.

"Sure. Go ahead, Johann"

CHAPTER 55: A SEPARATE PEOPLE

"*Gut!* Then I'll jump ahead to January 31ˢᵗ, 1933 when the party came into power. You might remember from our last visit that I had mentioned *The Daily Express of London.* They reported that a Jewish boycott was declared against Germany on March 24ᵗʰ of that year.

"The headline on page one read: *Judea Declares War on Germany.* I copied some text from that article that is interesting, *The whole of Israel throughout the world is uniting to declare an economic and financial war on Germany. The appearance of the Swastika as the symbol of the new Germany has revived the old war symbol of Judas to new life. Fourteen million Jews scattered over the entire world are tied to each other as if one man, in order to declare war against the German persecutors of their fellow believers.*"[1]

He finished reading with a flourish as if it were breaking news. "The party had been in power for only two months and hadn't passed any anti-Semitic legislation, but the press reported that every Jew in the world was declaring an economic war on us!"

"Whoa, Johann." I held up my hand and shook my head. "What did you expect them to do? Send well wishes and congratulations? Lena just took us through centuries of governments persecuting the Jews. These people were only trying to prevent that from happening again. You're lucky she wasn't here to listen to this."

"Don't be a *Klugscheißer,* Willi. My point is that this article and the boycott were the first shots fired! Jewish and Capitalist leaders as well as the Western press didn't wait to start defaming our government and taking hostile actions against us."

I couldn't believe my ears and almost laughed out loud until I saw his face was dead serious. "But, Johann, can't you see they did this only because your party had been threatening them for the last ten years?"

"Ach," Johann waved away my comment dismissively. "The party only said those things to win votes. They needed a scapegoat to blame all our problems on. But after they assumed power, Hitler never mentioned the Jews in any of his speeches until a year or so later. His government didn't take any action against the Jews until this boycott was announced. In fact, after the party came into power, they began working immediately with the Zionist Federation of Germany and the Anglo-Palestine Bank to prepare and sign the Haavara Agreement. This agreement was signed on August 25th, 1933, and allowed approximately sixty-thousand German Jews to migrate to Palestine between 1933 and 1938.

"After that Agreement was signed, Kurt Tuchler, from the German Zionist Federation's management committee, reached out to Leopold von Mildenstein, an SS officer, to visit British Palestine and witness Zionist development. Mildenstein went in 1933 and stayed for six months. He came back in 1934 and wrote a series of twelve articles called *A Nazi Travels to Palestine* in *Der Angriff*, a Nazi Party newspaper. Goebbels minted a coin with the Swastika on one side and a Star of David on the other to commemorate the importance of the visit and encourage further emigration."

All this was news to me: the boycott, the Haavara Agreement, an SS officer going to Palestine, and a Nazi coin with the Star of David. Once again, Johann presented another side of history that never made it into the mainstream. At least not as far as I knew of.

"But wait a minute, Johann. Wasn't all this self-serving? After all, the Jews were being persecuted, and now they were being put on notice they had better leave the country."

"It was self-serving, but for both parties. The Zionists wanted to go to Palestine to restore Israel, and we were helping them to do that. Each side had an interest in making that agreement as successful as possible. Did any other country do as much for the Jews over the years? In the past, many countries just threw them out with no place to go."

"But didn't this all lead to the Holocaust? Wasn't that the Nazi's final solution for removing the Jews?"

"We'll get to that in a bit, but first, let me finish with the thirties," Johann said and turned back to his iPad. "The next significant thing that happened was the passage of the Nuremberg Laws on September 15th, 1935. These laws stripped German Jews of their citizenship. There was an article in the *Jüdische Rundschau*, the largest Zionist weekly newspaper in Germany at the time, that actually supported these laws.[2]

"Georg Kareski, who was head of both the Revisionist Zionist State Organization and the Jewish Cultural League, as well as the former head of the Berlin Jewish Community, was interviewed by *Der Angriff* at the end of 1935. He basically said the same thing as the *Jüdische Rundschau* article." [3]

Johann stopped to grab his coffee while I reflected on what he had just said. I was aware that a rift existed between the German Jews. On the one side, there were those who elected to stay and make the best of it. On the other side, there were those who saw the writing on the wall, left before things got worse, and then protested loudly over what was happening.

I put a star by Kareski's name in my notes. I found out later there were stories about his colluding with the Nazis. One article performed exhaustive research into his using Nazi connections to achieve internal Jewish political goals. However, in the end, it came to no clear conclusions whether he was a collaborator or not. [4]

"Well, all that would've been fine, Johann, if the Jews could choose between peacefully coexisting or leaving. But the first option didn't exist. I saw the pictures and films of Germany in that time. You should know that the whole notion of treating people separate but equal has never worked."

CHAPTER 56: NOBODY IN THEIR RIGHT MIND

He grimaced. "You may be right about that. However, it became increasingly impossible for us to live peacefully with the Jews since so many demagogues on either side continued to rail against each other. The rhetoric escalated as time passed and led to increasing violence on both sides. Since you've seen those pictures and films from our side, let me share some examples from the other side.

"Samuel Untermeyer was a lawyer and close friend of presidents Wilson and Roosevelt. On August 7th, 1933, seven months after the party came into power, he gave a speech on WABC radio in New York City. He likened the boycott to a war and denigrated our people.

"Listen to some of what he said." He looked down into the iPad and began reading, *It is a war that must be waged unremittingly until the black clouds of bigotry, race hatred and fanaticism that have descended upon what was once Germany, but is now medieval Hitlerland, have been dispersed... benighted Germany, which has thereby been converted from a nation of culture into a veritable hell of cruel and savage beasts ...*

Revolting as it is, it would be an interesting study in psychology to analyze the motives, other than fear and cowardice, that have prompted Jewish bankers to lend money to Germany as they are now doing. It is in part their money that is being used by the Hitler regime in its reckless, wicked campaign of propaganda to make the world anti-Semitic; with that money they have invaded Great Britain, the United States, and other countries where they have established newspapers, subsidized agents and otherwise are spending untold millions in spreading their infamous creed.[1]

"How would you feel, Willi, if your family and friends were called *cruel and savage beasts?* Also, how could the party, in seven short months, manage to invade Great Britain, the United States, and other countries with newspapers, and agents and then spend *untold millions* to spread our propaganda? Our country was broke!" He threw his arms up in the air and exclaimed, "So, you can see both sides were equally guilty of lying and slandering.

"And then there was Bernard Lecache, president of the *International League against Racism and Anti-Semitism*. He was another Jewish leader railing against the Nazis. On November 9th, 1938, in that organization's issue of *Right to Life*, he wrote that *Germany is our public enemy number one. It is our object to declare war without mercy against her. One may be sure of this: We will lead that war!* So, you can see, Will, where all this was heading."

"You said that Lecache made that statement around the same time that *Kristallnacht* happened. If that's true, then I can't blame him for saying that. That was really the first shot fired."

"You're right about the date, Willi. *Kristallnacht* started on the evening of November 9th and lasted through November 10th. It's been established that it was all coordinated through the government, but the first shot to be fired was by a Jew. Were you aware of that, Willi?"

"What are you talking about?"

"A Polish Jew shot a German government official in our Paris embassy on November 7th. He was upset over how his family was treated in Germany. His parents were Polish immigrants, and they were arrested along with thousands of others and forced to return to Poland.

"Our official died two days later, which happened to be the anniversary of the Munich Beer Hall Putsch. All the party leaders were there for the celebration and heard the news. Goebbels told the attending party members that there should be violent reprisals. And right before midnight, Gestapo chief Heinrich Müller sent a message to police across the country telling them that *in shortest order, actions against Jews and especially their synagogues will take place in all of Germany. These are not to be interfered with.*" [2]

"Do you remember any of that?" I asked.

"I do, even though I was only eleven at the time. We all knew the Jews were being persecuted, but *Kristallnacht* was a big deal, almost like the Russian *pogroms*. My parents weren't comfortable with all the violence, and their fear upset me." He stopped to gather his thoughts. "I can tell you, Willi, that as bad as it was, nobody in their right mind would have ever imagined that millions of Jews would be killed only a few years later."

I looked down at my notebook and felt like a break was needed. Johann must have felt the same way. "Would you like to grab a cookie and a fresh cup of coffee, Willi?"

CHAPTER 57: UNCOVERING THE BEAST

We left the Garden Room and walked down the hallway to the dining room. Wheelchairs lined each side of the hallway and reminded me of the hospital where I recovered from the stroke.

"Willi, are you sure you want to continue with this?" Johann stopped and turned to face me with a look of concern. "It's all over and done with."

"I don't think it is, Johann." I struggled to find the right words to answer him and remembered Zinn. "It all relates back to everything we were taught about other people and about ourselves." I paused to gather my next words.

"Johann, I've heard things from you that I never heard before. Nobody mentioned these things in any books I read or in classes I attended. And you must have had the same experience after you started your research. And I have to ask myself why some things are recorded and why some are kept hidden? Things might have turned out different if people were made aware of the truth at the time." I thought again about the Eloi blindly consuming what the Morlocks brought them. "I just want to know the truth about what happened to me and my country."

He screwed his face up into a squint. "What do you mean, Willi?"

"I mean, something went wrong. I've been thinking about my past as well as yours, and it seems like everything bad that happened to Germany during your war also happened to America during my war in Vietnam. It seems like we were both lied to and led into doing the wrong things by bad people. I'm still bitter about it. Aren't you?"

He turned away and started walking down the hall. "I don't feel that way, Willi. I was raised well. I know that bad things are always done by bad people, but I never felt like I was led into doing anything wrong. I never felt like a victim. I never felt bitter or discouraged like you do. I held onto my beliefs."

We kept walking, and his expression took on a stoic cast.

"*Meine Ehre Heisst Treue.*"

"What did you say?"

"I said, my honor is loyalty." He took a few more steps. "And I never broke either."

It was the first time he gave a hint of what drove him. I knew that was the motto of the SS, and he must have seen the apprehension on my face as I turned to look at him.

He kept looking forward as he replied. "We can talk more about that later, but only after we finish with this topic." The finality of his tone made it clear that the subject was closed for now.

"Okay, Johann." I wasn't going to press him any further since he said it would come up later.

We continued walking down the hall, and the eerie sense of being back in the hospital returned. As we walked in silence, I remembered the time before my stroke. I was at the peak of my career then, but the constant overseas travel, the stress of my job, and the time away from Cynthia drained my physical, mental, and moral well-being. I finally found an outlet to provide temporary relief. But I had to keep it hidden, which only served to make a bad situation worse.

I remembered the day I came home from work and found Cynthia waiting at the door. This was unusual, and she wasn't smiling. She looked at me as if she had just turned over a rock and saw the most repelling thing in her life. She asked if it was true, and I knew what she was talking about. My heart dropped into my stomach, and I admitted it was.

After I confessed, her face expressed all the anger, fear, and shame I had experienced over a lifetime. The words spewing out of her mouth wavered between the wrath of God and the passion of Christ. She had gazed upon the beast and saw the antithesis of all that she believed in. When I saw the effect on her, it was the first time I could feel someone else's pain. It eclipsed all the suffering that I had endured during my lifetime.

When she asked why I did it, I could only manage a feeble excuse with the promise not to do it again. I couldn't speak about it then and still can't now. I broke down and cried in front of her, knowing my actions had permanently scarred her, just as my father had done to me. Everything we had as a joined couple was lost in that moment. A chasm opened between us that could never be crossed.

For several days thereafter, I was left void and purposeless. There was no amount of wit or charm I could muster to gain my redemption. I was lost and mired in guilt. I canceled all my business trips and stayed home.

CHAPTER 58: INFARCTION

A week after uncovering the beast, Cynthia and I sat on the couch, watching the morning news. She hadn't been speaking much to me since then, but she finally broke the silence by asking about our plans for the day. I was surprised when I couldn't respond. I could hear her but couldn't move a muscle. I was paralyzed. She asked again and finally got up to check on me. She shook me, but it was to no avail. She left the room to call 911.

I had no idea what was happening. There was no pain, only the sense of life slowly leaving me. Death seemed imminent when a sudden and insistent "get up, get up" clamored inside me. I exerted all my willpower to comply but only made it halfway when I crashed to the floor. The EMTs arrived soon after and began asking me questions. I lay stretched out on the floor, and no matter what they asked, all I could answer was: "I'm okay."

After treating me in the ER, I was checked into the hospital. I don't remember much of my stay. I do know that Cynthia was by my side the whole time. She told me later that my first words to her were, "You really do love me." She was surprised, not only because it came out of nowhere but because I said it with such conviction. She said it sounded like I just realized it. And, in fact, I did.

Before the stroke, I was too focused on myself. Whatever I said or did to others was only to get what I wanted. My heart and mind was closed to them. After the stroke, both opened. Up to this time,

I had been trained in the needs of the war, but now my senses were tuned into the needs of others.

My attention turned back to the present as Johann and I entered the dining room. There was a row of windows on our left. I looked outside and saw the sky was darker than when I first arrived. A storm was definitely coming. We grabbed a couple of cookies from a large tray and poured ourselves a cup of coffee. Neither of us said anything as we sat down and ate our cookies.

The gloom around us took me back to the past. The stroke had totally stripped away my *persona*. All the wit, charm, and confidence I expressed on the job had left me. But, on a positive note, all the fear, shame, and anger had left me as well. I was like a shattered Humpty Dumpty, never to be put back together.

I stumbled my way through recovery as if I were walking through a fog. Each step forward moved me onto unknown ground. An MRI revealed brain damage. The neurologist sent me to a speech pathologist to rebuild my cognitive abilities. I also went to a psychiatrist to help with a debilitating depression. I had to learn to be gracious to people as they provided comfort whenever I felt lost and helped me recover. I often had to beg for their indulgence whenever I tried communicating with them.

Cynthia's love carried me through this period. She never lost faith in me, even after seeing the beast. She must have seen some traces of goodness in me and trusted they would prevail. She nursed me back to health: physically, mentally, and spiritually. One day, I asked for her forgiveness. She said she couldn't do it and never wanted to discuss the topic with me again. I couldn't blame her.

After my rehab was complete, the neurologist took another MRI of my brain. It was the first time that I had seen the damage. The image showed a mass of dull, gray matter on the left temporal lobe that was surrounded by glowing, white matter. The gray matter was dead brain tissue.

He asked whether I felt like returning to work. I shrugged. How the hell did I know if I was capable of doing my old job, and besides, what other choice did I have? A few months earlier, Cynthia quit her job to care for her parents. We couldn't afford to lose my income, so I sucked it up, stared back at the doctor, and said, "I'm okay."

Johann finished his cookie, grabbed his cup of coffee, and gave me another nudge. "Ready to go back, Willi?"

CHAPTER 59: INVASION

We were about to enter the Garden Room when we saw Lena wheeling down the adjoining hallway. We stopped to wait for her, but she rolled right past us and parked by Johann's empty chair. Johann and I looked at each other with raised eyebrows and followed in her wake.

Johann nodded at Lena when we sat down and didn't waste any time picking up where he left off. "Okay, where were we?" He took out his iPad to look up something. "Here it is, while the German Zionists worked with our government to emigrate to Palestine, there were other Jewish leaders that didn't agree with the Zionists and derided the Haavara Agreement.

"The Simon Wiesenthal Center's online *Museum of Tolerance* posted an article about this this opposition. Here's a bit of it: *The non-Zionists opposed the Haavara Agreement because they hoped that the boycott would pressure the Nazis to restore Jewish rights. In contrast, most Zionists worked from the premise that the Jewish position in Germany was irrevocably lost and that emigration to Palestine was their only option...*

"The author goes on to say that, as a result of the Haavara Agreement, German exports to Palestine increased so rapidly that by 1937 they exceeded those of Great Britain. She wrote that her research showed that Great Britain put pressure on Palestinian Jews to cancel their German orders and to reorder them from the UK."[1]

Lena sat up, clearly upset. "Johann, as I said before, all this doesn't matter. We all know that Germany wanted to get rid of its Jews no matter what, and the Jews wanted to get rid of the Nazis no matter what. And no country in the world was going to help us; they had their own problems during the Depression. You can say whatever you want about your theories, but the fact of the Holocaust remains, and don't you dare try to deny it."

"Lena, I have never denied it. Just ask Willi what I said to him."

Johann got up from his chair and paced around. Lena sipped from her water bottle, and I looked at my watch to avoid getting caught in the middle of this. It was now past the time when I planned to leave, but I wasn't about to go anywhere until this subject was concluded. I tried to move things along. "So, when did you learn about the Holocaust, Johann?"

He stopped pacing to stroke his chin. "I didn't know about the Holocaust until after the war, Willi, but my research showed it started shortly after Britain and France declared war on us for invading Poland. Chaim Weizmann, President of the Jewish Agency, announced that *the Jews stand by Great Britain and will fight on the side of the democracies.*[2] This statement put every European Jew at risk as they all became enemies of the German state whether they were involved in the fighting or not."

Lena was shaking her head in disbelief as Johann sat back down. "Johann, if you and all the other German people didn't realize that Hitler planned to get rid of all the Jews sooner or later, then you all had your heads in the sand. And, by the way, Weitzman didn't put anyone at risk. We've been at risk, ever since the Romans destroyed our temple and took us from our homeland as slaves almost two thousand years ago."

She paused to gather her breath. "And did you know that when the Romans charged into our temple, they killed unarmed, peaceful people before destroying it? They butchered them like animals. Josephus wrote about this shortly after it happened. You should read his book some time!"

Johann ignored her rebuke and continued. "As soon as the invasion was over, Germany launched Operation Tannenberg to imprison or execute its political enemies in Poland; this happened around the end of 1939. The *A-B Aktion* program followed in 1940 and had the same objective. Neither of these two programs specifically targeted the Jews. They were focused on political enemies opposed to the occupation.

"However, Heydrich did issue an order on September 29, 1939 to send the Jews into ghettos or work camps, stating *the reason to be given for the concentration of the Jews in the cities is that the Jews have taken a decisive part in sniper attacks and plundering.*[3] So, you can see the Jews were already involved in fighting a partisan war against us."

Lena sat up in her wheelchair. "And what do you think we were going to do, Johann? Just roll over? And where were you when all this was happening?"

"I was only thirteen years old! I was in the Hitler Jugend in Breslau, and you were about one hundred- and fifty-miles due east of us."

"That's right. I was standing on the sidewalk in Łódz when the Germans marched in. Within two weeks, the persecution began against the Poles, but the greatest venom was reserved for the Jews. We were immediately ordered to wear an armband with a Jewish star. By the end of 1939, a slum area was cleared, and orders came to move us into the ghetto. You could only take what you could carry. By 1940, ghettos were set up in all the larger towns and cities, and we were put on a train to Warsaw."

Johann nodded. "I remember the Jewish community in Breslau. There were about twenty thousand people living there. As I said before, they were every bit as German as the rest of us, but they had established their own separate schools, cultural institutions, and even their own hospital. We never mixed with them, but I remember their community grew smaller and smaller as the war went on." He shook his head quietly. "There was so much anger on both sides before the war; it was like an inflamed boil that just burst open once war was declared."

He looked over at me. "Willi, I put this topic off because I really didn't want to discuss it. After learning about it, I couldn't believe any country would be capable of committing such an evil act. It became another reason to dig and dig to find out what happened. I can share what I found if you like."

Lena watched him and scrunched down in her wheelchair. Her head shook to dismiss the whole subject, and she grabbed her wheels, preparing to wheel away. "You two should know that things get ugly once war begins. There's nothing good about it. I had enough of this discussion. I *know* what happened."

She took a deep breath and stared right at me. "Will, remember this fact, in the Twentieth Century, in one of the most cultured centers of Europe, unimaginable atrocities took place, and my entire family was lost because of them. And then, only twenty years later, the same atrocities were being committed against the Vietnamese by one of the most advanced countries in the world ... and I lost my son, my only child, there, in that awful war."

She stopped to gather her breath, and it looked like she was about to weep. "It's become so easy to spread hate and kill people these days," she said sadly. She turned and left just as suddenly as before.

We were both at a loss for words. We sat in silence, watching her wheel out the door. Neither of us had heard about her son before. Johann sighed and turned back to face me. We looked into each other's eyes and knew there was nothing left to say.

CHAPTER 60: *INTERMEZZO*

Lena's disclosure about her son hung over me like a specter. It surfaced memories of the dead and wounded being carried off Biên Hòa's airstrip and then of my daughter who died shortly after birth. My body began to shake, and I closed my eyes.

"Are you okay, Willi?"

"I'm sorry, Johann. Bad memories."

He stood up and patted me on the shoulder. "I understand, Willi. Take your time. I have to go to the bathroom, anyway. Please excuse me."

I closed my eyes again and opened them seconds later to see his empty chair. I stood up and went outside for some fresh air. It was quiet. The clouds had mostly cleared, and the sun was inching toward noon, leaving a narrow shadow trailing behind me. It made me think of Lena's son.

She didn't tell us his name or how he died, and my thoughts went back to *Biên Hòa*. It was August 1st, 1972. I'll never forget that day. A rocket attack came somewhere between 0-five hundred and 0-six hundred, and the explosions jarred us awake. We threw on our utilities, pulled on our socks and boots, grabbed our helmets and M-16s, and ran to the area where the remains of the ordnance shop were burning.

It was completely destroyed. There were a few damaged planes nearby that were illuminated by the flames. Several men were outlined by the blaze, as they pulled the bodies away and tended to them. I learned later that one of the casualties came from our barracks. He was killed while on duty that night, and there were twelve other Marines that were wounded. I remembered thinking one of them could have been me.

I thought of Lena. She was undoubtedly sitting alone in her room, harboring memories of her parents, her sister, and her son. I didn't know what placed her in that wheelchair, but I wouldn't be surprised if the weight from all those years of suffering had pressed her into it. She was probably asking herself why all this happened to her.

I looked in the Garden Room for Johann, but he hadn't returned. I turned around and looked at the woods bordering the facility and realized it's been years since I thought about my baby or about *Biên Hòa*. After making the decision to leave Alicia and my past behind, I made a conscious effort to suppress any thoughts concerning the two. It was a real struggle until the night when I fell in love with Cynthia.

I remember that night clearly. We had been out together only a few times before. We were having dinner. I drank more wine than I should have and began thinking that I could never live up to the image I was trying to portray to Cynthia. I was fearful that the façade would collapse one day, and that would end everything.

Cynthia sat there watching me stare into space and asked what was wrong. I was irritated that she broke into my thoughts and appeared to be probing into my defenses.

"I'm just tired, that's all."

"Tired of what, Will?"

"You wouldn't understand."

At that point, she became angry, and I soon learned that wasn't a good thing. "Why wouldn't I understand? Tell me about it." No one had ever challenged me to open up that way before. She gave me the impression that she wasn't going to be easily dismissed.

"Well, it's just everything I've been through: my childhood, the war. It just gets the best of me sometimes, but it's probably just the wine. I'll be alright tomorrow." I put on a weak grin to fend her off.

Cynthia pulled my wine glass away and leaned over the table. "You're not the only one who's had to suffer in life, Will."

I'll never forget when she said that because it made an impression. I had never thought about that before. And later on, I realized how right she was. Who's to say whether one's suffering is greater than another's? But, at the time, her remark made me angry, and I clammed up, more out of fear than resentment. I was afraid of losing her if I said anything more.

She wasn't about to let up, however. "Your time in the war must have been difficult, Will. But it wasn't any more difficult than someone who has had to suffer through a terrible car accident or the loss of a loved one."

I remember staring at the tabletop, so angry I couldn't say a word. I wasn't angry at her. I was pissed off at everything that happened in my life. "You don't understand."

She reached out to pick up my chin. Her face was stern. "*You* don't understand, Will," she said evenly. "You're no different than anyone else. You're not special. Everyone suffers in life. Do you have any idea how much I had to suffer to get where I am?"

I held her gaze, and my eyes narrowed. "I have no idea."

"And that's exactly my point." She withdrew her hand from my chin and clasped it with her other on the tabletop. "Stop wallowing in the past. If you have to think about suffering, think about how others are suffering now and how you might help them."

She locked onto my eyes. "Look at me. You survived. You're bigger than everything that's been done to you. You can overcome it. I can see that in you." She smiled, and that's when I fell in love with her.

I smiled at the recollection, then looked through the glass walls of the Garden Room and saw that Johann was back.

CHAPTER 61: IDA

"Now, where were we? Oh yes, we were talking about Poland. Tell me, Willi, have you ever heard of the Katyn massacre?"

"Yes, I remember reading something about it a few years back. Wasn't that where the Russians admitted to executing a bunch of Polish people and burying them in mass graves?"

"Yes, that's it. And it's an interesting story for a lot of reasons. German soldiers originally uncovered the mass graves in 1943 and blamed the Russians. I believe there were over twenty-two thousand victims. And, of course, Russia denied it and blamed Germany.

"Of course, the Allies heard about it and told the entire world that it was another example of German war crimes. It was only after the Soviet regime collapsed in 1991 that the new Russian government investigated the massacre and accepted responsibility. That's when you probably read about it. The story fueled speculation about the truth of other Soviet charges made at Nuremberg."

I jumped in at the mention of the Tribunal. "I've looked into some of the charges made at Nuremberg and had some surprises myself. I read the first charge against Germany for preparing and starting the war, but I stopped there. I never got up to the Holocaust. I wanted to hear from you first."

"Willi, probing into that period is like wading into a murky cesspool," Johann said sadly. "It's dark, ill-defined, and offensive to the senses. Things will get rough from this point. Are you sure you want me to continue?"

Cynthia warned me you can't unhear things, but what did I have to lose at this point? I had already regurgitated most of my painful past. Why shouldn't I listen? I looked over and nodded, resigned to seeing where all this would take me.

"Okay then. Let's get into it. I have a lot of notes on this, so bear with me; we may be at this for a while,"

"That's okay, Johann, but first, let me call Cynthia and tell her I'll be here a while longer." I called Cynthia, and she thanked me for checking in.

Johann was watching me carefully. "Willi, is everything okay?"

"Sorry, my wife worries about me. I guess that's not a bad thing, is it?"

"No, it's not. My wife, Ida, was the same way. She died eight years ago of pneumonia, and I still miss her every day. She was always after me for spending too much time researching this stuff once I retired. I even went down to the National Archives to do some research."

When he mentioned his wife, I took the opportunity to ask again how they met.

He leaned his head back and laughed. "Ach, you're a persistent one, aren't you? Well, that's a long and peculiar story, but I will try to keep it short; we have a lot of ground to cover."

He took a sip of coffee and began. "I told you before that several of us in the *Waffen-SS* used to get together after the war to keep one another company. We were labeled as war criminals by the Allies and even our own government. We were even denied any military benefits or pensions. We joined other veteran groups to form the HIAG and lobbied the government for our benefits as well as for our comrades' widows.

"Anyway, I was just as outspoken then as I am now and became friends with this older fellow in the group who told his wife about me. His wife was friends with Ida and thought we would be a good match since she was so quiet, but strong-minded. She felt Ida would keep me contained. They got the two of us together, and we never separated."

He stopped for a moment to think of her. "She became a nursing assistant during the war and lost her family just as I did. We were a good couple; she kept calm and stayed out of politics while I got all worked up about post-war Germany. We were, as you said, treated like red-headed stepchildren in our own country because of my service."

"But she stayed with you, didn't she, despite your record?" I just blurted it out, and he stared at me like I was from another planet.

"Yes, she did. I think she saw something good in me. You know, Willi, the last time you were here, I told you what a good person she was. When we got to the States, we went to see *Gone with the Wind*, and I thought she was just like Melanie, not a mean bone in her body."

"So, how did you two get to the States?"

He threw his hands up and smiled broadly. "Well, that's the peculiar side of this story, Willi. While I was in the PoW camp, there was an American guard named Jacob Kleinhaus. He told me about a family named Knoske back in Pennsylvania. Jacob lived on a farm there and told me what a good life it was. Everyone left you alone, including the government, as long as you paid your taxes."

"Was that in the Lehigh Valley, Johann?"

"Why yes, it was. Why do you ask?"

"When I was doing research on our line, I found other Knoskes who lived there in the 1800s, along with a lot of other German immigrants. That's a funny coincidence. So, how did you wind up moving over here?"

"Well, Jacob and I got close. I helped him with his German, and he helped me with English. When I was released, he passed on his personal information and told me to contact him if I ever wanted to come to the US. After Ida and I had Auggie, we decided it would be best for him to grow up in America, so I contacted Jacob, and he sponsored us.

"We came over in 1956 when I was thirty. Auggie was two years old then. Jacob found me a position as an apprentice machinist, and I eventually became a tool & die maker. But things changed over time. The farms went away, the developers came in, and it became too crowded. We retired up here in the Finger Lakes to get away from it all, and things went well until Ida died."

He suddenly stopped, waved his hand to clear his emotions, and looked away from me. I decided to switch to another topic.

"Did you ever meet that other Knoske family?"

"I did, but that was a long time ago. As I remember it, we never figured out if we were related."

"What were their names?"

"I believe it was Frederik and Wilhelmina. They told me their great-grandparents came over on a ship from Hamburg around 1850, but that's all I can remember about them."

"I think I remember seeing those names, and I think they do tie back to a common ancestor of ours. I'll have to look them up."

"*Ach*, don't bother. The past is the past. Tell Auggie if you like, but I'm not interested." He abruptly broke away from the discussion to open his iPad. "Anyway, let's get back to where we were, or we'll be here all day."

I quickly wrote the two names down while he continued.

CHAPTER 62: *GENERALPLAN OST*

"Ok, we left off with your wanting to hear what led up to the Holocaust. Do you still want to continue, Willi?"

"Yes, I'd like to hear about it. Tell me, how did Germany ever get to that point?"

"Well, I have my own theories, but there's no definitive answer. However, I can tell you what I learned, and the best place to start is with *Generalplan Ost*. This plan was designed to develop Germany's *lebensraum* in Eastern Europe and Russia after they were conquered. It was reportedly written in 1940 by Doctors Hans Ehlich and Konrad Meyer.

"The original was never found, although references were made to it in other government documents. A memo written on April 27, 1942, by Erhard Wetzel, director of the NSDAP Office of Racial Policy, entitled *Opinion and Thoughts on the Master Plan for the East of the Reichsführer SS* was used by historians after the war to reconstruct its general outline.

"The reconstructed plan had two components: the Small Plan, which specified the immediate deportation of people from Poland, Belorussia, Ukraine, and the Baltic States to Western Siberia to make room for German resettlement. The second component, the Big Plan, addressed the occupation and development of Russia; it would take another twenty-five to thirty years to complete."

I interrupted him at this point. "Wait a minute, Johann. You haven't mentioned anything about the Jews in this plan, but didn't the Small Plan go right through The Pale of Settlement?"

"You're listening. Good. And you're right. The plan only mentioned 'racially undesirables,' and this was everyone who was not considered an Aryan. It was basically the same three-step plan used by other Western countries to build out their empires: invade, occupy, and plunder."

I put down my pen. His last point about the other countries didn't sit well with me. "Lena mentioned this before, Johann. Just because others did it in the past doesn't make it right."

"Agreed, Willi." He smiled with a knowing grin. "But apparently, when you're successful at it, you can write your own history and make it all sound heroic."

I nodded, thinking that Western imperialism had been at it for over 400 years, but mankind has been at it forever.

"Anyway, the Little Plan started with the invasion of Poland in September 1939, and the Big Plan began with the invasion of Russia on June 22, 1941."

I stopped writing. "But didn't Germany and Russia have a non-aggression pact of some sort? Wasn't Germany being deceitful by launching a surprise attack?"

He began laughing while shaking his head from side to side. "That pact was just a delaying tactic for both sides while they got ready to attack one another. After Russia invaded Poland in 1939, they began spreading their troops along the entire eastern border of Germany.

"On June 28, 1940, Russian troops occupied Bessarabia and Northern Bukovina, both of which were close to the Romanian oil fields, a vital commodity for Germany. Romania, fearful of Russia, joined the Axis on November 16, 1940, and Germany dispatched twenty-two thousand troops to protect them. During that same year, Russia also occupied the Baltic States.

"Furthermore, in April 1941, Russia signed a Treaty of Friendship and Non-Aggression with Yugoslavia. This allowed them to station Russian troops there. This last move effectively sealed off the whole of Germany's eastern border. By June 1941, Russia had deployed two-million and seven-hundred-thousand men around that border."[1]

"Wow, I never heard about that before." I wrote down as much as I could remember and asked him to confirm the names and dates so I could confirm later. "Okay, thanks. That puts a little more perspective on that invasion. Go ahead and continue."

CHAPTER 63: RUSSIA

"Well, our initial advance into Russia was so rapid that we captured most of those roughly two-and-a-half-million troops that were stationed on Germany's borders. No one had ever planned on capturing so many prisoners in such a short time. There were significant challenges in handling all of them, but then the rear-guard partisan effort began. The intensity and brutality of the civilian resistance led to significant problems for German forces.

"The US Army wrote a 1956 pamphlet entitled *The Soviet Partisan Movement, 1941-1944* that best describes how non-uniformed agents of the NKVD and other civilian partisans began resistance almost immediately after the invasion began.[1]

"This was no longer conventional warfare, Willi, and it was brutal. It didn't take long for the German forces to respond in kind. On July second, Reinhard Heydrich, an SS general who reported to Himmler, ordered the *Einsatzgruppen* to find and execute all Comintern officials, including commissars and other ranking members of the Communist Party. As far as I know, this order never mentioned Jews specifically."

"Well, their resistance shouldn't have been a complete surprise, Johann. You invaded their country. It was like us fighting in Vietnam."

"You're right about that, Willi. And you were right about our invasion going right through the Pale of Settlement, where most of the Russian Jews lived. The atrocities began happening almost immediately – on both sides. Kurt Meyer, who later became my Regiment commander, wrote about the brutality of one partisan attack as early as July seventh, only two weeks after the invasion began: *for the first time we found an abandoned German weapon on the battlefield. A few steps away from the gun there was a looted ambulance. Its doors were wrenched, and blood smeared … The naked bodies of a brutally butchered company of German soldiers were before us. Their hands were fastened with wire. Wide staring eyes gazed at us. The officers of this company had met an end that was perhaps even more cruel. They lay a couple of meters away from their comrades. We found their bodies torn to pieces and trampled underfoot."* [2]

I stopped him short. "You mentioned the *Einsatzgruppen* earlier. Weren't they the mobile Death Squads who went to all the towns executing the Jews during the first wave of the Holocaust?"

He stiffened up in his chair. "First, let me say that the term *Einsatzgruppen* translates to an Operational Group or a Task Force; someone has since mangled that term to mean any number of other things. These groups operated behind our lines to kill political enemies per Heydrich's orders. Your Phoenix program operated the same way in Vietnam, I believe. Correct me if I am wrong, Willi."

"You're right, Johann. Their mission was to go into the villages, identify and eliminate VC leaders while our troops were out fighting in the field."

Johann nodded. "That's what I read. The program operated in every province of South Vietnam and reportedly eliminated eighty-thousand people."

I was tired of these deflections. "That sounds about right, Johann. But I never supported what they were doing. It sounded like murder to me." I was pissed off because of his deflections and unloaded on him. "We were wrong for doing it, just like the Germans were wrong for doing what they did. Lena was right. Shit happens in war."

He shrugged off my comments and continued. "Anyway, as I said, our troops went through the Pale of Settlement and were under constant attack by partisans. On July eighth, a week after his first order, Heydrich ordered all Jews to be regarded as partisans and any male Jews between the ages of fifteen and forty-five were to be executed. During August, that order was modified. He included Jewish women, children, and the elderly because they were supporting their effort.

"We reached Kiev by September 19, 1941, and, shortly after that, partisans planted bombs around the city. One exploded in Army Group South Headquarters, killing a colonel on the General Staff, among many others. Retribution was ordered, and on September twenty-ninth and thirtieth, over thirty-three thousand Jews were executed at Babi Yar, in northwest Kiev. By the end of October, more than a hundred thousand were shot."

I shook my head, overwhelmed by the numbers, and remembered my war. "This sounds like all the civilian killing we did in Vietnam, although we didn't do it all at once. We set up these 'free-fire' and "H&I' zones and went on 'search-and-destroy' missions. We didn't round up people to kill them, but we sure as hell shot or bombed anything that moved in those areas."

I regretted saying that almost immediately and thought of Lena. She was right about the ugliness of war. I should have left when Lena did. Perhaps the unexamined life wasn't so bad after all.

"You're right, Willi. We were responding to civilian resistance just as the Allies did, both before and after the war. The English committed atrocities against the Boers in South Africa. The French did it against the Arabs in Algeria. The Russians did it in

Afghanistan and the Americans in the Indian Wars, the Philippines, and later, in Vietnam. There's no simple military solution to dealing with civilian resistance. You're faced with the choice of either penning them up in camps or killing them."

I decided to stop him right there. "Well, maybe Germany should have pulled out when it got so bad, Johann. Lots of other countries did when they ran into trouble, just like we did in Vietnam. Germany might have saved itself and others a lot of grief if you had."

I could see regret written all over his face. "But this was nothing like Vietnam, Willi. We couldn't pull out like you did. FDR, Stalin, and Churchill wouldn't allow it. They wanted to destroy National Socialism, and that became very clear when they demanded our unconditional surrender during the Casablanca Conference in January 1943."

CHAPTER 64: THE DEVIL'S CHOICE

Johann gently rubbed his eyes and looked away from me. Both of us were getting emotional. I flipped through a few pages of my notebook while he gathered himself.

"You have to understand, Willie, that the partisans were killing our soldiers, and the Allies made things worse by supplying them with money, arms, and equipment to do their fighting for them. We had to do something to survive."

He reminded me of McNamara in the movie *The Fog of War* when he was trying to rationalize his actions during the Vietnam war. I almost blurted that out but knew the clock was ticking and wanted to keep us on track. "Well, what happened next, Johann?"

"A month after the invasion began, at the end of July, Hermann Göring wrote a memo to Heydrich. The memo said to start planning for the *final solution of the Jewish question*' It was written in July of 1941 when we were moving swiftly through Russia on all fronts, and confidence was high for successfully executing *Generalplan Ost*.

"Goering's memo mentions emigration and evacuation, part of *Generalplan Ost*, but makes no mention of any other action. Here's an official translation of that memo, so you can see for yourself what was written."[1] He handed his iPad over to me and waited while I read.

The Reichsmarschall of the Greater   Berlin, 31 July 1941
          German Reich
Plenipotentiary for the Four-Year Plan
        Chairman
of the Ministerial Council for the
      Defense of the Reich

       To
          the Chief of the Security Police
              and the SD
          SS-Gruppenfuehrer HEYDRICH

                    B E R L I N

    As supplement to the task which was entrusted to
you in the decree dated 24 January 1939, namely to solve
the Jewish question by emigration and evacuation in a way
which is the most favorable in connection with the
conditions prevailing at present, I herewith commission
you to carry out all preparations with regard to organization, the material side and financial viewpoints
for a final solution of the Jewish question in these
territories in Europe which are under German influence.

    If the competency of other central organizations is
touched in this connection, these organizations are to
participate.

    I furthermore commission you to submit to me as soon
as possible a draft showing the administrative material
and financial measures already taken for the execution
of the intended final solution of the Jewish question.

                (signed) GOERING.

         CERTIFICATE OF TRANSLATION

    I, Wolfgang Von Eckardt, hereby certify that
I am thoroughly conversant with the English and German
languages and that the above is a true and correct
translation of the Document No. NG-3945.

          Signature: W. Von Eckardt
                     U.S.Civ.A.165634.
     - END -

71

I read it and handed the iPad back to him. He was right about the date and the content. He didn't wait for me before taking off once again.

"As victory over Russia was anticipated, Heydrich was ordered to work with other party officials to begin moving the Jews to Western Siberia. The conditions in the existing camps and ghettoes were rapidly deteriorating due to overcrowding.

"In the meantime, our invasion continued. We only stopped in December of 1941 due to supply issues and the weather. We were eighteen miles from Moscow when fresh Russians troops arrived from Siberia. They launched their first counter-offensive, and by January 1942, we were pushed back over sixty miles from Moscow. The invasion had failed."

He stopped to sip his coffee, and I quickly jumped in to move us along. "But what about the Jews in Western Europe, Johann?"

"Well, after the Allies declared war on us in 1939, you need to remember that Chaim Weizmann wrote to Chamberlain and pledged Jewish support for the fight against Nazi Germany. And our German leaders took him at his word." [2]

"You mentioned this earlier, Johann. Are you implying that the Jews were responsible for everything that happened after that?"

"No, I'm not. But some of those Jewish leaders were just as responsible as ours for escalating tensions that led up to the war, beginning with their boycott in 1933. One thing is certain, Willi. Once those leaders on both sides decided to go to war, the Devil was there to help them. But in the end, he always demands his due."

He stopped to scroll through his iPad while I waited. "Ah, here we are. After Poland was defeated, we offered to negotiate a peace with the Allies but were refused. We invaded Western Europe in 1940, and that battle ended very quickly. However, partisan resistance in the West began almost immediately. Britain established a Special Operations Executive group to support them and had Churchill's orders to '*set Europe ablaze.*'[3]

"The struggle with the French resistance became as intense as it was in the East, but not as savage. German Field Marshal Keitel described it at the Nuremberg trials: *During the summer of 1941, the civilian population's resistance to our occupation forces intensified perceptibly in every theater of war, with sabotage incidents and attacks on Germany security troops and installations… Acts of sabotage became horrifyingly frequent in France and even in Belgium.* [4]

"Remember, Willi, this was an ideological war, and most of the resistance in Western Europe came from the Communists and the Jews. In June 1941, various French Communist groups banded together to increase their effectiveness. The Jews also fielded nine guerilla groups to operate in France. Two of the most prominent were the Jewish Scouts and the Jewish Army.

"In 1942, Germany began deporting Jews, Communists, and other political enemies from Western Europe to camps in the East. There are lists that show the number of arrivals and deaths at each camp, and some show their countries of departure. However, none of these lists came from German records. None showed the nature of their death. Those deaths could have come from gassing, from disease, malnutrition, exposure, or starvation.

"Meanwhile, the failure to take Moscow took *Generalplan Ost* off the table. However, the SS had already gathered people into ghettoes and camps for deportation in anticipation of victory, but now they had nowhere to send them. The number of prisoners continued to grow each day as the war ground on. Our existing camps and ghettoes were already overwhelmed by the influx. Key resources to house and care for prisoners became strained. Remember, Willi, that even German citizens were on food and supply rationing since 1939.

"Rudolf Hoess, the commandant of Auschwitz from 1940-1943, described the camp's situation at Nuremberg like this: *Until the outbreak of war in 1939, the situation in the camps regarding feeding, accommodations, and treatment of internees, was the same as in any other prison or penitentiary in the Reich. The internees were treated severely, but methodical beatings or ill treatments were out of the question…*

When the war started and when mass deliveries of political internees arrived, and, later on, when prisoners who were members of the resistance movements arrived from the occupied territories, the construction of buildings and the extensions of the camps could no longer keep pace with the number of incoming internees… And, furthermore, rations for the internees were again and again severely curtailed by the provincial economic administration offices. This then led to a situation where internees in the camps no longer had the staying power to resist the now gradually growing epidemics." [5]

I stayed quiet and continued writing notes. The Commandant of Auschwitz was hardly a neutral observer. He was an SS officer who had been a party member since the early twenties and was on trial for his life. Hoess' description was probably accurate, but why would he continue to oversee this increasing horror? I couldn't see myself doing it. There was no ideology, no system in the world that could ever justify that for me.

Perhaps Lena was right. Maybe we should just forget about ideology and go about living our lives in peace. Is that what the partisans should have done? Were they right to fight back against the Nazis? Their doing so placed all their neighbors and communities at risk of reprisals. Perhaps they should have just accepted things as they were and saved everyone a lot of trouble.

And then I remembered Johann's point about one evil begetting another evil; it was all just a never-ending cycle of violence.

"In the end, Willi, we were forced into making a Devil's Choice. We could either let the massive overflow of prisoners die slowly of disease and neglect, or we could dispose of them as quickly and humanely as possible. It would have been suicide for us to release them."

I couldn't respond to that. I stopped writing and just shook my head.

Johann paused and then added. "There was a lot at stake in that war … for all sides."

"But there must have been another option, Johann. You have to draw the line somewhere."

"We'll discuss that later. Perhaps at our next visit. But as 1941 ended, so did our plans for conquering Russia and emptying our camps by emigration."

"So, I guess this when the gassing program began, Johann?"

He looked down at the floor for a moment and then raised his head. "Yes, that's when we started building the killing centers. But I will tell you, there's not too much documented that would tell us why or how it started. I'd like to think that it started because our leaders felt *Generalplan Ost* was no longer feasible. They saw that people were dying of unsanitary conditions in the overcrowded camps and ghettoes. Perhaps they thought death by gassing was a more humane alternative. No one will ever know for sure, Willi. Nor will anyone know how many in these camps died from gassing or from neglect or disease."

Johann put his iPad down and took a final drink, draining his cup. I began to feel queasy about what he was going to say next. "The one thing that always stuck in my mind, Willi, was that none of this was done before the war." He cleared his throat, smacked his hands on his thighs, and then stood up. "But that's enough of that for now. Let's take a break. Can you stay and have lunch? I have us covered." I wasn't hungry in the least, but I welcomed the break.

We must have hit peak time for lunch because there was a long line of antsy seniors waiting outside the dining room as we approached. We joined the line and quietly shuffled forward, each of us tied up in our own thoughts. We finally made it through and sat down to eat without much conversation. After finishing, we grabbed a cup of coffee and headed outside.

CHAPTER 65: PURGATORY

As we left the building, the immensity and brightness of the blue sky made us stop and squint. It felt comforting after the morning gloom. I looked up and felt its warmth blanket my face. I suddenly missed Lena. I wondered when, where and how her son died in Vietnam. She had looked deeply into my eyes when she mentioned him, radiating a maternal concern that touched me.

"What's on your mind, Willi? You were quiet during lunch."

"I was thinking about the time I had a stroke." Although I mentioned it to Lena, I never spoke to him about it.

"You had a stroke?" He stopped in his tracks and turned to stare at me with a wide-eyed look of surprise. "When was that?"

"I was forty-nine, at the top of my game and I just collapsed on the floor. I was lucky to be with my wife when it happened."

"*Gott sei Dank!* You seem all right now, though."

"Well, that all depends on how you define it. I guess I am. I lost a lot back then. By the way, what did you say in German just now? Something about God?"

"*Gott sei Dank?* It means: Thank God. And I make it a point to thank Him every night for each day spent on this earth." He grinned and patted me on the shoulder. "I can relate to how you felt, Willi. The end of the war was like that for me. I lost everything, including my family, and then I had to undergo the humiliation of de-Nazification before being released. I know what it feels like to start all over again." His voice trailed off as he bowed his head.

"So do I, Johann." I mouthed *Gott sei Dank* in a feeble whisper as we resumed walking down the pathway. I liked the sound of it.

The mention of his humiliation reminded me of my own. The stroke hit me hard like a bolt of divine retribution. I felt broken and defeated afterward. When the neurologist approved my returning to work, it was like opening a door into a dark, endless passage. There were, at least, fifteen years until I reached retirement age. It was a long slog. I wondered if I would make it.

When I first arrived at work, it was like a condemned man approaching the gates of Hell. I had no confidence, drive, or desire to be there. I half expected to see Dante's sign hanging over my office door: *Abandon hope all ye who enter here.* I felt like an unarmed gladiator entering the arena, knowing it was only a matter of time before I fell.

The practice had suffered during my absence; revenue was down with no promising prospects in the pipeline. Worse yet, I had no interest in pursuing either. It didn't take long for my partners to notice and become concerned. They said they knew I needed to recover but they could only keep me around if I took a huge pay cut. They gave me a month to think about it.

Cynthia was worried sick after I told her. I never mentioned how dispirited and disinterested I was, but she must have seen it. She always tried to lift my spirits and bolster my confidence during this time. She never voiced her concerns, probably because she was afraid it would put undue pressure on me.

Within a few days after meeting with my partners, a recruiter called. He represented another consulting firm and said they were looking for a leader to help build their practice; they obviously knew my record but were unaware of my circumstances. I met with them, and they returned with an overly generous offer. It's amazing what people can overlook when they're desperate. I accepted, knowing it was only a delay in the inevitable, but it got me that much closer to retirement. How much worse could it get? I soon learned.

The new firm turned out to be a body shop that wrung every penny of profit from its employees. This was a special kind of hell for me. I now worked for people who were driven by the same ravenous beast that left me.

They were disappointed when I didn't bring any of my clients over and became upset when I failed to land any new ones. They sent me to Detroit to manage a large project for a Fortune 50 client. I had to leave Cynthia each Sunday night to fly out and drag myself back home on Thursday night.

Each week there was a terrible gauntlet of congested airports and clogged highways to reach the client site and then back again. I had to work twelve-hour days trying to keep the project afloat.

Every day was spent fighting a demanding client on one side and a demanding set of executive owners on the other. Each night was spent in a lonely hotel room, feeling physically and emotionally drained. My nights alone were very different from what they had been before the stroke. The fear of failure had disappeared but in its place the pain of what I had done to Cynthia haunted me. No amount of suffering could ever atone for what I had done.

As I reached the second anniversary of working in Detroit, I was almost at the end of my rope. I felt myself slipping away into oblivion as I sat on the edge of the hotel bed, remembering what landed me here in the first place.

I opened the nightstand drawer, hoping to find a Bible and wasn't disappointed. As I picked it up, the image of Jesus knocking on a door appeared. It came from a memory when I was confirmed. The church gave a framed picture of this as a gift to all the confirmands. There was something written at the bottom, but I couldn't remember what it said. I searched the Internet for "Jesus knocking" and quickly found the inscription: *"Look! I stand at the door and knock. If you hear my voice and open the door, I will come in."*

I looked at the bottom of the hallway door and saw the light streaming in. I felt like a lost child, anxious and scared, waiting for his father. I bent over, rested my head in my hands, and surrendered to God. I tried to pray the Lord's Prayer but didn't remember the words, so I simply thanked God for His help that day and asked the same for tomorrow. And, like Johann, I've done that every night since.

They say souls in Purgatory can leave anytime they want, provided they have corrected the flaw that got them there in the first place. Although I knew my sin, I didn't know how to correct it. The beast was gone, but it had left a hole behind that needed filling.

Johann jarred me back into the present when he announced, "look, Willi. Here's our bench; let's have a seat."

CHAPTER 66: INITIATION

We sat on the bench and sipped our coffee silently. I was savoring the aroma and taste.

"You look as if you're lost in thought, Willi."

"I was thinking about my recovery after the stroke, Johann. It was the hardest thing I've ever done … even harder than getting through the Marines."

"But you made it through, Willi." He smiled and nodded.

"Not quite, Johann. I lost everything back then. And after that happened, there was nothing left to build on." I couldn't tell him about the beast and what I did to Cynthia.

"But since I met you, I've been rethinking things, trying to understand the decisions I made in life and what to do with what's left of it." I paused, knowing there was more to say, more to talk about, but I was mentally exhausted.

"I've tried to show you what I learned, Willi … you have to look for the truth if you want to find peace."

"I know. You made me want to learn the truth about my life but it's not a good story."

"We've been together only five times, Willi, but … " he paused as if trying to think of what to say next, "I'm glad I got to know you. It's like I have my old friend back."

I didn't know how to respond to that, but he didn't wait for me.

"The one thing you need to understand is that everyone has something bad that happens in life. Maybe something bad was done to you by someone or you did something bad to someone else, but the important thing is what you do with it... whether you drown in it or try to overcome it."

I chuckled.

"Did I say something funny?"

"No, Johann. It reminds me of something we used to say in the Marines: *Improvise. Adapt. Overcome.* It's one of those things you don't forget. That phrase helped get me through anything I set my mind to but I'm not so sure I can do that anymore," I confessed tiredly. "But I'm trying, God knows, I'm trying."

"Well, Willi, He knows that, and He will help. Just keep asking for His help and don't give up. Keep trying."

I nodded. I learned the truth of that statement in Detroit. Once I started praying, the two-year project was put on-hold a short time later and I returned to our office in mid-town Manhattan. There were no projects waiting for me when I got there. I wondered how long I would be kept on the payroll.

I walked alone each lunch hour and, one day, passed St. Patrick's Cathedral. I walked up to its massive doors and saw the list of scheduled services. Mass was conducted every day at noon. I wanted to go in, but I was raised a Protestant.

A queasy feeling overcame me and prevented me from passing through those massive doors. I mustered the courage two days later and went in to attend service. I went each day thereafter and watched each parishioner carefully to learn the proper sequence of events. I listened earnestly, so I knew what to say and when.

It didn't take long for me to lose a sense of self-consciousness and fall into a sense of being with God. There was a certain kind of joy in being with Him each day. The gospels say the well-educated scribes and Pharisees rejected Jesus' teaching and miracles because their hearts were closed to anything that threatened their control of the status quo. The Bible says only humble people with open hearts can receive God's message. Well, at that point, I was as humble as anyone could get.

After several months of attending Mass, I decided to take two major steps. First, I got rid of my guns since I had no intention of ever using them again. Second, I decided to convert to Catholicism.

There was a Catholic chapel near our home; it was an old wooden structure built in the nineteenth century. I met the priest, who was about my age, and told him why I was there. He asked about my intentions. I told him everything that led up to the stroke and how I wanted Christ to fill my heart. There was no fear of failure or shame left in me anymore. I was accepted as a candidate for the program.

The day before the Rite of Initiation into the Church, the priest took the candidates to a local monastery. We were told to go off on our own, reflect on our intentions and then return to discuss our feelings with the group.

I found a small nook with a single stained-glass window. A small wooden kneeler was placed in the middle of the space. I approached it with the same trepidation that I did at the doors to St. Patrick's. I crossed myself, dropped to my knees and offered a prayer. After some time, I stopped thinking, and a vision came. The floor opened beneath me, and I fell into a bottomless well lined with cobblestones. Each stone seemed to symbolize one of my many sins. As I fell, I felt lightened and wasn't scared in the least.

My descent slowed until it came to a complete stop and then my ascent began. I looked up and saw a bright light shining from a round opening above. At that point, my eyes opened, and there was a solid floor beneath me. I went back to the group feeling as if I was on the right path, but I had no idea of where it might lead me.

Although my conversion happened thirteen years ago, I was still walking down that path with no end in sight. It struck me that this journey was longer than the one Odysseus took to find his way home. I exhaled loudly, spiritually exhausted by the many years it took.

"Willi, what are you thinking about?" Johann's question jolted me back to reality.

CHAPTER 67: RING OF TRUTH

"Sorry Johann, I was thinking about what you said earlier, that there was a lot at stake in World War II. What exactly did you mean by that?"

He looked out over the grounds before answering me. "Well, I can tell you right now that it never was a case of good versus evil. War is violent conflict. Lena was right to say that morality goes out the door once war starts and people start killing each other."

He turned his eyes down, looking frail and defeated. "All the people who died and all the resources wasted during our two generations of war were due to the powerbrokers on both sides. They drove their followers into war by using propaganda to stir up the people and gratify their needs. Lena was also right when she said people should just focus on their daily lives and forget about blindly following leaders with their half-baked ideologies."

"Maybe so, Johann, but what about the bad guys? Do you just let them go?"

He straightened up and his voice began to rise. "Who's to say who's bad? You see how we were labeled and treated by people who committed the same crimes as we did. These wars didn't need to happen, and they shouldn't have. There are always other ways to solve conflicts without resorting to violence."

He paused to look into my eyes as if he were about to confess something. "All my research helped me to understand the events that led up to my war, but it didn't help with my understanding why men keep going to war generation after generation despite its cost. It's like they never learn and now I realize it's all human nature, a concern for the self rather than for others. It's all about greed, Willi. As long as people won't acknowledge that and cloak their feelings in false ideologies, then we'll be fighting forever."

We both sat in silence after that negative note. I wasn't quite sure what to say to him.

He looked over at me, and his eyes were piercing. "I will tell you this one thing, Willi, while I deeply regret what happened during the war, I don't feel guilty about it."

"What do you mean by that?"

"I mean that I fought for a cause and not for myself. I kept my honor and loyalty to that cause all along."

He surprised me. He had just agreed with Lena's position about blindly following an ideology and now he seemed to be contradicting himself.

"But that cause was wrong, Johann."

"Was it? Do you think it was wrong to get rid of that Treaty? To help our people get out from under it and rebuild our country? Perhaps Lena was right when she said our system was wrong for setting our Jewish citizens aside and stripping them of their rights, but this was nothing new. Other countries, including your own, did the same. Our system was imperfect, but it worked!"

He suddenly stopped and his face went blank. He looked away and softly spoke to no one in particular. "Nobody on either side ever imagined what the war would bring, or we would never have fought in it."

There was a ring of truth to what he said. I watched him ponder his thoughts and realized that Lena had uncovered his beast just as Cynthia had uncovered mine.

He must have seen how his anger and sense of injustice had driven him to blindly follow the party's cause. He must have seen that his system acted no differently than all the other systems he had been railing against. And he fought for it to the bitter end.

I looked down at my notepad and reflected on his past. The Germans did what they felt needed to be done in order to survive, regardless of the consequence to others. Nothing new there. I closed my eyes, realizing I had just summed up my life.

He leaned forward and put his hand on my knee. "Should we wrap things up by discussing the end of the war, Willi?"

I looked at him with arched eyebrows. I couldn't face any more of his past or mine. "No need to do that, Johann. I know what happened."

Johann nodded and slowly closed his iPad. I was about to get up and leave when he grabbed me by my shoulder.

"Before you go, Willi, let me finish. We started today by saying there's no justification for evil to exist. And in the end, it always consumes itself, just as it did with my country." He looked into my eyes as a father would to his son. "Frankly, I'm worried about you and Auggie. I fear America may be headed down the same path."

CHAPTER 68: SQUARE PEGS INTO ROUND HOLES

I turned to face him, and his hand fell off my shoulder. "What are you talking about?"

He looked away from me and replied. "Let me ask you something, Willi. When you came home after the war, were people talking about the Phoenix Program or the war crimes being investigated by the Winter Soldier Investigations?"

His eyes swung back to meet mine. "They probably weren't," he said grimly. "They probably didn't know about it or, even if they did know, they didn't want to talk about it. Would it then be fair to call them accessories to the war crimes in Vietnam? Based on how Germans were treated after the war, I would say it was. Most Americans didn't actively resist the war, and they all paid taxes to keep it going."

I was checked out of this conversation and didn't want to encourage him with an answer. However, he went on anyway. "Yet every single German after the war was labeled as accessories to genocide. And many still live with that shame today." He squinted at the sun as if remembering the harshness of that time.

"So, what do you think, Willi? Why do you think our German leaders were charged with war crimes and crimes against humanity while the Allies were never called to account for the same crimes committed over the last four hundred years? How fair was it to hold every German accountable when most of us were never aware of these crimes?"

I finally gave in under the barrage of questions. "It's obvious the Allies wanted to make a point. They wanted to make sure nobody ever did that sort of thing again, Johann."

"Well, Willi, I can tell you that it never happened again in Germany or in Japan. But the Western Allies continued to brutalize their colonies after the war. France did it in Algeria and Vietnam, while Britain did the same in Kenya and Ireland. America wanted to expand its influence by fighting a proxy war against Russia in Vietnam. Russia reciprocated by doing the same in Afghanistan ten years later. And now the US is back at it again in the Mideast."

He paused to reflect a moment. "And this is why I worry about your future. The dimensions of war have expanded, Willi. Technology has sanitized it and made it more anonymous for the people who wage it. It's like Lena said, it's become too easy to kill people. My fear is this pattern of evil will consume those who pursue it, like a snake eating its tail. One day, this country will reap the whirlwind."

Johann looked exhausted and his voice dropped to a whisper. "You asked me before about Ida. She was a good example of what Lena was talking about. She just lived her life unwed to any ideology. I wish that Auggie had grown up to be more like her than me. She looked outward and lived in the present. She didn't try to make sense of the world or mold it into her own image.

"She just wanted to help everyone and everything in it, just as Lena said. She would help anyone regardless of who they were or where they came from. But I wasn't like her. I fought with the party to obtain justice for our people and then, toward the end, to help our system survive another day.

"I never felt sorry for doing that. But now, after our discussions and hearing from Lena, I can see where we let the party do our thinking for us. They made it easy for us to understand a changing world by labeling other people as our enemies. It's no wonder we were doomed to fail because every person on this earth shares a common humanity, regardless of which system they belong to. It's a useless exercise for people to go on fighting each other, Willi. It's like trying to slam square pegs into round holes."

He paused again as if he were sifting through old memories. "If Ida knew what was happening to those poor people in the camps and ghettoes, I know she would have tried to help them. And if it was in her power, I know she would have opened the gates and freed them. She would have done the right thing regardless of her safety. She would have freed them and hoped for the best."

CHAPTER 69: UNFINISHED BUSINESS

I looked at my watch. It was long past the time for me to leave. This day had been traumatic. It began with reading Zinn's comments about rethinking *long held ideas*. Well, Johann and I had surely done that. We plowed through our past and turned around to face the victims resting in the furrows. There was nothing left to discuss. I needed to go home, sort through today's notes and see if any more visits were necessary.

"I should be leaving, Johann. It's getting late." I stood up from the bench and extended my hand. "C'mon, I'll walk back with you and then I'll hit the road."

The quiet of the well-kept grounds was calming as we walked back. We reached the rear entrance, and I opened the door for him. He turned to say goodbye. "It's been an awfully long day, Willi. There is one more point that I just thought of, but it can wait. I'm exhausted and it's getting late."

He had me curious, but I didn't want to tax him further. I started to leave but then stopped and turned around. "You know, Johann, when I got back from Vietnam, everyone called us baby killers. They treated us like criminals, just as you were." I paused, thinking about what to say next. "Most of that has been forgotten by now. They're actually saying thank you for our service now." I looked into his tired eyes and added. "But that hasn't happened for you yet."

He put his hand on my shoulder. "I know what you're trying to say, Willi. After all, we're related." He managed a slight smile and then entered the building. "I look forward to our next visit and hope it will be soon."

I returned his sentiment and watched as he walked to his room. The door closed behind him, and I turned around to leave by the side exit. I was headed toward the parking lot in front of the building when I spotted Lena sitting in the sun and reading a book. I approached her to say goodbye.

"Are you boys done talking?"

I gave her a disarming smile; glad she had not participated and hoping she would leave it at that. "Yes, we had lunch and then spoke a little more after that."

"What did you conclude about the Holocaust?"

I didn't want to get into it with her. "As you said, we all know what happened." I looked for my car and then checked my watch. "I need to leave, Lena. I'm already late."

"I want to tell you one more thing before you leave, Will." She sat up straight in her wheelchair. "You have seen war and know what it's like."

She turned her head to face the woods. I waited patiently since it seemed important. She turned back to face me. "You heard what happened to me in Europe and my son in Vietnam. Tell everyone you know to avoid ideologies. They only serve to set one group of people against another and that leads to war. You should always turn away when one group starts pointing fingers at other groups and spewing hatred against them. We all have our differences. Just live the life God gave you and let others live theirs."

I was confused by her remarks. "But how can you say that, given what happened to you and your family?"

She looked up and touched my hand. "The thing is, Will, we Jews have always tried to keep to ourselves, live our lives, and keep our faith, but we have always been under attack. Look where we are today: fighting for the right of Israel to survive. Right here in America, our temples are being attacked, our cemeteries are being desecrated, and we are being massacred in mass shootings. My friends live in fear as they watch Orthodox Jews being beaten up in New York City. Many of us went to our deaths in Europe without a fight, but now, believe me, when we are attacked, we will fight to the end, both for Israel and for our right to exist as a people."

"But, Lena, you just said to stay away from war and avoid hating others."

"I said you should live your life and avoid people who hate and attack others. But when people don't let you do that, then you must fight back. If you let evil go, it will not only destroy everything in its way, but in the end, it will also destroy itself." Her eyes were severe as she spoke but then turned maternal after she finished.

Her last sentence about evil destroying itself made an impression. It was the same point that Johann had made earlier. It also reminded me of myself before the stroke.

"I can understand how you feel, Lena."

She lifted herself up and said emphatically, "Willi, you have to do more than understand. You have to fight against hatred at every level of our society. But you must do it judiciously. After all, we are all human beings."

I thought of Martin Luther King and Gandhi. Both said violence only begets more violence. But Lena's words seemed to be contradictory. She just talked about fighting hatred, but her earlier advice was to live your own life and let others live theirs. I wanted to explore this further with her, but it was already late.

"Lena, thanks for sharing your thoughts, but I told my wife I was leaving over a half hour ago. I'd like to spend more time with you, but I really need to be going. I'll be back again soon."

She nodded and settled back in her chair. I patted her hand and left.

I walked to my car in a funk. I sat there for a few seconds before calling Cynthia to tell her that I was finally leaving. This visit was devastating but there was more unfinished business to close out. Johann had completed rehashing his war, but then he said there was one more point left to discuss. And Lena gave me contradictory advice that I needed to explore further with her. And, finally, there was the nagging question of how, where and when her son had died in Vietnam.

As I drove out of the facility's exit, I visualized piles of corpses lining either side of the road. They seemed to be bookmarking all my visits up here. I dreaded coming back. But I knew one more visit was necessary.

CYCLE IV: TRUTH

Therefore, having put away falsehood,
let each one of you speak the truth with his neighbor,
for we are members one of another.
Ephesians 4:25

~ AT HOME ~

CHAPTER 70: A LEGAL SHAM

I made it home in time for dinner. Cynthia was quiet while we ate. I could tell something was on her mind. I could well imagine what it was, and it wasn't long before it came.

"You look tired, Will. Why were you there so long today?" She didn't look angry, just concerned.

"You're right. I'm exhausted. Johann spent a lot of time discussing what led up to the Holocaust and then Lena showed up."

Her mouth and eyes opened wide. "This is the Jewish woman who was at Auschwitz?"

"The very same."

"What did she have to say about all of this?"

"We were doing okay until we got to the point where the war started. She said she knew what happened after that and just left. I saw her again when I was leaving. She pulled me aside and told me to avoid anybody or anything causing hatred toward other people. And then she started talking about how the Jews were still being persecuted today and how they wouldn't roll over anymore; they would fight back."

"Well, I agree with her. You should stay away from anything having to do with hatred. Forget all this Nazi stuff and stop sticking your nose into places where it doesn't belong. Do what normal people do when they retire."

Sticking your nose into places where it doesn't belong? The last person who told me that was Lulu. And that was forty-six years ago. "Let me think about that. Anyway, I probably need only one more visit. There are a few open questions I have for each of them. Let's forget about this for now and relax on the couch. I can clean up after dinner. C'mon, I'll pour you a glass of wine."

The next day, like clockwork, Doris and Daisy woke me at 4:00 am. We went outside and then came inside after they finished their business. I turned on the morning news then warmed up their breakfast and had mine. I waited for the sky to lighten a bit before heading out for our walk.

I was almost finished with our walk when I saw my neighbor, Larry, loading boxes into his car. He was probably heading to court. I remembered how much he loved to talk and braced myself.

"Good morning, Will. How's life treating you?"

"Real good, Larry. I'm just finishing up my walk. How are things with you?"

"Good. I haven't seen you lately. What have you been up to lately besides not working?" He knew I had recently retired and often told me how jealous he was .

"Oh, I've been busy doing what I always wanted to do – reading and writing."

"About what?"

I laughed, knowing one question led to many others with Larry. "Well, I started exploring my family history. And I found this long-lost relative, a German fellow who lives close by. This guy was actually in the war...World War II... on the other side."

"Really?" He seemed genuinely interested.

"Yeah, he's a real survivor."

"You know, I mentioned when we got together with the wives that I did a paper on Nuremberg. My thesis proved it was a real legal sham. I won a prize for it while I was in law school." He slammed down the trunk and headed toward the driver's door.

I followed in his wake. "Really?"

"Yeah, the Allies wanted to set a new legal framework for trying international criminals. Nuremberg was to serve as a precedent for prosecuting future war crimes and crimes against humanity." He dropped into his seat and left the car door open. "The Allies set themselves up as judge, jury, and executioner. They wanted to cement their position as lords over the new international order. Well, their framework survived the trial, but ultimately it had no legs to stand on."

That surprised me. "Whoa, that should take the wind out of Spencer Tracy's sails." I thought about all the gravitas he portrayed as a judge in the film, *The Nuremberg Trials*.

He chuckled as he started the car. "Their system lost all credibility once the Allies started committing the same type of war crimes as Nazi Germany did. The real eye-opener for me was the trial of Klaus Barbie. He had a helluva defense lawyer and you ought to read how he presented his case."

He checked his watch and then put the car into gear. "I have to get going, Will, but we should sit down over a beer sometime and I can tell you more about it."

I agreed and he left. I walked the last few blocks home, thinking about Lena. She was right about war. Once it starts, it becomes the devil's playground. How can there be rules and regulations when you're fighting for your life? All bets are off. And if anybody thinks otherwise, they haven't been there.

Cynthia was already awake when I entered the house. "How was your walk?"

"It was good. I ran into Larry on my way back. He told me a little bit more about the paper he wrote on the Nuremberg Trials."

"You brought that up with him?"

"Well, he asked me what I was doing, and I mentioned family history, then meeting Johann and it just came up."

"People are going to start talking if you don't cut out this Nazi business, Will. They'll start thinking you're some kind of a nut."

"Let them talk, Cynthia. I'm just studying history. Maybe they can learn something."

"Yeah, they'll learn you've lost your mind. Seriously, Will, you have to stop this. Move on."

"You know I love history. It's always been interesting to me."

"Well, study some other country then, like Spain and the Aztecs. You've been at this too long. I thought you said the other night you were going to stop seeing this Nazi guy. You know, this kind of thing attracts a whole nutty following. If you're not careful, you'll get tagged by some radical left- or right-wing group. Or maybe the government itself."

I barely kept myself from laughing. She must have seen the slight smirk on my face. "What's so funny? You think that won't happen? And what about me? This could affect both of us. Why don't you just leave things alone?"

"I'm sorry. I shouldn't laugh, but you make it sound like we're living in a police state, for God's sake."

"That's no joke. Everybody is on edge these days, with all these terrorists and all these conspiracy theories."

She sounded eerily like Johann did when he said, "We felt surrounded by our enemies." I hoped her words didn't prove to be prophetic.

"I'll be careful, honey. I promise."

Lulu. Lena. And now Cynthia. They all told me to leave things alone. But I couldn't.

CHAPTER 71: AN "INHERITED BIAS"

There were two things to do after my conversation with Larry: first, look up the Klaus Barbie trial; and second, discover why German soldiers, in both world wars, referred to their enemies on the Western Front as "Latins." I noticed they did this during my research but never took the time to find out why.

I had studied the Roman Empire in college and knew there was a long history of conflict between Rome and Germany. It made me curious if there was some kind of "cultural memory" that caused the Germans to use this label several millennia later. To my amazement, I searched for "cultural memory" on the Internet and found several hits.

Jeanette Rodriguez and Ted Fortier co-authored a book in 2007 called *Cultural Memory, Resistance, Faith, and Identity*. They defined a cultural memory as *those transformative historical experiences that define a culture, even as time passes, and it adapts to new influences*. They proved their case by identifying *inherited biases* that held up over time and existed among different cultures.[1]

There were numerous conflicts between the Romans and Germans that began with the Cimbrian wars in 113 BC and ended with the Byzantine–Lombard wars in 750 AD. An article in the *Smithsonian* magazine qualified the Battle of Teutoburger Wald in 9 AD as one of those *transformative historical experiences*.

This article quoted an archaeology expert as saying, *This was a battle that changed the course of history... It was one of the most devastating defeats ever suffered by the Roman Army, and its consequences were the most far-reaching. The battle led to the creation of a militarized frontier in the middle of Europe that endured for 400 years, and it created a boundary between Germanic and Latin cultures that lasted 2,000 years.* [2]

An email from *History.Com* about ancient Rome arrived several days earlier. I retrieved it and the subject line read: *This Day in History. September 4, 476. Western Roman Empire Falls.* The message's content started by saying: *Romulus Augustus, the last emperor of the Western Roman Empire, is deposed by Odoacer, a German barbarian who proclaims himself king of Italy.*

Odoacer turned out to be no barbarian. He was an officer in the Roman Army who led the German *foederati*, a Roman term for foreign troops. He was selected by his military peers to become the "King of Italy" after the Roman governor ignored the Army's petition to grant them permanent quarters and land in Italy.

He marched his troops into Ravenna and compelled Emperor Romulus to abdicate. He spared the emperor's life, exiled him to the countryside, gave him a pension, and allowed him to live with his family. Why then would the writers at History.com label him a *barbarian?* It was a *prima facie* case for inherited bias.

Both the Latins and Germans appeared to have carried this "inherited bias" against each other over the years that led to ongoing conflicts. This bias may have influenced several modern events. It may account for the "Latins" distrust of the Germans when they deceptively promoted the Fourteen Points in order to get the Armistice signed. It may also be why the "Latins" felt it necessary to strongarm the Germans into signing the Versailles Peace Treaty.

But what about the Germans' distrust of the Latins? Perhaps it was their distrust of the Latins that led them to start the First World War. And it may have been their vehement frustration with correcting the Latins' Versailles Peace Treaty that led to the Second World War.

I paused reading when I heard Emmy Lou Harris singing *I'll Be Faithful to You*. The title reminded me of the *Treuelied*, a song that Johann had mentioned during my first visit. I looked it up and found that it was originally written in 1814 and adopted by the SS as their loyalty song. I scanned through the lyrics and found they were about men keeping faith with one another and with their God. The last line made me pause: *We will preach and speak of the holy German Empire.*

I had never heard of a *holy German Empire*. I looked it up and found that it was another name for the First Reich, which began with Otto I, king of the Eastern Franks. Otto was crowned Holy Roman Emperor in 962 by Pope John XII for saving Christendom from pagan invaders, the Hungarian Magyars. During his reign, he consolidated power over the outlying German duchies and formed the Holy German Empire. The First Reich lasted almost nine hundred years, ending in 1806 when Napoleon defeated Emperor Franz II at Austerlitz.

This made me curious about the origins of *Gott Mit Uns*, the phrase imprinted on German army belt buckles during both world wars. The oldest reference I could find was at the time of the Crusades. It was used by the Order of Brothers of the German House of Saint Mary in Jerusalem, more commonly known as the Teutonic Order, which was founded in 1190.

The Teutonic knights displayed a black and white cross on their tunics. That same cross was displayed by the German military during both world wars and by the Bundeswehr today.

I stopped and realized that both sides, the Latins, and the Germans, had a common and strong belief in Christianity over the centuries. If only both sides had held true to their religious beliefs and rethought their *long-held ideas*, then they would have recognized their *inherited bias* against each other and avoided the two world wars.

But, in the final analysis, Johann may have been right after all. He said it was self-interest that was the cause of any conflict. It blinds people and nations to the needs of others, to the shared humanity they have in common with their opponents.

I closed the book on ancient history. It was time to switch gears and read about the Klaus Barbie trial.

CHAPTER 72: A "HEAVY SILENCE"

I was surprised to find that the best material on the Barbie trial came from the Jewish Virtual Library (JVL). It offered an extensive background and insight into the proceedings.

Barbie headed the Gestapo unit in Lyon from 1942 to 1944. He was responsible for suppressing the French resistance effort. His group captured, interrogated, and neutralized civilians involved in partisan warfare. He was arrested for overseeing the deaths of some 4,000 persons and the deportation of 7,500 others to camps in the East. Johann's reference to the Phoenix program came to mind. It ran twice as long and had ten times as many victims as Barbie's.

Barbie was captured after the war by the British. He worked in counterintelligence against the Russians from 1947 to 1951, first with the British and then with the Americans. After that, our country secretly released and sent him and his family to Bolivia. He was tracked down by a Nazi hunter and captured in 1972. He was returned to France in 1983 to face charges as a war criminal. The US issued a formal apology to the French for hiding Barbie from French justice.

The JVL had extensive information on Jacques Vergès, the defense attorney for Barbie. Vergès had fought with the French Resistance during the war. After the war, he became a lawyer and defended the Arab guerillas charged with insurrection in French-occupied Algeria.

Larry was right about Vergès. His defense was hard-hitting. The JVL website summed it up well: *Vergès would discover the truth about the inseparability of French nationalism and French imperialism. For the French, the smooth transition from a war of liberation to a war to protect the colonies seemed natural, but for Vergès, it was not. When the natives of the Algerian city of Constantine rose up against the French just one week after Hitler's suicide, the French reaction was swift and brutal. The Algerians counted 40,000 victims of the repression, but the French admitted to only 1,500. As Vergès later recalled, he was horrified by the repression of the Constantine revolt: "I was still in the Resistance, and I was terribly shocked. I didn't understand how they could fight Hitler then turn around and do that. Two years later, there was a similar repression in Madagascar. The Nuremburg trials were taking place at the time. I simply could not understand how nations could hold these trials so that the sort of thing the Germans did would never happen again. It was clear that the victorious colonial nations were doing exactly what the Germans had done in France."* [1]

Johann had basically said the same things about the Allies during the Nuremberg Tribunal. I went back to skimming through the trial records until Vergès began cross-examining Eli Wiesel.

Vergès asked the famous Nazi hunter if he felt Israel was just as guilty as Nazi Germany in torturing and massacring Palestinian civilians at Dair Yassin during the war for its independence. The author who wrote the JVL article described what happened next: *After a long pause, Wiesel, this time his voice trembling, had an attack of his own: "I find it especially regrettable that the lawyer of the defense dare accuse the Jewish people of the very crimes committed against them. Is that all he has to say today in 1987?"*

Cerdini [the judge]... *wanting to avoid national embarrassment over what might happen next, shouted, "We are getting distracted from our trial ..." But in mid-sentence, the much louder voice belonging to*

323

Jacques Vergès took over, " [our defense is to show] *that all peoples are considered the same!"*

What followed was described by the papers as a "heavy silence." The silence … was not the empty stillness of shock but the pensive silence of reflection and understanding. From that moment on, the court understood … how little the trial had to do with Klaus Barbie … Could the charge of "crime against humanity" be levied against France for what it had done, both to foreigners and her own citizens, over the past fifty years? Was imperialism a crime against humanity? Was the Holocaust unique or just another 'consequence' of war and human nature? [2]

Critics of Vergès accused him of using the *tu quoque* argument to invalidate the charges against his client, accusing France of committing the same crimes that they charged Barbie with. The JVL said as much as well, asking: *Were the French any different than Nazis? Were the Jews any different than Nazis? Was anyone any different than the Nazis? Down to his very core, Jacques Vergès believed the answer was no.* [5]

Johann's third point, all men are alike, dovetailed perfectly with Vergès defence. However, Johann's fourth point took it further: all men are alike because their life-giving spirit comes from God and God gave us the free will to decide whether to serve Him or not.

Both Barbie and Hoess opted to serve an ideology rather than God. Once that choice is made, the sanctity of life is no longer considered. Anyone who is not inside their ideological circle is judged as real or potential enemies. Saint Paul warned against separating yourself from God and then judging others. He cautioned the Romans *whatever you judge in others, you condemn in yourself; for you who judge, practice the same things.* It sounded like Vergès and Johann took a page from St. Paul's playbook.

I wondered what followed this verse and reached for the Bible. St. Paul continued writing that God *will repay each person according to what they have done. To those who by persistence in doing good … he will give eternal life. But for those who are self-seeking and who reject the truth and follow evil, there will be indignation and wrath, tribulation and anguish on every soul of man who does evil ...*

I not only saw the truth in those words but also realized that my life was a prime example of that truth.

CHAPTER 73: "WHITHER GOEST THOU?"

I closed the Good Book when another phrase popped into my head, *"Whither goest thou?"* I knew it wasn't from the Bible. I searched the Internet and found it came from Jack Kerouac's novel, *On the Road*. His novel was first published in 1957 when America was emerging as a global superpower, and the cold war was ramping up. I was curious about the context of his question and purchased a digital copy of the book and found the passage: *What kind of sordid business are you on now? I mean, man, whither goest thou? Whither goest thou, America, in thy shiny car in the night?*

Americans in 1957 probably would have replied with a cut from the Superman theme; they were on *a never-ending battle for truth, justice, and the American way,* But the truth about our country's direction was best expressed by President Eisenhower in his farewell speech when he left office in 1961: *Until the latest of our world conflicts, the United States had no armaments industry... But now we can no longer risk emergency improvisation of national defense; we have been compelled to create a permanent armaments industry of vast proportions...*

In the councils of government, we must guard against the acquisition of unwarranted influence, whether sought or unsought, by the military industrial complex. The potential for the disastrous rise of misplaced power exists and will persist.[1]

I pulled on the military-industrial complex thread and found that subsequent facts proved Eisenhower knew what he was talking about. The June 2014 issue of the *American Journal of Public Health* stated: *Although we acknowledge that there are various causes of war, we focus on the role of militarism and its pervasive influence on US public policy… Although war is a global public health issue, this article focuses on the United States, in part because of the extent of the global role and influence of the United States in war.*[2]

The Journal made two important observations in this article. First, from the end of World War II up to 2001, the U.S. was responsible for launching 201 out of the 248 armed conflicts in the world. Second, U.S. military spending dwarfed all other countries in 2014, with 41% of the world's total military spending. The next largest was China, with 8.2%.[3] By 2017, US arms sales rose to $398.2 billion. The next closest was Russia, with $37.7 billion, one-tenth of ours.[4]

I found another article published by *The Council on Foreign Relations* entitled *The Military-Industrial Complex, Fifty Years On.* It was a 2011 interview with Leslie Gelb, and it was even more telling than the other article. Gelb was the assistant secretary of state and director of the Bureau of Politico-Military Affairs during the Carter administration from 1977 to 1979. He was also president of the Council on Foreign Relations from 1993 to 2003.

Gelb stated that America's "military-industrial complex" had grown significantly over the last 50 years. He stated, *We are spending on the military today… about seven-hundred and fifty billion dollars a year. If you compare the Eisenhower budget in today's dollars, it would be a little more than half, or four hundred billion. So, there is a huge difference.*[5]

General Smedley Butler was right after all; war is a racket. The Cambridge Dictionary defines *racket* as "a dishonest or illegal activity that makes money." It seemed like Johann was right when he said that wealthy powerbrokers were underwriting the politicians who kept the racket growing. Even though these wealthy individuals contributed to various charities, it hasn't helped to level the playing field or affect their racket.

I wondered how skewed the playing field really was. The website *Worldometers* puts the earth's population at 7.6 billion people. The *Oxfam* website states that 62 of the wealthiest people in the world hold as much material worth as 3.6 billion of the poorest people.[6]

I grabbed my calculator and tried to calculate the percentage of 62 over 3.6 billion. The calculator choked. There wasn't enough space to hold all the zeroes trailing the decimal point. The adage that the rich get richer while the poor get poorer seemed truer than ever. But there was an addendum: the rich convince the poor to do all the fighting and dying to keep them and their system in play.

The huge gap between the privileged and poor made me think about the marginalized refugees in the Middle East who became terrorists. Why would any sane person strap on a vest with explosives? Was it an act of terrorism or desperation? I think it was the latter.

I thought again about Zinn's comment about rethinking "*long-held ideas*" and wondered what the context of this remark was. I did a quick search and found this: *What does it take to bring a turnaround in social consciousness—from being a racist to being in favor of racial equality … from being in favor of the war in Iraq to being against it? We desperately want an answer because we know that the future of the human race depends on a radical change in social consciousness.*

It seems to me that we need not engage in some fancy psychological experiment to learn the answer but rather to look at ourselves and to talk to our friends. We then see, though it is unsettling, that we were not born critical of existing society... embedded there by years of family prejudices, orthodox schooling, imbibing of newspapers, radio, and television.[7]

I continued reading. I was gobsmacked again by one of his observations, *Certain facts appeared before us, startled us, and then caused us to question beliefs that were strongly fixed in our consciousness.* This is exactly what happened to me when Johann began his discourses.

But was this a blessing or a curse? As Johann remarked to Auggie, we can all live comfortably in our system without ever thinking about how it impacts others. But Kerouac's question remained. Where were we heading? And what happens if our system breaks down? What if America loses a war and faces judgment by our enemies? How do we account for all the drone assassinations, commando raids, and other violent violations of another country's sovereignty? To paraphrase James Carville, *It's the economy, stupid.*

I turned away from the PC, disheartened, and noticed the Bible lying on my desk. I reached for it like an alcoholic groping for a drink. It was still open to Saint Paul's letter to the Romans. I paged through it aimlessly until I found a verse that promised to break the perpetual cycle of violence: *Repay no one evil for evil … live peaceably with all. Beloved, never avenge yourselves, but leave it to the wrath of God, for it is written, 'Vengeance is mine, I will repay, says the Lord.'…if your enemy is hungry, feed him; if he is thirsty, give him something to drink… Do not be overcome by evil but overcome evil with good.*

What if people recognized their common humanity and followed this simple lesson? If they did, none of my generation or Johann's would have participated in all of the evils we had discussed during my last five visits.

CHAPTER 74: "A SORRY SCRUB"

Cynthia walked into my study and saw me hunched over the desk, holding my head. She asked what was wrong. I looked up and told her I was tired. She sat down and leaned over the desk. "No, you're not. You know it's more than that. You may think you're over the past but you're not. You keep going back and torturing yourself over things in the past."

She always knew me better than I know myself and I nodded in agreement. "You're right and I know it. It's no fun for me either, but I have to work this out, honey. I'm almost there. I'm sorry."

Cynthia waited for more. When it didn't come, she broke the silence. "Well, don't be sorry, Will, do something about it. Move on."

She was right. I needed to wrap this up and get beyond the past. "I know, Cynthia. I'll get it done."

She got up, put her hand on my shoulder, and silently left. She was never one to rub my nose in it.

As she walked out, I recalled the sign hanging over Carl Jung's doorway: *Bidden or unbidden, God is always present.* And then I felt the weight of that statement. God had always been there with me, regardless of what I did or thought. I was part of Him. Pure and simple.

I first felt His presence when I was twelve, at confirmation. It was comforting and I was filled with joy. However, those feelings vanished with my father's next outburst. Shame and anger arose in his wake. Afterward, I wondered if the joy of His presence would ever come back.

We were studying the Puritans at that time. We were introduced to *The Pilgrim's Progress* and learned that it was about leaving the evils of the Old World to find salvation in the New. At the time, I thought it would be a good idea to read it, thinking it would show a way back to feeling His presence. The text was not only dense but written in 17th-century English. It was like wading through knee-high muck for a twelve-year-old boy. I remembered jumping to the end, hoping to find a solution there, but nothing made any sense to me, and I quickly forgot about the whole effort.

I decided to try reading it again to see if I could find anything of value. I found a free online version and skimmed through the pages until something made me stop. Christian, the main character, was on a pilgrimage and recognizes another character named Faithful, who is fleeing the Valley of the Shadow of Death. I stopped reading. The name "Faithful" and the "Valley of the Shadow of Death" reminded me of Johann and Germany after the surrender.

I started reading again but quickly stopped after Christian shouts to Faithful to wait for him and hears a frantic response: *No, I am upon my life, and the avenger of blood is behind me.* I immediately thought about the German POWs in the London Cage who feared for their life while they were being tortured.

I shook it off and went back to reading. Christian hurriedly catches up to Faithful and the dialogue between the two caught my attention:

FAITHFUL. But, good brother, hear me out. So soon as the man overtook me, he was but a word and a blow, for down he knocked me and laid me for dead. But when I was a little come to myself again, I asked him wherefore he served me so.

He said, because of my secret inclining to Adam the First: and with that, he struck me another deadly blow on the breast and beat me down backward; so I lay at his foot as dead as before. So, when I came to myself again, I cried him mercy; but he said, I know not how to show mercy; and with that knocked me down again. He had doubtless made an end of me, but that One came by and bid him forbear ...

CHRISTIAN. Who was that that bid him forbear?

FAITHFUL. I did not know Him at first, but as He went by, I perceived the holes in His hands, and in His side; then I concluded that He was our Lord ...[1]

I kept reading until the two pilgrims reached the town of Vanity Fair, where they became involved in a dispute with the townspeople. At that point, I quit reading the original and switched over to Cliff's Notes for a summary of what happened.

But what particularly irks the townspeople is their attitude toward the goods displayed at the fair. When called to look at them, they turn away, putting their fingers in their ears and crying out, 'Turn away mine eyes from beholding vanity.'

When mockingly asked what they might be interested in buying, they 'gravely' reply, 'We buy the Truth.' A crowd gathers to taunt and revile them, 'some calling upon others to smite them,' which leads to a great hubbub and the arrest of the Pilgrims for disturbing the peace. After being questioned, they are severely beaten and locked up in an iron cage.[2]

Following their internment and torture, the two pilgrims are taken to trial. *Three witnesses are brought forward — Envy, Superstition, and Pickthank. Swearing falsely, Envy testifies that he has long known Faithful, that he has always been a troublemaker, persistently denouncing the laws and customs of the town ... The jury, having heard the false witnesses and Faithful's reply, retires to discuss what should be done.*

'I see clearly that this man is a heretic,' says Mr. Blind-man, foreman of the jury.

'Away with such a fellow from this earth,' cries Mr. No-good; Mr. Malice, Mr. Love-lust, and Mr. Live-loose agree.

'Hang him, hang him!' exclaims Mr. Heady.

'A sorry scrub,' says Mr. Highmind.

'Hanging is too good for him,' Mr. Cruelty insists.

After Mr. Liar and other jurors have expressed similar views, Mr. Implacable sums up: 'Let us forthwith bring him in guilty of death.'[3]

I stopped reading at this point, unnerved by the similarities between my research and this passage. It also dawned on me that Christian and Faithful shared a relationship similar to the one Johann and I had.

I stopped reading and quickly called Johann to ask about visiting tomorrow. I was anxious to test whether my impressions about the relationship between the characters in the book and ours were correct. I also wanted to tell him that his sponsor's neighbor, Frederik Knoske, was a distant relative to both Johann and my mother. All three were descended from Karl Knoske, who was born in Silesia in 1796 and died there.

He agreed to the visit but didn't sound so well. I was glad I called. I made some updates to our family tree and stuck it in my notebook.

~ 6TH VISIT ~

CHAPTER 75: *AUSGELÖSCHT*

When I arrived at the nursing home, I went directly to the Garden Room, but Johann wasn't there. I went to the Reception Desk, and they told me he had a TSI, a small stroke, last night. He was doing well and resting in his room. I asked about Auggie, and they told me that he came right away but left a few minutes ago. They told me it was okay to visit Johann but not to do or say anything that might excite him.

I walked into his room. The blinds were open, and I could see the clear sky outside. The wind was still, and the trees were at rest. He was lying on his back, half-elevated, when I entered. He must have heard me coming down the hall because his head was turned toward the door.

"Willi! It's good to see you. *Wie geht's dir?*"

"Johann, I'm fine. *Bist du in ordnung?* I heard you had a little trouble?"

"Ach, just a little scare. You expect these things when you get to be my age."

"I'm glad to see you. I'm sorry it's been a while, but I've been reading."

He smiled broadly and reached out to grasp my hand. "*Guter junge!* Good boy! What have you been reading?

"Oh, any number of things, including some ancient history about Germany and Rome on one end and the Klaus Barbie trial on the other."

"*Mein Gott!* That covers a lot of time, Willi." He grimaced as he forced himself up with both arms. He looked over at me with a forced smile after he finished. "Let's go outside and talk more about it. But first, help me get into that wheelchair over there."

I wheeled him out and picked up coffee for us. He held a cup in each hand with the iPad cradled between his legs. We stopped at the same bench where we had sat before. It was a beautiful day with barely a cloud in the sky. The sun beamed down on us and painted a warm hue over our faces.

"What a nice day, Johann. I'm glad you're feeling better."

"It is a nice day, Willi. Thank you for the coffee and for wheeling me out here. They said I could start walking a little tomorrow." He sipped his coffee, looked into the distance, and muttered *"Ich fühle mich wie scheiße."*

"What was that, Johann?"

"I said I feel like shit. I didn't walk this morning and didn't get much sleep last night. I feel washed out."

He appeared quite pale in the daylight. I was concerned about his condition and how much time he had left. I thought it was best to finish our family history first before taking on any other subjects.

"So, Johann, we talked about world history during the last few visits, but we didn't talk too much about our families. I know you lost your family in the war, but do you know anything else about your relatives or any other Knoskes in Europe?"

His expression changed abruptly. I should have known better. "I don't know anything about your mother's side of the Knoske family, Willi. As for my side, the only way to describe them is

Ausgelöscht." He looked out at the breeze, which began stirring the trees. Then he swiveled his head up to look at the clouds.

"Do you know what that word means, Willi? It means obliterated. As far as I know, my mother and sister both died in Breslau sometime during 1945. I don't know what happened to them or any other relatives after that." He sipped his coffee and used his other hand to scroll through the iPad. "I did hear about my father, though. His name was August Knoske. I named my boy after him. I wrote to the *Volksbund* after the war. They said he died on June 20, 1945, in a Soviet labor camp. It was built in Stakhanov, Ukraine, for German POWs.

"He was buried there in a cemetery with one hundred and forty other POWs. He was fifty-six years old. My guess is that he was probably pressed into the *Volksturm* during the battle for Breslau. He was probably captured and sent to the Ukraine for forced labor."

"I'm so sorry I brought it up, Johann."

"Ach, no need. Nobody cared what happened to the Germans in Breslau or how they were treated after the war. In fact, if they said anything, it was that we got exactly what we deserved." I kept my mouth shut; those were exactly my thoughts before I met him.

He paused, looking away as if he wanted to drop the subject but then turned to face me. "I can tell you a bit more about Breslau, though. It was a good place to be during most of the war. We were too far east for the bombers to reach us but that changed in 1944. During the summer of that year, Hitler declared that Breslau would become a *Festung*, a fortress to be held at all costs, down to the last man. And after that, no one was allowed to leave the city.

"As the Ivans came closer and closer, they started shelling the city. The *Gauleiter*, Karl Hanke, finally allowed women and children to evacuate in January 1945. They had to leave on foot since all roads and rails out of the city were destroyed by Soviet bombing. The winter of 1944 to 1945 was one of the worst on record in Europe. It was bitterly cold but fifty- to sixty-thousand German civilians managed to leave. I read there were eighteen thousand frozen bodies recovered on the exit route after the spring thaw.

"I don't know if my mother and sister left with the others in January or stayed. Since my father was probably pressed into the *Volksturm*, I imagine that they stayed there with him, but I don't think anyone will ever know. Supposedly, two-hundred thousand civilians remained in Breslau after January. The first attack on the city came on February sixteenth. The Germans fought the Ivans block by block. By late March, all German military organization was gone. Individual soldiers from the *Hitler Jugend* and *Volksturm* kept fighting from house to house as the Ivans moved deeper into the city.

"Finally, on May sixth, four days after Berlin fell, the Russians agreed to a conditional surrender of Breslau providing for the safety and medical attention of civilians and soldiers. The Soviets tossed aside those provisions after it was signed, much as the Allies did to Wilson's 14 Points at Versailles.

"For the next two months, the Soviets went house to house raping, murdering, and stealing. Some survivors said there was a murdered, disfigured, or disemboweled German hung on every lamppost in the city. I heard how the Russians were amazed at how much the Germans had. They took watches, dishes, utensils, basically everything that wasn't nailed down, and they sent it all back home.

"All of Silesia was occupied by the Soviets after the war, and they had a terrible reputation for raping German women. You can look this up, Willi, if you don't believe me. Madeleine Pauliac was a doctor with the French Red Cross. She was the chief doctor for the French Hospital in Warsaw after the war and took notes of the women in maternity units who were either raped during labor or moments after giving birth.

"I read one of her reports about one-hundred and eighty-two Catholic nuns who were raped in Neisse and sixty-six nuns found pregnant in the diocese of Kattowitz. She wrote twenty-five nuns in one convent had been raped, some as many as forty times in a row. The French recently made a movie about this called *The Innocents*. He paused to fill his lungs after that long discourse, then he looked away from his iPad and over at me. "Did you have a chance to read *After the Reich*, Willi?"

"Yes, I did, Johann, several weeks ago. I never knew about the atrocities committed against the Germans after the war and, frankly, it was very hard to read."

"*Ja*, but it's all true. It finally took someone seventy-two years to write it all down, but this fellow did a good job of it."

I put my pen down and watched as he swung his gaze up to the sky. There was no anger or bitterness in his eyes, nor in his posture or in the set of his jaw. After hearing about the tragedy of Breslau, I realized the truth of his first point: evil begets more evil and there's no end to it.

CHAPTER 76: IN REVERSE

"Johann, I still can't believe that there's so much about Germany that I had never heard before. It's very peculiar that everything you said wasn't more generally known."

He quickly latched onto my comment. "Well, Willi, there's much more for you to know. Some people have estimated more Germans died in the year following the war's end than during the five years of the war itself. When the three Allied leaders met at Potsdam in 1945 and agreed to turn Silesia over to Poland, it was like negotiating the Versailles Treaty all over again – except this time, the resident Germans weren't left to stay behind. All of them were expelled from their homes and told to return to Germany.

"All over Eastern Europe, more than ten million German-speaking residents from other countries were forced to return to Germany.[1] It was like putting *Generalplan Ost* into reverse. Some of these expelled Germans were initially interred in Polish concentration camps, like Camp Jaworzno, Camp Potulice, Camp Lambinowice, Camp Zgoda, and others. Like my father, many were sent to the gulags in Russia for forced labor.

"Any street, park, town, or anything with a German name in Poland was replaced with a Polish or Russian name. The German language was forbidden, and any civil rights for Germans were immediately suspended. The Poles returned and took over the homes and jobs of the expelled Germans.

"There were two-hundred thousand Germans left in Breslau at the start of 1945, and this was reduced to a handful by the end of 1945. By the 1950s, Breslau was resettled with Poles and renamed Wrocław. By 2010, there were only one-thousand people in the city who claimed to have German roots."

He leaned back in his chair to ponder his next thought. "This is not a nice thing to say, Willi, but if the Allies wanted us dead, then maybe they should have just killed us off after the war instead of having us die a slow death or enduring such misery. Konrad Adenauer, the first Chancellor of West Germany, wrote about this expulsion in his book. He wrote, *According to American estimates, some 13.8 million Germans were expelled from Eastern Germany, Poland, Czechoslovakia, Hungary, etc. 7.8 million arrived in the eastern and western zones. 6 million Germans disappeared from the face of the Earth. They are dead and gone.*[1] Other organizations pegged the total number of expelled Germans at sixteen million, which would raise the number of missing people."[2]

He took a deep breath, exhaled slowly, and continued. "Those were the civilians, Willi. The West German government found over three million soldiers were taken prisoner by the USSR, and over a million of them died in captivity, many of them declared to be 'missing.' Tens of thousands of soldiers died from hunger, exposure, or neglect in the American *Rheinwiesenlager* POW camps. These camps were just fenced-in open fields along the Rhine River with no facilities at all. They only had holes in the ground for shelter.

"The Allies never designated our surrendered forces as POWs. Eisenhower had us classified as 'disarmed enemy forces' instead. This allowed him to avoid compliance with the Geneva Convention. The Allies couldn't or wouldn't provide us with the nutrition, medical care, or shelter required by that treaty. The Allies also violated the Hague Treaty when they funded and supplied civilians with military equipment to fight on their behalf as non-uniformed combatants. Yet they turned around and convicted our officers for violating both of these documents."

He paused to wait for my reaction, but I was busy writing notes. He sipped on some coffee and then looked off into the woods. After I finished, he was still looking off into the distance. It was like he was lost in the present moment, as if he was seeing the be-all and end-all of his long life.

CHAPTER 77: *DER LETZTE SEINER ART*

"Johann, you never told me what happened to the 12th after the war ended." As soon as the words came out of my mouth, I remembered I wasn't supposed to get him upset.

It didn't. Johann answered calmly. "We surrendered to the Amis, that's what we called the Americans, near Steyr, Austria, on May eighth. We were exhausted from weeks of constant combat and lacked rations and sleep. We were herded into an open field near Mauerkirchen with a bunch of other prisoners.

"It didn't take long for the Amis to separate the *Waffen-SS* from the other prisoners. We were forced to jog to Altheim, about ten miles down the road, through the heat. There were women alongside the road who offered us water, but the Amis beat them back with rifle butts. Over twenty of us died on the way, and it came to be known as the Death March of the SS. When we arrived, we were told to stay in a soggy meadow next to a creek and lived there for some time. We were starving, but so was the entire country. We boiled grass to ease our hunger pains.

"Later, they moved us to several different camps: Ebensee, Lichtenfels, Winkel, and then, in May 1946, to my last stop in Camp Auerbach. I volunteered for agricultural labor to get outside until they finally released me in June 1946.

"I read that Patton was so disgusted with the treatment of German POWs that he noted it in his diary. Let me read that for you." He scrolled through his iPad and found it. "*It is amusing to recall that we fought the revolution in defense of the rights of man and the civil war to abolish slavery and have now gone back on both principles."[1]*

Johann took a deep breath and then brought his eyes back to meet mine. I spoke first. "So, after all that, Johann, do you think it was worth it? Do you still believe in everything you fought for?"

Johann cocked his head as if he had misheard me. "I told you before that I fought for my country, Willi. It is what I knew and how I was raised. My beliefs were built upon each other like stones in a pyramid; family, then country, and finally God. These things never change, and I'll never forget them."

I shook my head in disbelief. After all we had been through, was he back at square one?

"What's wrong, Willi?"

"Do you still consider yourself a Nazi, Johann? They started the war and committed one of the worse crimes in history, the Holocaust." I immediately regretted my question. It was poorly worded, and I was afraid it might upset him.

It didn't. Johann slowly pushed himself up in the wheelchair, leaned forward, and pulled up the sleeve of his robe, revealing a small tattoo inside his left arm. It was his blood type written in German script. It was applied by the *Waffen*-SS in case a transfusion was needed on the battlefield.

"Do you see this, Willi? Some tried to scratch or cut it out when the war ended to avoid being identified. I never did."

He slowly exhaled and sank back into his chair. "Our cause unfolded like Wagner's *Gotterdamerungen*; first, we were tricked into starting a war and then we were killed for our beliefs, just like Siegfried." His eyes squinted, and then he bolted back up. "And all because of your President Roosevelt!"

"What do you mean by that?" I was surprised at his outburst and concerned that he was getting too excited.

"Well, first, he gave Britain and France a promise of military support if they issued that guarantee to Poland, which stopped them from negotiating with us. Then, after Britain declared war on us, he baited our U-boats by using American ships to send arms and munitions to them. And, finally, he made sure that our system would be totally eliminated by demanding an unconditional surrender. This announcement put us in the position of either fighting to the very end in the hope of maintaining our freedom or surrendering and being made into another colony of the Allies.

"Generals Marshall and Eisenhower tried to get FDR to change his mind. They felt his unconditional surrender announcement would stiffen German resistance and lengthen the war. And they were right. Goebbels came on the radio shortly after the Casablanca Conference and said the demand for unconditional surrender left no alternative for Germany but total war."

He finished his coffee with a long sip that seemed to recharge him. "There's one more thing to mention, Willi. When the war ended, we accepted defeat. There was no resistance. We were tired of fighting, of bombing, of killing. We were thoroughly beaten and knew we had to pay penance, but no mercy ever came."

He ran his fingers through his white hair and sighed. "After the war, some people called the 12th SS Division *der letzte seiner art*, which translates to the 'the last of its kind.' I always took it as a compliment. To me, it meant we were the last of the believers in a noble cause, and there was honor in our loyalty."

He paused for a moment to gather his thoughts. Any thoughts I had of a connection between us and the two characters in *The Pilgrim's Progress* quickly passed as it seemed he was falling back into his old mindset. I had thought he was seeking redemption. But now, it was like he was regressing. However, I didn't say anything for fear of upsetting him.

"But let me go back to your original question, Willi. I never considered myself a Nazi as such, but I did believe in justice for my country and my people. I fought willingly for those beliefs and then tried for the next 70 years to understand what went wrong. I wanted to piece together everything that led to that war and then…"

His voice trailed off. He paused as if his original train of thought was derailed. I waited a moment for him to continue.

CHAPTER 78: THE NEEDS OF OTHERS

"And then, I saw that Lena was right. Our pride had blinded us." He paused to take a deep breath and then looked down. "We were only thinking of ourselves. We only wanted our country to survive. We didn't see war for what it was, a selfish act to get what you want regardless of others. We never asked if our actions served God or not."

This was a major turnaround. I was glad that I held off speaking my earlier thoughts about his regressing. I watched as he leaned back into his chair and smiled. I felt a closeness to him that I never felt before. He gazed over at me and gave a weak nod in return.

"Ach, but that's water over the dam now. But as I told you and Auggie before, I'm afraid that America is following the same path."

He didn't say anything about evil destroying itself, but he did bring back recollections from my recent research on America's recent record since World War II: the frequency of our wars, the size of our military budget, and the volume of our arms sales. He also brought to mind the *Avenger of blood*, the evil being in *The Pilgrim's Progress* who chased down and beat Faithful within an inch of his life. Have we become that *Avenger of blood*? Suddenly, I too was fearful of America's future.

Johann took a deep breath and continued in a weaker voice. "At our first meeting, you said that you wanted to learn more about our family history. And when you mentioned your father and asked me about the war, you were startled when I mentioned the SS. You thought I was evil. And then when you mentioned enlisting in the Marines and serving in Vietnam, I could see you wondering whether you were as evil as me."

He paused for a moment to study my face as if he were trying to read my thoughts. "You seemed lost, Willi, and that's why you kept coming back to visit me. You saw that I wasn't as lost as you. You came back because you needed someone to show you a way out. You needed to find something to believe in, something that would ground you. Am I right?" His head tilted slightly, waiting for a response. He had hit the nail on the head. I was dumbstruck but still managed to give him a nod. "You were stuck in the ditch, Willi. You needed someone or something to pull you out."

"I was, Johann. And all politics aside, you helped me see outside myself. And when I did, I saw how much shit I put myself and others through." A sudden wave of emotion overcame me. I struggled to hold back my tears. "You know, my mother always believed in me and pushed me to become a minister. But I knew I wasn't good enough. My father made sure of that. It must have broken her heart when I joined the Marines and came out as damaged goods. But she acted like nothing was wrong after I came home. She didn't want to deal with what I went through. And it was the same way with her marriage. She ignored everything bad around her. I think she felt it would all go away if she waited long enough."

Johann broke into a fatherly smile. "Well, I can tell you this, Willi. None of us are born evil. Some of us get lost or damaged along the way, but no one is perfect. We need to see the flaws in ourselves and others. We need to be humble enough to forgive both. Kurt Meyer, our Regimental leader, said it best. He told his prosecutors, *Humans, not angels, fought on both sides.*" [1]

He paused and inhaled deeply. "And this is the last point I want to share with you, Willi. I thought of it the other day when you were leaving. Even though we are all born of God, we're all imperfect."

His hand reached out to cover mine. His voice suddenly softened and took on a spiritual tone. "I've been thinking about this ever since our last visit, Willi." He took another deep breath. I was starting to think that the mini-stroke provided him with an impetus for finishing his story. You see, Willi, each of us is part of Him. It's the way that He participates in His creation. But we are mortal. We're all constrained by time and space. We can't know everything there is to know. How could we? After all, we are the created, not the Creator."

He squeezed my hand as if to stress the importance of what came next. "Listen to me, Will. The awareness of these limitations brings a degree of suffering to all of us. We suffer because we want to know everything about Him, His Creation, and why we are here. But we never will. People try to alleviate this suffering by developing or following ideologies to fill that void. But when those ideologies turn from serving God and His creation, that's when trouble begins."

He paused again to catch his breath and his resolve. "This is why you need to be strong in your beliefs, Willi. But you have to be humble in applying them." He shook his head and smiled as if he were amused by some thought.

"How can you feel lost, Willi, when you're part of God and all His creation? This world is so big, and we can only know so much. That's why we must always seek the Truth before saying or doing anything that may affect others. We need to learn to forgive one another's imperfections just as we ask God to forgive ours. Until we understand the needs of others, there's always the chance we'll do more harm than good."

I suddenly felt a deep connection with him. I imagined it was like the one Christian shared with Faithful.

He stopped and locked his eyes onto mine. "Do you remember what was printed on our belt buckles, Willi?"

He took me by surprise with that one. "Yes, I do. It was *Gott mit Uns*. I looked it up and saw it went back to the Teutonic Knights."

"*Ja*, that's right … 'God is with us.' Like most people, we believed in God and prayed for His help during both wars. We never lost faith in God, but we lost sight of Him."

Johann appeared exhausted, and his voice dropped to a whisper. "Lena was right to say you should just live your life. We don't need a Hitler, a Roosevelt, or a Nixon to tell us what to do, what's right or wrong. God gave us the free will to seek out the truth. He also provided us with reason to determine the truth of what our leaders are telling us. Whenever our leaders start threatening others, we need to closely examine the needs of both sides before deciding what to do.

"You see, Willi," he spoke softly as he leaned forward in his chair, "you can still believe in God but sin out of ignorance, fear, or desperation."

He paused to watch the wind stirring the trees. "God always provides, yet people forget that. Instead, they place their faith in systems to get them whatever they want when they want it. They don't trust that God will provide them with justice. Instead, they take matters into their own hands, irrespective of the needs of others. And that's when conflicts begin."

CHAPTER 79: *WU-WEI*

He paused to sip some coffee while I thought about my relationship with God. I stopped listening to my conscience, which I believe is that part of God within me, shortly after joining the Corps. My fears of surviving boot camp drove the frequency and volume of the beast's urgings until it overshadowed everything else, just like it did to Germany during the '30s. And look where it got us.

Johann reached out to touch my shoulder. "Willi, bad memories?"

"Yes," I said. "I know what you mean about people forgetting about God. Some people never get past their own needs to care about anything else." I shook my head and looked down the pathway. "I'm not much better. Since we met, I've been looking back on my life. I can't believe all the pain I inflicted on myself and others. I listened to my own demons rather than to God." This was the second time I humbled myself to another, but this confession ran deeper than the one I had with the priest.

"Willi, remember *Gott Mit Uns*. He is with us every step of the way. You don't need a belt buckle to remind you of Him. Be strong and trust in God."

I closed my eyes and smiled at a long-forgotten memory. "Johann, we had a saying in the Marines: they can kill you, but they can't eat you."

"*Ja*, that's it!" He smiled broadly and nodded. "That's a good one to hold onto."

"Yes, it is," I agreed.

He nodded several more times to emphasize his agreement. "We have finally reconciled ourselves to the truth, Willi. We shouldn't let any system separate us from God; that is the original sin. And that's it, Willi. That was the last point I wanted to make. Striking out at others only provokes revenge, and revenge is evil. It is only done to satisfy the self and doesn't provide lasting peace or justice. Trusting in God will provide both, but only if we have patience and faith in Him."

He gave me a weak smile and nodded. I watched as he slowly laid his head back and closed his eyes.

"Thanks, Johann; you're right. I've been too wrapped up in my own problems to appreciate the problems of others. Thank you for helping me to see that."

I looked out at the field lying on the other side of the pathway. It stretched out a hundred yards and ended at the tree line. It reminded me of my father's day in the Ardennes and my first deer hunt. The fear, shame, and anger associated with both events had left me. I wondered how different my life would have been if I had only trusted in God and let His will be done. I bowed my head, knowing there was no answer.

The wind picked up, and the trees began swaying back and forth. I turned around to check on Johann. He was resting peacefully with his eyes closed. I closed my eyes as well, and an image of Lulu appeared.

She was standing by the hotel window on my last night of R&R. Her body was outlined by the shimmering city lights in the distance. She explained *wu wei* to me that night. She said it was the action of non-action, of watching the cycle turn from one extreme to the other, of being detached from it all and accepting each moment.

She slammed the door shut on me when I offered my help. She said my intentions for her were no better than America's were for Vietnam. Both were worth shit to her. And she was right. After America left, Southeast Asia turned to shambles, and so did I.

Forty-five years later, Lulu's words still haunted me. She not only spoke of *wu wei* that evening but also of *wu nien*, the Thought of Non-Thought, and *wu hsin*, the Mind of Non-Mind. She negated everything about the self. Nothing was left but the Cycle, and it kept turning with or without me.

I sat on the bench feeling like a stationary hub inside a turning wheel. Both Johann and Lulu said I was part of something greater than myself, but I was too focused on my own worries to see that.

After a few moments, the wind tapered off, and the sun grew hotter. It was time to take Johann back for lunch. I turned to him and said it was time to go. When he didn't respond, I lightly touched his shoulder. No response. I felt for his pulse. There was none – he was gone.

CHAPTER 80: A LESSON TO BE LEARNED

I wheeled Johann to the front desk and asked for a nurse. One came and confirmed what I already knew.

I immediately thought of Auggie. They would be contacting him, so I wrote a brief note expressing my sympathies. I asked the person at the front desk for an envelope and tucked the note in along with a copy of the family tree. He sent me an email the next day thanking me and inviting me to Johann's funeral.

I was about to leave when I saw Lena coming down the hallway. She looked at Johann's lifeless body in the wheelchair and then at me with questioning eyes. "What happened, Willi?"

"He's passed, Lena. I was just sitting with him outside, having some coffee and talking. He closed his eyes, and I thought he was sleeping." I couldn't go on.

"I'm sorry, Will. He was a relative, yes?"

"Very distant, but we became very close over the last few months. He was like a father to me."

She seemed to be wondering what to say next. "Can we go outside for a minute to talk before you leave?"

We left the building and went to a bench as far away as possible from the entrance. I sat down, and she wheeled over to me. "I'm sorry for your loss, Will. He seemed like a good man."

"He was … at least to me."

"He was to me, as well; there was just too much history between us, and it got in the way." She seemed to be struggling with what to say next as she wrung her hands.

"Will, I don't want history to put up a wall between us as well. I wanted to tell you about my son Isaac, who died in Vietnam. I mentioned him before but just couldn't talk about it at the time."

She sighed as if unloading a long-standing burden. "He was killed on May 15, 1969, on Hamburger Hill. You probably heard about it. It was a senseless battle. I felt so devastated. It was all so tragic."

Who hadn't heard of it? There was a movie about it, and Congress had a huge political debate over incurring so many casualties to take a hill with no military value. And when it was over, we just walked away. And the enemy came back to occupy it. What a fucking way to go.

"My husband was angry when our son was drafted. He called all kinds of people and contacted politicians to get him deferred, but nothing helped. The system just took him. After Isaac was killed, my husband was enraged about the war and railed at the government, but nobody would listen. I couldn't take his anger or Rand's views on Vietnam any longer. My husband and I divorced soon after that. That whole time was, as you well know, tragic."

"I'm sorry to hear that. But what were Rand's views on the war?"

"Oh, she was very outspoken about Vietnam. I still followed her in the media, and we kept in touch with one another. She was right about some things but wrong about others. She was right when she said that the United States wasn't fighting for any moral reasons in Vietnam. And she was right that American lobbyists were pressuring our government leaders to pursue that war.

"But she was wrong about America's leaders. She said they pursued that war and sacrificed our soldiers out of altruism, a sin, according to her. She said they had no will to win and shouldn't have sent our boys to fight without it. She felt the war was a moral and political failure. She said our troops performed heroically, but it was a war that never should have been fought."

She may have been old and bound to a wheelchair, but she could still summon the tone and bearing of a trial lawyer. "After they told us our son was killed, I was grieving, and it was hard for me to be around her. With Rand, everything was logic and reason;

354

there was no room for emotion or human empathy. She had no *Neshamah* if, you know what I'm talking about."

She stopped for a moment to see if I understood. I shrugged and shook my head.

"It means you have no heart or soul. Whenever she tried reasoning with me about how illogical the war was, all I could think about was my son. He died in some distant place without my being there to hold and comfort him before he passed."

She gripped the arms of her wheelchair and pulled herself up to bolster her point. "Rand was wrong about America's leaders. They weren't altruistic in any sense of the word. They didn't care about the Vietnamese, saving democracy, or anything else. They just wanted to make more money and keep expanding the economy. Just like they are doing today."

"I couldn't agree more. And Johann basically said the same as well."

"And, you know what, Will? Rand said that a formal investigation should be done over why the U.S. ever got involved in Vietnam in the first place." She started wriggling in her chair, becoming more animated, and raising her voice. "Then, she said this investigation should dig even deeper than Watergate to find exactly who said what and why, so it would never happen again."

Her voice rose from a place deep within her; the anger came out after years of living silently with grief, suffering, and death. "She said a thorough investigation would reveal the intellectual and moral crimes of the policymakers, and all the public humiliation they would suffer would be punishment enough."

She took a sip from her water bottle and began to calm down. "Rand concluded that no investigation was ever done because the people who would have been selected would have come from the same group responsible for it in the first place. And that, she said, was the only lesson to be learned from the Vietnam War. And she was absolutely right!"[1]

I didn't expect her to say that, but it made sense to me, especially after reading about the Nuremberg Tribunals. "I can see the logic in that, Lena."

"I saw it as well, Will." She paused to wipe her eyes. "However, her thinking that the American leaders were being too altruistic was pure *drek*."

I smiled. "Does that word mean what I think it does?"

She smiled. She appeared more relaxed than I had ever seen her. "You see," she said, her voice cracking, "you've already made me feel like I could talk to you like a son, Will."

Her eyes broke away to look down at her plain, black shoes. I heard her whisper "good" to herself as if she had just unloaded all her grief and finally put Isaac to rest.

CHAPTER 81: A SPIRITUAL STATE

"Well, that's all I have to say for now, Will, except for one more thing. Your Johann turned out to be a real *mensch,* after all. We met after your last visit, and he said again how sorry he was for what had happened. He said they had been misled and lost sight of God. I always had the impression that he didn't swallow all that hateful poison about races.

"And then he told me how much he cared about you and how he tried to share his life lessons with you. That made me feel closer to him."

I nodded in agreement and choked up. She had just crossed an invisible chasm to acknowledge his humanity. However, there was one thing that still nagged at me. "Lena, the last time I was here, you said something about fighting back against hatred. It didn't seem to square with what you said earlier about just living your life. Johann admitted you were right about that and staying out of politics. He said God was in all of us, and we shouldn't kill one another."

She grunted in acknowledgment. "I see. But he's an old man, and he's already fought and lost his battles. He can afford to say that. But I can't, and my people can't either. I can and will live my life without bothering others, but I will never again let anyone rob me or my people of our freedom."

"I understand how you feel." And I understood how Johann felt as well, but I was done with fighting. I got up from the bench and put my hand on her shoulder. "I have to get going, Lena." She looked at me with the same expression as Johann had at the end of my first visit. Her eyes were imploring for a return visit. I reached out for her hand and gave it a gentle squeeze. "Thank you for your kind words today. I hope we'll see each other soon."

I held back my tears as I walked to the car. At least Johann had a peaceful death, and his last words were of God. I should be so lucky. I missed him already.

On my way home, I occasionally looked up at the clouds and thought about God. He had created my life and then prevented its demise several times: first, during the bombing at Biên Hòa; then when I was on the mountaintop contemplating suicide; and finally when He beckoned me to get up from the couch during my stroke.

The idea of dying never bothered me after I killed that deer. In fact, suicide haunted me as a way to end the beast's urges. I suddenly remembered *Thanatos*, Freud's concept of a death wish. We studied it in college. It was of great interest to me because I related to the urge.

In his later years, Freud wrote that the death wish was *a queer instinct… directed to the destruction of its own organic home*. Freud posited that organic matter had an instinctive urge to return to its original inorganic state. He never made provisions for a spiritual state, be it heaven or hell. Freud was an atheist. Freud said man's belief in God was a collective neurosis, i.e., a *longing for a father*. He didn't believe in a spiritual state because it couldn't be observed or studied.

But I had experienced it twice. Once when I "heard" the voice urging me to "get up" after the stroke. And the other was shortly before my conversion when I had a vision of the floor opening beneath the kneeler. Neither could be observed or studied, but each had its own reality for me.

I gripped the steering wheel as I recalled my life without God. It had been a desolate existence. I had to slog my way through the Marines, through college, through the death of my child, and then through a nerve-wracking and demanding career.

Last night, Cynthia told me to leave the past behind. I believe what she meant was to leave Johann. But, as it turned out, he left me first, but not before confirming my impressions after reading *The Pilgrim's Progress*. He was my Faithful, accompanying me on the path to salvation.

I immediately became curious about what happened to Christian after Faithful died. I needed to go back and finish the book. I also felt a strong need to reconcile my past transgressions with Cynthia after I got home. There was a hole in me that needed filling.

~ AT HOME ~

CHAPTER 82: A BELIEVER

My exit sign suddenly appeared. Unlike all the other trips, this one went by quickly.

I made it home a few minutes later and pulled into the garage. I turned off the engine and looked into the rear-view mirror. There was nothing moving outside. I sat there in silence. The whole experience with Johann seemed so distant. Yet, sitting here, I felt closer to him than I ever had. Johann may not have been the ideal voice to explain modern history. But, then again, the full truth of his war and mine will always be elusive.

I was getting out of the car when Cynthia opened the door to the garage. "I thought I heard you pull up. What took you so long today?"

"Well, a lot happened." I wasn't quite ready to tell her about Johann's passing yet. "Let's go in, and I'll tell you about it over a glass of wine."

I went into my study to drop off my notebook, wallet, and keys while Cynthia headed toward the kitchen. There were folders and papers scattered over the top of my desk, and then I noticed a package. It looked like a book. Cynthia must have dropped it off with the mail. It was a book, and the title was: *Kill Anything That Moves* by Nick Turse. It was about Vietnam. I forgot I had ordered it. I wasn't in the right frame of mind to open it and tossed it back on the desk.

Johann's voice came back and whispered the first line of the *Treuelied*: *When everyone else is unfaithful, we will remain true.* He was faithful to the end while I wasn't. I was lost. I tried so hard over the past few months to understand how he held onto his beliefs despite all the evil he had lived through.

He grew up under National Socialism, believing the community had more value than the individual. He fought to defend his volk, his culture, and his country. His war had a purpose for him. He spent years trying to understand why it ended in disgrace. And in the end, Lena explained it to him in a few short meetings.

On the other hand, I grew up under democratic capitalism, where individual freedom was valued more than the community. I too joined to fight in a war against Communism, but I enlisted solely for selfish reasons. I wanted to get away from my father and from a modern world that was threatening to marginalize me.

"Are you all right, Will?"

I looked up and saw Cynthia standing next to my desk. Her voice brought me back to the present.

"I am," I said plainly.

She looked concerned. "I was in the kitchen waiting for you. What have you been doing?"

I just blurted it out. "Johann died today."

"He died?" She appeared genuinely shocked. "I'm so sorry to hear that. Did it happen before you got there?"

"No, we were together. He had a mild stroke the day before and was in bed when I got there. I got a wheelchair for him, and we went outside for some fresh air. We were sitting there talking, and I thought he just closed his eyes to rest."

"So, he died while he was with you?" Cynthia put her glass down, and her hand went over her mouth.

"Yes, he did. I took his pulse, and there wasn't any. I still can't believe it." I just shook my head and exhaled as if I were unloading a heavy weight from my chest.

"Well, how do you feel now?"

I didn't know how to answer, so I walked around my desk to hug her. The smell of her hair and the warmth of her skin was comforting. "He was a good man. I'm glad he died peacefully and had someone with him when he went. On the way home, I thought about how he was closer to me than my own father, even though we only met a short time ago."

I paused to remember my father and what happened to him during the war. "I never told you, but I also researched my father's record during the war."

"Oh? What did you find?"

"It's a bit of a long story. Do you mind if we go into the family room so I can tell you about it while we have our wine?"

She agreed.

Once we were on the couch, I told her what had happened to my father during the war. I told her about the assault, the day he spent in the woods all alone, the retreat at dusk, and the dead soldier he ran into.

Cynthia leaned toward me on the couch. "You found all that out, Will?"

"Yeah, it wasn't that hard. Some of it was in a letter he wrote. The rest I got from army records or from other fellows in his unit. In any event, he was evacuated the next day with frostbitten feet. The shame of that day must have really gotten to him. He had to carry it for the rest of his life. It might explain why he was so angry all the time and why he lashed out at us if we showed any sign of fear or weakness."

"Well, you should be glad he made it out. Otherwise, you wouldn't be here."

I tried to stop the most ironic grin in the world from appearing on my face. "After I came home from the Marines, our relationship changed. He never belittled or criticized me again. He wouldn't even look me directly in the eyes. Instead, he would only glance at me out of the corner of his eye, like a beaten dog. The only thing that didn't change was the distance between us. We never became close; not like I was with Johann."

Cynthia sat back and reached for her wine. Her face took on a look of concern while she took a small sip. She put the glass down and replied, "You must have felt pretty weird after finding all this out, Will, but imagine how your father must have felt. He had to live with that memory for so many years. I feel so sorry for both of you."

I closed my eyes and finished off my wine. For the first time in my life, I felt compassion for him. "I see now how much he must have suffered that day and each day thereafter. I don't know if I could have lived with it."

Cynthia moved over to hug me and then broke away to look into my eyes. I saw her concern and reached for her hands. There was something else I had to say. "You know, Cynthia, Johann was not a bad person. He was a believer."

"A believer? In what?" Cynthia looked at me with some incredulity.

"In God. In people." I paused to watch her expression change back to one of concern. "He told me his regimental commander said, *Humans, not angels, fought on both sides.* He told me we're all imperfect, but we're all born as children of God, and we have to learn to live together since we're all parts of His Creation."

I looked down and felt Johann's presence. "He taught me a lot. I'm really going to miss him."

She was still watching me as if she knew there was more to come. And there was. "You know, when I was driving home, it struck me that civilians back in the Seventies hated servicemen. They called us baby killers. You would've avoided me like the plague back then, just like you reacted to Johann; it's kinda the same thing. At the end of the day, we're all human."

I smiled, looked into her eyes, and kissed her. "I love you, Cynthia."

"Will, I love you too. Now and always. But the past is over. I know we've had our problems, and it's been hard for you ever since the stroke, but I'll always be with you, no matter what. All that other stuff is behind us, so let's enjoy the rest of our life while we still have it. I do love you."

Cynthia always had the right words to say at the right time. She made me feel complete.

"I love you too, and we will."

CHAPTER 83: A SINNER

I took a slow, thoughtful sip of wine. "It's been a rough day."

"It must have been."

I put the wine glass down and looked at her. I thought of all those bleak nights in the hotel room before the stroke. I felt alone and unloved and didn't give any thought to Cynthia's sacrifices while she took care of her parents and our home while working full-time. All I heard was the beast's urging to find some relief.

I finally gave in and found some semblance of relief but soon discovered that once a mortal sin is committed, any illusion of peace disappears. My conscience pleaded with me to stop, but the urge would always return. I knew a day of reckoning was coming. I could envision the beast coming to demand its due and, once satisfied, would leave me behind as an empty shell.

That day arrived sooner than expected. I came home from work and saw Cynthia standing by the front door, brandishing a note in front of her. She found it inside my luggage. Her wrathful eyes burned a hole into my being, releasing the beast who fled with my spirit. The stroke came a few days later, delivering the *coup de grâce* that robbed me of my senses.

I stared at my wine glass, remembering Johann's discourse on how God endowed us with His spirit. He said that spirit gave us life, animated our bodies, and provided us with the free will to either serve God or to sin. And then another thought struck me. I finally found the flaw that caused me to sin and placed me in Purgatory for years.

"Will, are you doing okay?"

I picked up my wine glass and took a sip to gather my thoughts before replying. "You know, as I was leaving today, I saw Lena and told her what happened to Johann. She was startled but said he was a real *mensch*, a good guy, after all."

I paused again, thinking that now was a good time as any to reconcile with Cynthia. "I never expected that Lena would have said that, but perhaps St. Paul was right when he said, *Love conquers and forgives all.*'

Her expression turned grim. "You said Johann was a believer, but the world will never forget or forgive what he and the Nazis did." She looked down into her lap. "But it's interesting that Lena said that." She stopped and swung her eyes up to the ceiling.

"You know, Will, I always thought you and I would have a good future together until you destroyed everything. After that, I felt like I could never forget or forgive you for all the hurt you caused me."

She looked over at me, and I could see her eyes were moistening. "You broke our trust, Will. You broke the bond that made us one in this world, and I was left hurt and angry. You took part of my soul, Will."

She dabbed at her eyes and looked deeply into mine. "I can never forget what happened, Will, but I can forgive you now. I know you've been trying to change and how hard it's been for you since the stroke, both physically and mentally. But things change over time, and now I feel differently than I did back then. And I know love can forgive."

She reached out her hand to hold mine. I smiled, not only because of the joy she gave me but also because of the joy we shared as a couple. Whether she knew it or not, she just gave the answer to her oft-repeated question of what I hoped to get from all of this? The answer was Love.

I could feel it rush in, filling the hole left by the beast's departure and giving me a sense of fulfillment. It reminded me of a passage from Plato's *Symposium: ...when one of them meets the other half... the pair are lost in an amazement of love and friendship and intimacy ... becoming one instead of two, was the very expression of [an] ancient need. And the reason is that human nature was originally one and we were a whole, and the desire and pursuit of the whole is called love.*

I sat by her side and felt whole.

CHAPTER 84: AMEN AND ALLELUIA

Early the next morning, I skipped my walk. Instead, I made a cup of coffee and went to my study. I had to find my bearings after yesterday's storm of traumatic events.

I sat down at my desk and wondered again what happened to Christian after Faithful had passed. I turned to my computer and opened *The Pilgrim's Progress*. I picked up where the citizens of Vanity Fair had just executed Faithful. Christian stood off in the distance after escaping from prison and watched his friend's departing spirit soar off to heaven. And then he sang this farewell song:

> *Well, Faithful, thou hast faithfully profest Unto thy Lord;*
> *with whom thou shalt be blest, When faithless ones, with*
> *all their vain delights, Are crying out under their hellish*
> *plights, Sing, Faithful, sing, and let thy name survive; For,*
> *though they kill'd thee, thou art yet alive.*[1]

A chill passed through me. The second line sounded like the *Treuelied*, and the last line like my comment to Johann that *they could kill you, but they can't eat you*. I stopped reading at this point, convinced that we shared the same connection as Christian and Faithful.

Johann mentioned *Gott Mit Uns* on our first visit and again at our last. Everything about our relationship began falling into place. We were two pilgrims fleeing the *City of Destruction* to find the Truth, that God was with us.

I resumed reading to see what happens next. After Christian sang his farewell song to Faithful, he meets another pilgrim named Hopeful. They journey together and arrive at a river. Off in the distance, on the other side of the river, was a gate leading to heavenly Jerusalem. There were two men standing by the riverbank dressed *in raiment that shone like gold… their faces shone as the light*. These two men tell the pilgrims they must cross the river, *or you cannot come at the gate*.

Christian wades into the river and begins to panic as the rising water begins to pull him under. He cries out to Hopeful, fearful of losing his life. Hopeful encourages him to persevere: *These troubles and distresses that you go through in these waters are no sign that God hath forsaken you; but are sent to try you, whether you will call to mind that, which heretofore you have received of His goodness, and live upon Him in your distresses.*[2]

I closed my eyes and a vision of Cynthia appeared. She was my Hopeful, standing by me on the other side of the river. My chest began heaving and I started sobbing. God did send me the right person. She never abandoned her mission to save my soul, despite my transgressions.

I suddenly recalled Saint Augustine's *Confessions*. I read it during my recovery from the stroke. He also wrestled with the beast before finally accepting God as the Truth. I wanted to achieve the same, but it was ultimately Lena who brought Johann and I into accepting that same truth.

I opened my eyes and scanned the bookshelf for his book but stopped when I noticed his *Prayer Book*. I got up and opened it to the page that had his *Resurrection Prayer*.

All shall be Amen and Alleluia.
We shall rest and we shall see,
We shall see and we shall know.

We shall know and we shall love.

We shall love and we shall praise.

Behold our end, which is no end.

I turned to look out the study window but couldn't see a thing. It was too early in the morning. It was still pitch-black outside. And then it struck me. The Truth was as unknowable as the darkness itself; it encompassed the fullness of time and space in its entirety. No one can ever claim to know it, for that is the providence of God, where all is as one and will always be.

I closed the prayer book, picked up my empty coffee cup, and went to wake Cynthia. We would be as one to the end, which has no end.

EPILOGUE

Man has himself brought about the evil from which he suffers by transgressing the law of God, on obedience to which his happiness depended.

Evil is in created things under the aspect of mutability, and possibility of defect, not as existing per se: and the errors of mankind, mistaking the true conditions of its own well-being, have been the cause of moral and physical evil.

~ Definition of *Evil* from the *Catholic Encyclopedia* (*https://www.newadvent.org/*)

END NOTES

Chapter 1: The Unexamined Life

1.   Hubert Meyer, *The 12ᵗʰ SS, Volume One* (Mechanicsburg, Pa: Stackpole Books, 2005), pp. 357-358. The incident involved an SS-Pionier named Pelzmann; there was no first name given.

Chapter 2: Core Curriculum

1.   Daniel Fusfeld, *The Economic Thought of Franklin D. Roosevelt and the Origins of the New Deal* (New York, Columbia University Press, 1954), pp 112-113.

Chapter 5: A Matter of Terms

1.   Jon Latimer, *World War II: 12ᵗʰ SS Hitlerjugend Panzer Division Fought in Normandy.* historynet.com June 12, 2006. Originally appeared in the July 2001 issue of World War II.

Chapter 9: Johann's First Point

1.   Ralph Raico, *The Blockade and Attempted Starvation of Germany.* mises.org/library/blockade-and-attempted-starvation-germany 05/07/2010.

Chapter 13: *Das Biest*

1.   *Wikipedia. Communist Party USA, Criminal prosecutions.* https://en.wikipedia.org/wiki/Communist Party_USA

"When the Communist Party was formed in 1919, the United States government was engaged in prosecution of socialists who had opposed World War I and military service. This prosecution was continued in 1919 and January 1920 in the Palmer Raids or the red scare. Rank and file foreign-born members of the Party were targeted and as many as possible were arrested and deported;

leaders were prosecuted and, in some cases, sentenced to prison terms.

In the late 1930s, with the authorization of President Franklin D. Roosevelt, the Federal Bureau of Investigation began investigating both domestic Nazis and Communists. Congress passed the Smith Act, which made it illegal to advocate, abet, or teach the desirability of overthrowing the government, in 1940."

2.   Wikipedia. *Philippine–American War*, https://en.wikipedia.org/wiki/Philippine–American_War

Chapter 15: An Uncomfortable Sense

1.   Kurt Meyer, *Grenadiers* (Mechanicsburg, Pa: Stackpole Books, 2005), p. 212.

Chapter 17: Self-Deception

1.   Klaus Wiegrefe, *A New Openness to Discussing Allied War Crimes in WWII*, Der Spiegel, May 04, 2010.

2.   Theodore Solotaroff, *The Last of the Just,*, by Andre Schwarz-Bart, https://www.commentarymagazine.com/articles/the-last-of-the-just-by-andre-schwarz-bart/

Chapter 18: Exploring Common Ground

1.   Hubert Meyer, *The 12th SS, Volume One* (Mechanicsburg, Pa: Stackpole Books, 2005), pp. 518.

Chapter 19: We're Only Human

1.   Public Broadcasting Service, *The West. Episode 4: Death Runs Riot*, © 2001 THE WEST FILM PROJECT and WETA.

Chapter 20: Lena

1.   Lena's life up to 1948 is loosely based on a transcript of an interview with Holocaust survivor, Felicia Weingarten. This interview can be found at the online United States Holocaust Museum http://collections.ushmm.org Lena's life after 1948, described in later chapters, is entirely fictional and any resemblance to any real character living or dead is coincidental.

Chapter 22: Leon

1.   Michael Eric Dyson. *The Legacy of Muhammad Ali* Progressive Magazine, June 1, 2018. Ali made several speeches during 1967 while protesting the draft; there are no complete transcripts available. The quoted passages are taken from the above article. Also see Muhammad Ali and Vietnam, theatlantic.com/news/archive/2016/06/muhammad-ali-vietnam/485717 and Muhammad Ali's inspirational statement on why he wouldn't fight in Vietnam. nydailynews.com/sports/more-sports/muhammad-ali-statement-wouldn-fight-vietnam-article-1.2661120 Youtube has a video of Ali speaking several of these lines at https://www.youtube.com/watch?v=V2EfL1j4KYE.

Chapter 23: Reparations

1.   Three American reporters were in Berlin and recorded Jesse Owens' victory: (1) *New York Times,* August 25, 1936. Jesse Ownes was quoted as saying: *"Mr. Hitler had to leave the stadium early, but after winning I hurried up to the radio booth. When I passed near the Chancellor he arose, waved his hand at me and I waved back at him."* (2) *The St. Joseph News-Press,* October 16, 1936. Jesse Owens was quoted in this article as saying: *"Hitler didn't snub me; it was our president who snubbed me. The president didn't even send me a telegram."* (3) *Pittsburgh Courier,* August 8, 1936. Robert Lee Vann wrote: *"Monday, I saw another vast crowd of close to 100,000 people go 'literally crazy' as they saw Jesse Owens running with the effortless speed of an antelope, completely dominate his field to win 'going away' in the 100 meters . . . I saw Herr Adolph Hitler, salute this lad. I looked on with a heart, which beat proudly as the lad who was crowned king of the 100 meters event, get an ovation the like of, which I have never heard before. I saw Jesse Owens greeted by the Grand Chancellor of this country as a brilliant sun peeped out through the clouds. I saw a vast crowd of some 85,000 or 90,000 people stand up and cheer him to the echo. And they were mostly Germans! Make no mistake about it. These German people are mighty fine. They have a spirit of sportsmanship and fair play, which overrides the color-barrier."*

2. Sumner Welles. *Letter to FDR. Berlin, March 2, 1940.*
    http://docs.fdrlibrary.marist.edu/PSF/box6/t72f02.html

"He was dignified both in speech and movement, and there was not the slightest impression of the comic effect from moustache and hair which one sees in his caricatures.

"His voice in conversation is low and well-modulated. It had only once, during our hour and a half's conversation, the raucous stridency which is heard in his speeches--and it was only at that moment that his features lost their composure and that his eyes lost their decidedly "gemutlich" look. He spoke with clarity and precision, and always in a beautiful German..."

Chapter 29: Larry the Lawyer

1. Wikipedia. *Saint Patrick's Battalion.*
    https://en.wikipedia.org/wiki/Saint_Patrick%27s_Battalion

Chapter 30: Lulu

1. Wikipedia. *Saint Patrick's Battalion.*
https://en.wikipedia.org/wiki/Saint_Patrick%27s_Battalion
Following is a quote from George Ballentine cited in Wikipedia*: "I have good reason to believe, in fact in some cases I know, that harsh and unjust treatment by their officers operated far more strongly than any other consideration to produce the deplorable result."*

2. Juan Soto, *Desertion Handbill (June 6, 1847)*. Original handbill in the Beinecke Rare Book and Manuscript Library, Yale University, New Haven, Connecticut. Copy can be found on this website:
Https://www.historyisaweapon.com/defcon1/juansotodesertionhandbill.html

Chapter 32: A Lack of Integrity

1.   Yale Law School – Avalon Project, *Nuremberg Trial Proceedings Vol. 1, Charter of the International Military Tribunal*

2.   Today's Federal Rules of Evidence span over forty pages and provide clear instructions for governing the admissibility, authentication, relevance, identification, and handling of physical evidence. They require a chain of custody for each piece of submitted evidence including how each piece was obtained, who did the collecting, when it was collected, and other details to guarantee its integrity during the trial including details about transportation, storage, and general handling of the materials. They also address the admissibility of verbal testimony including hearsay, privilege, witnesses, opinions, and expert testimony.

3.   Educalingo website, *Black Propaganda.* https://educalingo.com/en/dic-en/black-propaganda

4.   Marc Wortman, *The Fake British Radio Show That Helped Defeat the Nazis.* Smithsonian.com 2/28/1017 https://www.smithsonianmag.com/history/fake-british-radio-show-helped-defeat-nazis-180962320. *"In August 1941, Prime Minister Winston Churchill consolidated previously disparate black propaganda operations under the 37-year-old English journalist, Denis Sefton Delmer, a German-language newscaster for the multilingual BBC European Service who knew Hitler personally and the German people intimately – and fiercely opposed Nazism. Delmer's PWE was a veritable fake news mill. Teams of artists, printers, and writers also published fake German newspapers and printed up thousands of illustrated leaflets full of believable, yet mostly false, 'news,' as well as pornographic illustrations, forged leave passes for soldiers, and other documents designed to crack apart German unity."*

5.   United States. Central Intelligence Agency, Center for the Study of Intelligence (U.S.), Studies in Intelligence. *The Defections of Dr. John. cia.gov/library/center-for-the-study-of-intelligence/kent-*

csi/vol4no4/html/v04i4a01p_0001.htm The CIA report stated that Otto John *"was turned over to Sefton Delmer... [and] according to Delmer; John lived with him for 10 months. In 1945 and 1946, John worked for the British in various capacities—with PID on intelligence matters, on the POW reorientation program at Wilton Park, and on research for XXXXXXXXXXXXX XXXXXXXXX XXXXXXXXX XXXXXXXXXXX XXXXXXXXXX XXXXXXXXX XXXXXXXXXXX.*

"After the surrender in May 1945, John did not return to Germany with the bulk of the political exiles. He worked for the British War and Foreign Offices, interrogating German generals in the Kensington cage and helping prepare legal documents for the approaching Nuremberg trials. At Nuremberg, he worked as an adviser to the UK prosecution staff, a fact omitted in his own curriculum vitae."

6.   Gerd Schultze-Rhonhof, *10/29/11 Speech on "The War that had Many Fathers". Anti-Zensur Koalition*
https://www.youtube.com/watch?v=Uvwb5QPrmc0
Here is an extract of a speech he gave describing this forgery: *"The British replaced complete pages in German documents, not knowing that their paper material was of different physical quality than the German originals. This was leading to a different discolouring process of the aging papers, so every page they replaced can now be identified, but the originals seem to be lost ..."*

Chapter 33: "Too Sanctimonious A Fraud"

1.   Ian Cobain, *How Britain tortured Nazi PoWs: The horrifying interrogation methods that belie our proud boast that we fought a clean war.* Daily Mail. October 26, 2012. dailymail.co.uk/news/article-2223831/How-Britain-tortured-Nazi-PoWs-The-horrifying-interrogation-methods-belie-proudboast-fought-clean-war.html
The following is an extract from the article: *"It was in 2005 during my work as an investigative reporter that I came across a veiled mention of a World War II detention centre known as the London Cage. It took a*

number of Freedom of Information requests to the Foreign Office before government files were reluctantly handed over ...

"The author outlined the process that occurred after the war at three different camps in London. One of the camp commandants and four of his officers were arrested for the deaths of their inmates. The commandant testified that... he had no idea the prisoners for whom he was responsible were being beaten, whipped, frozen, deprived of sleep and starved to death.

"This was the very defence that had been offered— unsuccessfully—by Nazi concentration camp commandants at war-crimes trials. But he was acquitted. The suspicion remains that he got off because, if cruelties did occur at Bad Nenndorf, they had been authorised by government ministers.

2.   Ibid.

3.   A.T. Mason, *Harlan Fiske Stone: Pillar of the Law* (New York: The Viking Press; 1st edition 1956), p. 716

Chapter 36: American Capitalism

1.   William Beach, *We're Spending More Than Ever and It Doesn't Work*. The Daily Signal, January 14, 2009

Chapter 37: "Corporate Socialism"

1.   Lewis v. United States, 680 F.2d 1239 (1982), John L. Lewis, Plaintiff/Appellant, v. United States of America, Defendant/Appellee. No. 80-5905, United States Court of Appeals, Ninth Circuit.

2.   Richard Pipes, *Survival Is Not Enough: Soviet Realities and America's Future* (New York: Simon & Schuster, 1984)

3.   Anthony Sutton, *FDR and Wall Street, Chapter 3* (http://www.reformation.org/wall-st-fdr-biblio.html (4 of 4)16.2.2006 10:06:29) Following is an extract from this book: *"Franklin D. Roosevelt was organizer and president of several speculative international financial enterprises linking Germany and the United States, and in particular one enterprise to profit from the*

ruinous German hyperinflation of 1922-23. In 1922 FDR became president and was one of the organizers of United European Investors, Ltd… formed to accumulate German marks deposited in the United States and to reinvest these marks in Germany by purchasing property from destitute Germans … This terrifying monetary inflation and the ultimate collapse of the German mark in 1923 ruined the German middle class …."

4. Arthur Meier Schlesinger, *A Life in the Twentieth Century: Innocent Beginnings, 1917-1950* (New York: Houghton Mifflin Harcourt, 2000), p.362

5. Anthony Sutton, *FDR and Wall Street, Chapter 12* (http://www.reformation.org/wall-st-fdr-biblio.html (4 of 4)16.2.2006 10:06:29)

6. David Dayen, *This is the Fed's Most Brazen and Least Known Handout to Private Banks,* New Republic, March 9, 2014.

The opening paragraphs of this article states: *"Rarely does a day go by when some House Republican doesn't demand an end to Federal Reserve funding of the Consumer Financial Protection Bureau (CFPB). But you will never hear about the Fed's direct subsidy to private banks that costs over three times as much as the total CFPB budget.*

"The subsidy comes in the form of a 6 percent dividend, paid on stock that over 2,900 banks purchase to participate in the Federal Reserve system. Very few places where ordinary Americans park their money offer such a risk-free benefit. In 2012 (the last year with available data), the Fed gave away $1.637 billion in dividends to banks, tax-free in the majority of cases. And the Fed has been doing this for the last 100 years. It's one of the many unknown ways the Fed extends special benefits to Wall Street."

Chapter 38: Ungloved

1. Anthony Sutton, *FDR and Wall Street, Chapter 10* (http://www.reformation.org/wall-st-fdr-biblio.html (4 of 4)16.2.2006 10:06:29).

Following is an extract from this book: "Far-fetched as this accusation may seem, we can isolate three major statements of fact: One. There was independent confirmation of General Butler's statements and in some measure unwilling confirmation by one of the plotters. Two. There existed a motive for Wall Street to initiate such a desperate gamble: the NRA-Swope proposal was foundering. Three. The alleged identity of the men behind the scenes is the same as those identified in the Bolshevik Revolution and in the political promotion of FDR.' "

2. *U.S. House of Representatives, Special Committee on Un-American Activities, Investigation of Nazi Propaganda Activities and Investigation of Certain Other Propaganda Activities, Hearings 73-D.C.-6, Part 1, 73rd Congress, 2nd session, (Washington, D.C.: Government Printing Office, 1935). p.4*

3. Ibid., p. 18

Chapter 39: "War is a Racket"

1. Smedley Butler, *War is a Racket* (New York: Round Table Press, 1935). The following is an extract from his book: *"War is a racket. It always has been. It is possibly the oldest, easily the most profitable, surely the most vicious. It is the only one international in scope. It is the only one in which the profits are reckoned in dollars and the losses in lives.*

"A racket is best described, I believe, as something that is not what it seems to the majority of the people. Only a small "inside" group knows what it is about. It is conducted for the benefit of the very few, at the expense of the very many.

"Out of war a few people make huge fortunes. In the World War, a mere handful garnered the profits of the conflict. At least 21,000 new millionaires and billionaires were made in the United States during the World War. That many admitted their huge blood gains in their income

tax returns. *How many other war millionaires falsified their tax returns, no one knows.*

"How many of these war millionaires shouldered a rifle? How many of them dug a trench? How many of them knew what it meant to go hungry in a rat-infested dug-out? How many of them spent sleepless, frightened nights, ducking shells and shrapnel and machine gun bullets? How many of them parried a bayonet thrust of an enemy? How many of them were wounded or killed in battle?"

2.   Wikipedia, Common Sense, https://en.wikipedia.org/wiki/Common_Sense_(magazine)

Chapter 42: A Loss of Standards

1.   Stanford Encyclopedia of Philosophy, *Ayn Rand.* https://plato.stanford.edu/entries/ayn-rand/ First published June 8, 2010, with substantive revision Sep 19, 2016. Lena's thoughts do not necessarily reflect the key tenets of Ayn Rand's Objectivism philosophy.

Chapter 43: People Need to Know

1.   *Daily Express.* London, March 24, 1933, pp. 1-2.

Chapter 47: Fact Checking

1.   Maxine Yaple Sweezy, *Distribution of Wealth and Income under the Nazis,* The MIT Press. Source: The Review of Economics and Statistics, Vol. 21, No. 4 (Nov.,1939), pp. 178-184

Chapter 48: Abstract Difficulties

1.   Yale University. *The Avalon Project: Nuremberg Trial Proceedings Vol. 19 Day 187,* p.3 https://avalon.law.yale.edu/imt/07-26-46.asp

2.   UPI Archives, *Hitler orders military conscription in Germany. March 16, 1935/* https://www.upi.com/Archives/1935/03/16/Hitler-orders-military-conscription-in-Germany/5124911384073/

3.   Ibid.

4.   Patrick J. Buchanan, *Churchill, Hitler, and The Unnecessary War* (New York: Crown Forum; 1st edition July 28, 2009), p. 172

Chapter 50: False Flag

1.   Charles Tansill, *"The United States and the Road to War in Europe,"* article in *Perpetual War for Perpetual Peace* (Newport Beach, Cal.: Institute for Historical Review, 1993), p. 184 (footnote 292).

2.   Richard Blanke, *Orphans of Versailles: The Germans in Western Poland, 1918-1939* (Lexington, University Press of Kentucky; 1st edition (December 15, 1992), p.236

3.   Yale Law School, *Avalon Project, Address by Adolf Hitler, Chancellor of the Reich, before the Reichstag, September 1, 1939.* https://avalon.law.yale.edu/wwii/gp2.asp

4.   Henry Hemming, *WW2: Franklin Roosevelt reveals 'secret Nazi map' in 1941.* Smithsonian.Com Daily, Sept 7, 2019. https://www.smithsonianmag.com/history/untold-story-secret-mission-seize-nazi-map-data-180973317/

Chapter 51: Ouroboros

1.   Wikipedia. *Howard Zinn.* https://en.wikipedia.org/wiki/Howard_Zinn

Chapter 53: A Lot of *Mishegas*

1.   Joseph Jacobs, *Finance. Jewish Encyclopedia.* http://www.jewishencyclopedia.com/articles/6116-finance, p. 383-384

2.   Gotthard Deutsch, Joseph Jacobs. *Banking. Jewish Encyclopedia.* http://www.jewishencyclopedia.com/articles/2444-banking

3.   Joseph Jacobs, Isidore Singer, Frederick T. Haneman, Jacques Kahn, Goodman Lipkind, J. de Haas, I. L. Bril Gotthard Deutsch, *Rothschild. Jewish Encyclopedia.* http://www.jewishencyclopedia.com/articles/2444-banking

4. Galia Licht, *Who Was the Most pro-Jewish U.S. President?* Haaretz. Sep 25, 2013

Chapter 54: Social Compression

1. Robert Wilton, *The Last Days of the Romanovs* (Newport Beach, CA: Institute for Historical Review, 1992), pp184-190

2. Rafael Medoff, *What FDR said about Jews in private,* LA Times April 7, 2013. Following is an extract from this article: *"In 1923, as a member of the Harvard board of directors, Roosevelt decided there were too many Jewish students at the college and helped institute a quota to limit the number admitted. In 1938, he privately suggested that Jews in Poland were dominating the economy and were herefore to blame for provoking anti-Semitism there...In 1943, he told government officials in Allied-liberated North Africa that the number of local Jews in various professions 'should be definitely limited' so as to 'eliminate the specific and understandable complaints,' which the Germans bore toward the Jews in Germany.* "There is evidence of other troubling private remarks by FDR too, including dismissing pleas for Jewish refugees as 'Jewish wailing' and 'sob stuff'; expressing, to a senator, his pride that 'there is no Jewish blood in our veins'; and characterizing a tax maneuver by a Jewish newspaper publisher as 'a dirty Jewish trick.' But the most common theme in Roosevelt's private statements about Jews has to do with his perception that they were 'overcrowding' many professions and exercising undue influence."

Chapter 55: A Separate People

1. *Judea Declares War on Germany,* Daily Express. London, March 24, 1933, pp. 1-2.

2. A.I. Berndt, *The Nuremberg Laws: German News Agency on the Nuremberg Laws.* Jewish Virtual Library. Quotation from *Juedische Rundschau*, No. 75, September 17, 1935 reported: *"After years of struggle the new Laws passed by the Reichstag*

... establish absolutely clear relations between the German Nation (Deutschtum) and Jewry ... German people has no objection to the Jew as long as he wishes to be a member of the Jewish people and acts accordingly, but that, on the other hand, he declines to look on the Jew as a fellow-member of the German Nation (Volksgenosse) and to accord him the same rights and duties as a German.

"The International Zionist Congress has ... put an end very plainly to any talk of Judaism being simply a religion. The speakers at the Zionist Congress stated that the Jews are a separate people and once again put on record the national claims of Jewry.

"Germany ... is meeting the demands of the International Zionist Congress when it declares the Jews now living in Germany to be a national minority. Once the Jews have been stamped a national minority it is again possible to establish normal relations between the German Nation and Jewry."

3.   Herbert S. Levine, *A Jewish Collaborator in Nazi Germany: The Strange Career of Georg Kareski, 1933-37*, Central European History , Sep., 1975, Vol. 8, No. 3 (Sep., 1975), pp. 251-281, Cambridge University Press on behalf of Central European History Society. Quoted Kareski as saying the following: *"For many years I have regarded a complete separation of the cultural affairs of the two peoples as a pre-condition for living together without conflict... I have long supported such a separation, provided it is founded on respect for the alien nationality. The Nuremberg Laws ... seem to me, apart from their legal provisions, to conform entirely with this desire for a separate life based on mutual respect t... This interruption of the process of dissolution in many Jewish communities, which had been promoted through mixed marriages, is therefore, from a Jewish point of view, entirely welcome."*

4.   Francis R. Nicosia, *The Third Reich and the Palestine Question* (Abingdon, UK: Routledge, 2000), p.56

Chapter 56: Nobody in Their Right Mind

1.   The New York Times, Text of Untermeyer's Address. August 7, 1933, Page 4

2.   *Kristallnacht. Britannica Online Encyclopedia*, date published: 02 November 2021

Chapter 59: Invasion

1.   Sara Reguer, *Palestine and Nazi Germany.* http://www.museumoftolerance.com/education/archives-and-reference-library/online-resources/simon-wiesenthal-center-annual-volume-4/annual-4-chapter-17.html

2.   The Jewish Chronicle, *Zionists Faithful to Britain, Dr. Weizmann Repeats Pledge, Letter to Prime Minister.* September 8, 1939

3.   Rudolf Heydrich, *Instructions by Heydrich on Policy and Operations Concerning Jews in the Occupied Territories, September 21, 1939.* Shoah Resource Center https://www.yadvashem.org/odot_pdf/Microsoft%20Word%20-%201984.pdf

Chapter 62: *Generalplan Ost*

1.   Richard Tedor. *Stalin's Secret War Plans: Why Hitler Invaded the Soviet Union.* The Barnes Review. Nov./Dec. 2000 issue

Following is an extract from this article: *"The [Soviet] defense committee had been secretly transferring combat divisions there [Soviet Wester Zone] since the summer of 1940. In April 1941, the Ural and Siberian military districts were ordered to release more formations. On May 13, an additional 28 divisions, nine corps headquarters and four army headquarters were relocated from the Russian interior. By June, according to recent Russian archival estimates, the Soviet armed forces had deployed 2.7 million men near the western frontier; the equivalent of 177 divisions. "This enormous fighting force was allocated 10,394 tanks, over 1,300 of which were the formidable types KV and T-34. The army was supported by nearly 44,000 field guns and mortars. Over*

8,000 *combat aircraft occupied forward airdromes. The western military districts established command posts close to the frontier. Army staffs and front administrative personnel were ordered transferred there in mid-June. One hundred Soviet divisions were positioned in eastern Poland alone. A high proportion of armored and mechanized formations deployed near Bialystok ...*"

Chapter 63: Russia

1.   Edgar M. Howell, *The Soviet Partisan Movement 1941-1944.* Department of the Army Pamphlet no. 20-244. August 1956 *Following are two extracts from this publication:*

A. *"... the initial German attack in June 1941 was hardly under way before the first signs of guerrilla-like opposition appeared... before the first of July infantry units of Army Group North were harassed from all sides ... On 10 July, the Partisan Movement was officially organized and placed under the control of the Tenth Department of the Political Administration of the Army... which in turn was under the direct control of the Central Committee of the Communist Party."*

B. *"The initial German attack in June 1941 was hardly under way before the first signs of guerrilla-like opposition appeared ... Even as early as the first days of July their stubborn resistance to mopping up operations created many critical situations, and pockets continued to appear far to the rear as early as the third day of the campaign. "Army Group Center [German] reported that Red Army 'stragglers and guerrillas' were attacking supply routes and field hospitals and striking at elements of the security divisions. And before the first of July infantry units of Army Group North were harassed from all sides ... On 10 July the Partisan Movement was officially organized and placed under the control of the Tenth Department of the Political Administration of the Army, a portion of Mechlis' command as chief of the Main Administration of the Political Propaganda of the Red Army, which in turn was under the direct control of the Central Committee of the Communist Party. "Great emphasis was continually placed on the need to bring all the irregular units under the central control of Moscow at the earliest possible date. Almost immediately the effect of this centralized control was perceptible. On 11 July, Mechlis issued to the ranking political officers of all the army fronts and, apparently, to the Central Committee of the Communist Party in all the Soviet Republics endangered by the Germans detailed orders to form partisan units. These political leaders were directed to organize irregular groups in "the main zone of operations . . . where the principal units of the enemy troops [were] located."*

2.   Kurt Meyer. *Grenadiers (Mechanicsburg, Pa: Stackpole Books 2005), p. 74*

Chapter 64: The Devil's Choice

1.   *Translation of Document No. 2586 (E), "Letter from Hermann Goering to Reinhard Heydrich, Berlin, July 31, 1941".* Truman Library. https://www.trumanlibrary.gov/library/research-files/translation-document-no-2586-e-letter-hermann-goering-reinhard-heydrich

2.   Wikipedia. *Chaim Weizmann,* https://en.wikipedia.org/wiki/Chaim_Weizmann Following is an extract from this entry: *On 29 August 1939, Weizmann sent a letter to Neville Chamberlain, stating in part: "I wish to confirm in the most explicit manner the declarations which I and my colleagues have made during the last month and especially in the last week: that the Jews stand by Great Britain and will fight on the side of the democracies." The letter gave rise to a conspiracy theory, promoted in Nazi propaganda, that he had made a "Jewish declaration of war" against Germany."*

3.   Nigel Morris, *The Special Operations Executive 1940 – 1946.* BBC websute (Last updated 2011-02-17) http://www.bbc.co.uk/history/worldwars/wwtwo/soe_01.shtml.

4.   Wilhelm Keitel, *The Memoirs of Field-Marshal Wilhelm Keitel.* Cooper Square Press (New York: Square Press 2000)

5.   Professor Douglas O. Linder, *Famous Trials: Testimony of Rudolf Hoess, Commandant of Auschwitz on Monday, April 15, 1946,* https://www.famous-trials.com/nuremberg/1932-hoesstestimony. p. 7

Chapter 71: An "Inherited Bias"

1.   Jeanette Rodriguez and Ted Fortier, *Cultural Memory: Resistance, Faith, and Identity,* University of Texas Press, 2007

2.   Fergus M. Bordewich, *The Ambush That Changed History.* Smithsonian Magazine. September 2006. The author's quote continues with this interesting speculation: *"Had Rome not been defeated, says historian Herbert W. Benario, emeritus professor of classics at Emory University, a very different Europe would have emerged. 'Almost all of modern Germany ... would have come under Roman rule. All Europe west of the Elbe might well have remained Roman Catholic; Germans would be speaking a Romance language; the Thirty Years' War might never have occurred, and the long, bitter conflict between the French and the Germans might never have taken place."*

Chapter 72: "A Heavy Silence"

1.   Jewish Virtual Library. *Nazi War Crimes Trials: Klaus Barbie.* https://www.jewishvirtuallibrary.org/trial-of-nazi-criminal-klaus-barbie. JVL noted that Verges quote was found in Unhealed Wounds by Erna Paris (Grove Press, 1985). p. 148-149

2.   Ibid.

3.   Ibid.

Chapter 73: "Whither Goest Thou?"

1.   Yale Law School, *Avalon Project, Military-Industrial Complex Speech, Dwight D. Eisenhower, 1961.*
https://avalon.law.yale.edu/20th_century/eisenhower001.asp

2.   American Public Health Association, *The Role of Public Health in the Prevention of War: Rationale and Competencies.*

https://ajph.aphapublications.org/doi/full/10.2105/AJPH.2013.3017
78

3.   Ibid.. The first point was taken from the following extract:
*"Since the end of World War II, there have been 248 armed conflicts in
153 locations around the world. The United States launched 201
overseas military operations between the end of World War II and 2001,
and since then, others, including Afghanistan and Iraq" The second
point is taken from this extract: "The United States is responsible for
41% of the world's total military spending. The next largest in spending
are China, accounting for 8.2%; Russia, 4.1%; and the United Kingdom
and France, both 3.6%...If all military ... costs are included, annual
[US] spending amounts to $1 trillion ... According to the DOD fiscal
year 2012 base structure report, 'The DOD manages global property of
more than 555,000 facilities at more than 5,000 sites, covering more
than 28 million acres.' The United States maintains 700 to 1000
military bases or sites in more than 100 countries."*

4.   The Stockholm International Peace Research Institute,
*SIPRI Top 100 Arm Sales in 2017. https://www.sipri.org/media/press-
release/2018/global-arms-industry-us-companies-dominate-top-100-
russian-arms-industry-moves-second-place*

5.   Council on Foreign Relations, *Military-Industrial Complex,
Fifty Years On.* Interview by Leslie H. Gelb, Interviewee Bernard
Gwertzman, Interviewer, January 12, 2011. https://www.cfr.org

6.   Oxfam website, *62 people own same as half the world.*
January 18, 2016. http://oxfamapps.org/media/prhow

7.   Howard Zinn. *Changing Minds, One at a Time.* Progressive
Magazine. March 1, 2005. progressive.org/magazine/changing-
minds-one-time-Zinn

Chapter 74: "A Sorry Scrub"

1.   John Bunyan. *The Pilgrim's Progress* (Minneapolis: Desiring
God Press 2014), p. 80

2. Cliff's Notes. *Summary and Analysis Part 1: Section 7 - Vanity Fair.* https://www.cliffsnotes.com/literature/p/the-pilgrims-progress/summary-and-analysis/part-1-section-7

3. Ibid.

Chapter 76: In Reverse

1. The World Future Fund also cited the number of expelled Germans after the end of the war, which is a higher number than Adenauer cited, which means the numbers of deaths would be higher as well. The following numbers are rough estimates compiled from various census and rationing records by the Centre against Expulsion Organization (Zentrum Gegen Vertreibungen). https://www.ausstellung-verschwundeneorte.de/index.php

- Germany east of 1945 border (1944 ration office records) 9,758,000 (est)
- Poland (1944 ration office records) (1939 borders) 2,140,000 (est)
- Czechoslovakia (1930 census) 3,071,000
- Hungary (cited by Austrian government 1940) 845,000
- Romania (1930 census) 745,000
  Total 16,559,000 (est)

2. Adenauer quote is taken from the World Future Fund website; http://worldfuturefund.org/Articles/Germanwardeaths/germanworldwarciviliansdeaths.htm

Chapter 77: *Der Letzte Seiner Art*

1. Rense.com. *Gen Patton's Clear Vision - Why He Was Murdered.* December 5, 2009

Chapter 78: The Needs of Others

1. Kurt Meyer. Grenadiers (Mechanicsburg, Pa: Stackpole Books 2005)

Chapter 80: A Lesson to be Learned

1.   Ayn Rand, *The Voice of Reason: The Lessons of Vietnam* (New York: Penguin Books USA Inc. 1990)

Chapter 84: Amen and Alleluia

1.   John Bunyan, *The Pilgrim's Progress* (Minneapolis: Desiring God Press 2014, p. 109

2.   Ibid., p. 180